Exploring Luke

Personality Type
and Scripture

Exploring Luke's Gospel

Personality Type and Scripture

LESLIE J. FRANCIS
AND
PETER ATKINS

MOWBRAY
LONDON AND NEW YORK

Mowbray
A Continuum imprint
The Tower Building, 11 York Road, London SE1 7NX,UK
Suite 704, 80 Maiden Lane, New York, NY 10038, USA

First published 2000

British Library Cataloguing-in-Publication Data
A catalogue record for this book is available from the British Library.

ISBN 0-264-67524-X

Designed and typeset by CentraServe Ltd, Saffron Walden, Essex

Contents

Preface

Psychological type theory is already being set to work by the Christian churches in a variety of ways. It is being employed to promote personal and professional development among clergy during initial training and continuing ministerial education, to enhance collaborative ministry and body-building among local congregations, and to help individual pilgrims find their own preferred pattern of spirituality. This book sets psychological type theory to work in the study of scripture.

There are two very practical ways in which this approach to scripture may be of service to the Christian community. First, this approach provides a disciplined way in which individuals can be helped to meditate on the richness of scripture. It helps them to transcend the more limited focus of their own psychological preferences. Second, this approach provides a disciplined way through which preachers can become more aware of how different members of their congregation may respond to their preaching. It helps them to appreciate how different psychological types may hear and respond to different emphases within the same readings from scripture.

This approach addresses the same four questions to each passage of scripture. How does this passage feed the sense perceptions and establish contact with the reality of the situation? How does this passage feed the imagination and spark off new ideas? What does this passage say about human values and interpersonal relationships? What does this passage do to stimulate the intellect and to challenge the roots of faith? Many Christians may instinctively find one of these questions of greater value and interest than the others. Many Christians may well benefit from experiencing how the scriptures can speak to the totality of their personality, to their senses and their imagination, to their heart and their head.

Readers who are already well versed in type theory will benefit from knowing the psychological type of the authors.

Such information may alert them to the strengths and to the weaknesses of each author's own perspective. In the language of type theory, Leslie Francis is an INTJ. This means that he prefers *introversion* (I), *intuition* (N), *thinking* (T) and *judging* (J). Peter Atkins is an ESTJ. This means that he prefers *extraversion* (E), *sensing* (S), *thinking* (T) and *judging* (J). Readers who are not already well versed in type theory will find these concepts defined and discussed in the series introduction.

Having carefully planned this book together we decided that it would be appropriate to allow our two independent voices to be heard through the text. We divided the fifty-one chapters into two sets, working in blocks of five. Leslie drafted Chapters 1 to 5, Peter drafted Chapters 6 to 10, and so on. While we have critiqued the content of each other's chapters, we have given variety to the text by not writing in the same style.

Index of Sundays (Year C)

Series introduction

Personality Type and Scripture: Exploring Luke's Gospel is part of a series of books which reflect on scripture in a disciplined way using insights from personality psychology. Readers as yet unfamiliar with the language and theory of personality type may benefit from a brief introduction to that theory. It is for this reason that each volume carries the series introduction.

For the preacher

Looking over the edge of the pulpit into the faces of the congregation, it is not difficult to see that people differ. At the simplest level it is obvious how people differ by age and sex. Most preachers will observe the gender and age composition of their congregation and take this information into account in structuring and delivering their message. Without wishing to sort people too rigidly into categories, it seems just good common sense to recognize that one presentation might be more appropriate for the local Cubs or Brownies, another more appropriate for the Mother's Union, and yet another more appropriate for the Pensioners' Guild. It is clear that the experience and the expectations of the specific groups have to be taken into account.

In many ways preaching to a homogeneous group like the local Cubs or Brownies may be easier than addressing a large and mixed congregation. In one presentation the preacher is required to address the needs of the ageing widow, to acknowledge the concerns of the business executive, and to capture the attention of the restless child chorister. People differ and the preacher needs to be aware of the differences.

A particularly intriguing and useful account of how people differ is provided by Carl Jung and his theory of psychological type. The theory of psychological type suggests that it is helpful for preachers to take into account not only how the members of their congregation differ in outward ways, but also how they differ in their psychological preferences. Different psychological types may hear sermons in very different ways, and this has important implications for preachers.

For personal study

When a group of people meet to study a passage of scripture, it often becomes clear very quickly how different individuals may study the same passage in very distinctive ways. One member of the group may want to focus closely on the details of the text itself. Another member of the group may want to draw the wider implications from the text and make links with other or contemporary issues. Another member of the group may concentrate on lessons for practical living and for personal relationships. Yet another member of the group may wish to explore the theological implications of the text and the problems and challenges which it raises for faith.

Bible study groups which contain such a rich mix of people can be exciting for many Christians and open their eyes to the different ways in which scripture can enrich the lives of the people of God. When individual Christians meditate on scripture in the privacy of their own home they need to have their eyes opened to the variety of perspectives which can be brought to the same passage by other Christians who see things in a different way.

Carl Jung's theory of psychological type not only opens our eyes to the ways in which people differ, but also to the rich variety of perspectives within ourselves. The theory makes us more conscious of those parts of ourselves which we may undervalue and underexercise. Type theory concerned with the richness of our own psychological composition has important implications for how we allow ourselves to be nurtured and nourished by scripture.

The Myers-Briggs Type Indicator

It is Jung's theory of psychological type which stands at the heart of the Myers-Briggs Type Indicator, a psychological tool being increasingly used by the Christian churches. This theory identifies two main mental processes. The first process concerns the ways in which we gather information. This is the *perceiving* process. Some people prefer *sensing* (S); others prefer *intuition* (N). According to the theory, these two types look at the world in very different ways.

The second process concerns the ways in which we make decisions. This is the *judging* process. Some people prefer *thinking* (T); others prefer *feeling* (F). According to the theory, these two types come to decisions about the world in very different ways.

Jung also suggested that individuals differ in the *orientation* in which they prefer to employ these two processes. Some people prefer the outer or extraverting world (E); others prefer the inner or introverting world (I). According to the theory, these two types are energized in very different ways. Extraverts draw their energy from the outer world of people and things, while introverts draw their energy from their inner world.

Finally, individuals differ in their *attitude* to the outer world. Both introverts and extraverts need to deal with the outer world and both may prefer to do this with a *judging* (J) or a *perceiving* (P) process. According to the theory, these two types display a very different attitude to the outer world.

What the theory demonstrates by these preferences now needs to be explained in greater detail.

Introversion and extraversion

Introversion and extraversion describe the two preferred orientations of the inner world and the outer world. Introverts prefer to focus their attention on the inner world of ideas and draw their energy from that inner world. When introverts are tired and need energizing they look to the inner world. Extraverts prefer to focus their attention on the outer world of people and things, and draw their energy from that outer world. When extraverts are tired and need energizing they look to the outer world. Since this text is being written by an introvert, the author prefers to present this perspective first, followed by the extravert perspective.

Introverts like quiet for concentration. They want to be able to shut off the distractions of the outer world and turn inwards. They often experience trouble in remembering names and faces. They can work at one solitary project for a long time without interruption. When they are engaged in a task in the outer world they may become absorbed in the ideas behind that task.

Introverts work best alone and may resent distractions and interruptions from other people. They dislike being interrupted by the telephone, tend to think things through before acting, and may spend so long in thought that they miss the opportunity to act.

Introverts prefer to learn by reading rather than by talking with others. They may also prefer to communicate with others in writing, rather than face-to-face or over the phone; this is particularly the case if they have something unpleasant to communicate.

Introverts are oriented to the inner world. They focus on ideas, concepts and inner understanding. They are reflective, may consider deeply before acting, and they probe inwardly for stimulation.

Extraverts like variety and action. They want to be able to shut off the distractions of the inner world and turn outward. They are good at remembering faces and names and enjoy meeting people and introducing people. They can become impatient with long, slow jobs. When they are working in the company of other people they may become more interested in how others are doing the job than in the job itself.

Extraverts like to have other people around them in the working environment, and enjoy the stimulus of sudden interruptions and telephone calls. Extraverts like to act quickly and decisively, even when it is not totally appropriate to do so.

Extraverts prefer to learn a task by talking it through with other people. They prefer to communicate with other people face-to-face or over the phone, rather than in writing. They often find that their own ideas become clarified through communicating them with others.

Extraverts are oriented to the outer world. They focus on people and things. They prefer to learn by trial and error and they do so with confidence. They are active people, and they scan the outer environment for stimulation.

Sensing and intuition

Sensing and intuition describe the two preferences associated with the *perceiving process*. They describe different preferences used to acquire information. Sensing types focus on the realities of a situation as perceived by the senses. Intuitive types focus on the possibilities, meanings and relationships, the 'big picture' that goes beyond sensory information. Since this text is being written by an intuitive, the author prefers to present this perspective first, followed by the sensing perspective.

Individuals who prefer *intuition* develop insight into complexity. They have the ability to see abstract, symbolic and theoretical relationships, and the capacity to see future possibilities. They put their reliance on inspiration rather than on past experience. Their interest is in the new and untried. They trust their intuitive grasp of meanings and relationships.

Individuals with a preference for intuition are aware of new challenges and possibilities. They see quickly beyond the information they have been given or the materials they have to hand to the possibilities and challenges which these offer. They are often discontent with the way things are and wish to improve them. They become bored quickly and dislike doing the same thing repeatedly.

Intuitive types enjoy learning new skills. They work in bursts of energy, powered by enthusiasm, and then enjoy slack periods between activity.

Intuitive types follow their inspirations and hunches. They may reach conclusions too quickly and misconstrue the information or get the facts wrong. They dislike taking too much time to secure precision.

Intuitive types may tend to imagine that things are more complex than they really are: they tend to over-complexify things. They are curious about why things are the way they are and may prefer to raise questions than to find answers.

Intuitive types are always striving to gain an overview of the information around them. In terms of an old proverb, they may prefer to pay attention to the two birds in the bush rather than the one in the hand.

Intuitive types perceive with memory and associations. They see patterns and meanings and assess possibilities. They are good at reading between the lines and projecting possibilities for the future. They prefer to go always for the 'big picture'. They prefer to let the mind inform the eyes.

Individuals who prefer *sensing* develop keen awareness of present experience. They have acute powers of observation, good memory for facts and details, the capacity for realism, and the ability to see the world as it is. They rely on experience rather than theory. They put their trust in what is known and in the conventional.

Individuals with a preference for sensing are aware of the uniqueness of each individual event. They develop good techniques of observation and they recognize the practical way in which things work now.

Sensing types like to develop an established way of doing things and gain enjoyment from exercising skills which they have already learnt. Repetitive work does not bore them. They are able to work steadily with a realistic idea of how long a task will take.

Sensing types usually reach their conclusion step by step, observing each piece of information carefully. They are not easily inspired to interpret the information in front of them and they may not trust inspiration when it comes. They are very careful about getting the facts right and are good at engaging in precise work.

Sensing types may fail to recognize complexity in some situations, and consequently over-simplify tasks. They are good at accepting the current reality as the given situation in which to work. They would much rather work with the present information than speculate about future possibilities. They clearly agree with the old proverb that the bird in the hand is worth two in the bush.

Sensing types perceive clearly with the five senses. They attend to practical and factual details, and are in touch with physical realities. They attend to the present moment and prefer to confine their attention to what is said and done. They observe the small details of everyday life and attend to step-by-step experience. They prefer to let the eyes tell the mind.

Thinking and feeling

Thinking and feeling describe the two preferences associated with the *judging process*: they describe different preferences by which decisions are reached. Individuals who prefer thinking make decisions by objective, logical analysis. Individuals who prefer feeling make decisions by subjective values based on how people will be affected. Since this text is being written by a thinker, the author prefers to present this perspective first, followed by the feeling perspective.

Individuals who prefer *thinking* develop clear powers of logical analysis. They develop the ability to weigh facts objectively and to predict consequences, both intended and unintended. They develop a stance of impartiality. They are characterized by a sense of fairness and justice.

Individuals with a preference for thinking are good at putting things in logical order. They are also able to put people in their place when they consider it necessary. They are able to take tough decisions and to reprimand others. They are also able to be firm and tough-minded about themselves.

Thinking types need to be treated fairly and to see that other people are treated fairly as well. They are inclined to respond more to other people's ideas than to other people's feelings. They may inadvertently hurt other people's feelings without recognizing that they are doing so.

Thinking types are able to anticipate and predict the logical outcomes of other people's choices. They can see the humour rather than the human pain in bad choices and wrong decisions taken by others. Thinking types prefer to look at life from the outside as a spectator.

Thinking types are able to develop good powers of logical analysis. They use objective and impersonal criteria in reaching decisions. They follow logically the relationships between cause and effect. They develop characteristics of being firm-minded and prizing logical order. They may appear sceptical.

Individuals who prefer feeling develop a personal emphasis on values and standards. They appreciate what matters most to themselves and what matters most to other people. They develop an understanding of people, a wish to affiliate with people and a desire for harmony. They are characterized by their capacity for warmth, and by qualities of empathy and compassion.

Individuals with a preference for feeling like harmony and will work hard to bring harmony about between other people. They dislike telling other people unpleasant things or reprimanding other people. They take into account other people's feelings.

Feeling types need to have their own feelings recognized as well. They need praise and affirmation. They are good at seeing the personal effects of choices on their own lives and on other people's lives as well.

Feeling types are sympathetic individuals. They take a great interest in the people behind the job and respond to other people's values as much as to their ideas. They enjoy pleasing people.

Feeling types look at life from the inside. They live life as a committed participant and find it less easy to stand back and to form an objective view of what is taking place.

Feeling types develop good skills at applying personal priorities. They are good at weighing human values and motives, both their own and other people's. They are characterized by qualities of empathy and sympathy. They prize harmony and trust.

Judging and perceiving

Judging and perceiving describe the two preferred attitudes towards the outer world. Individuals who prefer to relate to the outer world with a judging process present a planned and orderly approach to life. They prefer to have a settled system in place and display a preference for closure. Individuals who prefer to relate to the outer world with a perceiving process present a flexible and spontaneous approach to life. They prefer to keep plans and organizations to a minimum and display a preference for openness. Since this text is being written by a judger, the author prefers to present this perspective first, followed by the perceiving perspective.

Judging types schedule projects so that each step gets done on time. They like to get things finished and settled, and to know that the finished product is in place. They work best when they can plan their work in advance and follow that plan. Judging types use lists and agendas to structure their day and to plan their actions. They may dislike interruption from the plans they have made and are reluctant to leave the task in hand even when something more urgent arises.

Judging types tend to be satisfied once they reach a judgement or have made a decision, both about people and things. They dislike having to revise their decision and taking fresh information into account. They like to get on with a task as soon as possible once the essential things are at hand. As a consequence, judging types may decide to act too quickly.

When individuals take a judging attitude towards the outer world, they are using the preferred *judging process*, thinking or feeling, outwardly. Their attitude to life is characterized by deciding and planning, organizing and scheduling, controlling and regulating. Their life is goal-oriented. They want to move towards closure, even when the data are incomplete.

Perceiving types adapt well to changing situations. They make allowances for new information and for changes in the situation in which they are living or acting. They may have trouble making decisions, feeling that they have never quite got enough information on which to base their decision.

Perceiving types may start too many projects and consequently have difficulty in finishing them. They may tend to postpone unpleasant tasks and to give their attention to more pleasant options. Perceiving types want to know all about a new task before they begin it, and may prefer to postpone something new while they continue to explore the options.

When perceiving types use lists they do so not as a way of organizing the details of their day, but of seeing the possibilities in front of them. They may choose never to act on these possibilities. Perceiving types do not mind leaving things open for last minute changes. They work best under pressure and get a lot accomplished at the last minute under the constraints of a deadline.

When individuals take a perceiving attitude towards the outer world, they are using the preferred *perceiving process*, sensing or intuition, outwardly. They are taking in information, adapting and changing, curious and interested. They adopt an open-minded attitude towards life and resist closure to obtain more data.

Personality type and preaching

The Myers-Briggs Type Indicator provides information about the individual's orientation (introversion or extraversion), perceiving process (sensing or intuition), judging process (thinking or feeling) and attitude towards the outer world (judging or perceiving). The crucial information for the preacher, however, centres on the two processes, that is to say on the two distinctions between sensing and intuition (the perceiving process) and between thinking and feeling (the judging process).

According to the theory, every individual needs to draw on all four functions of the two processes: sensing and intuition, thinking and feeling. But at the same time one of these four functions is preferred and becomes dominant. The four functions of sensing and intuition, thinking and feeling, when dominant, approach the world in very different ways. These different approaches will be attracted by very different perspectives in preaching.

At its most basic level, the sensing type needs to respond to facts and information, to details and clearly defined images. The intuitive type needs to respond to challenges to the imagination and arresting ideas, to theories and possibilities. The feeling type needs to respond to issues of the heart and to the stuff of human relationships. The thinking type needs to respond to issues of the head and to the stuff of logical analysis.

Of course, left to their own devices preachers will emphasize their own type preference. The preacher who prefers intuition will preach a message full of fast-moving ideas and imaginative associations. The sensing types in the congregation will quickly lose the thread and accuse those preachers of having their heads in the air and their shoes high above the ground. The preacher who prefers sensing will preach a message full of detailed information and the close analysis of text. The intuitive types in the congregation will quickly tire of the detail and accuse those preachers of being dull and failing to see the wood for the trees.

The preacher who prefers feeling will preach a message full of human interest and of loving concern for people. The thinking types in the congregation will quickly become impatient with this emphasis on interpersonal matters and accuse those preachers of failing to grasp the hard intellectual issues and the pressing challenges and contradictions of the faith. The preacher who prefers thinking will preach a message full of theological erudition and carefully argued nuance of perspective. The feeling types in the congregation will quickly become impatient with this emphasis on theological abstraction and accuse those preachers of missing the very heart of the gospel which cries out for compassion, understanding and human warmth.

Responding to the challenge

The theory of psychological types helps to clarify and to sharpen one of the problems confronting the preacher. There is no one simple solution to this problem, although being aware of the problem is itself an important step towards addressing it.

One suggestion is to try to include within the majority of sermons components which will speak directly to each of the four types: sensing, intuition, thinking and feeling. The problem with this solution is that the time generally allowed for preaching makes it difficult to develop all four perspectives in any depth. Evenly distributed, a ten-minute sermon would allow two and a half minutes on each perspective. A second suggestion is to try to vary the preaching style from week to week. In this sense perhaps an ideal preaching team should include four preachers representing the four psychological types. Few churches, however, may have such a resource readily available!

Our aim in this book has been to take 51 gospel passages from Luke included in the *Revised Common Lectionary* and to interrogate each passage from the distinctive perspectives of the four psychological types. For all 51 gospel passages we have followed the same disciplined pattern of exploring the four functions in the same fixed order: sensing, intuition, feeling and thinking. There is a logic in this order. We need the sensing function to ground us in the reality of the passage of scripture. We need the intuitive function to draw out the wider implications and to develop the links. We need the feeling function to become attuned to the issues of values and human priorities within the narrative. We need the thinking function to face the theological implications and to struggle with the intellectual issues.

We cannot imagine preachers wishing to follow this pattern slavishly week in and week out. But we can imagine preachers using this material in two main ways. On some Sundays we envisage sermons being preached which self-consciously present four different perspectives on the one gospel passage. We envisage congregations, as well as preachers, being aware of the reason for this. We envisage this process leading to a wider and better-informed discussion of the relevance of type theory for appreciating the diversity of perspectives and the diversity of gifts within the local congregation.

On other Sundays we envisage the preacher deliberately targeting one of the perspectives and developing that consistent line of presentation. We envisage individuals in the congregation representative of all four types being challenged to listen and to respond. We envisage this process leading to a deeper spiritual awareness as individuals gain closer contact with the less well-developed aspects of their inner self, and come to appreciate more deeply how the God who created us with diversity of gifts and diversity of preferences can be worshipped and adored through sensing as well as intuition, through thinking as well as feeling.

1

Luke 1:26–38

²⁶In the sixth month the angel Gabriel was sent by God to a town in Galilee called Nazareth, ²⁷to a virgin engaged to a man whose name was Joseph, of the house of David. The virgin's name was Mary. ²⁸And he came to her and said, 'Greetings, favoured one! The Lord is with you.' ²⁹But she was much perplexed by his words and pondered what sort of greeting this might be. ³⁰The angel said to her, 'Do not be afraid, Mary, for you have found favour with God. ³¹And now, you will conceive in your womb and bear a son, and you will name him Jesus. ³²He will be great, and will be called the Son of the Most High, and the Lord God will give to him the throne of his ancestor David. ³³He will reign over the house of Jacob for ever, and of his kingdom there will be no end.' ³⁴Mary said to the angel, 'How can this be, since I am a virgin?' ³⁵The angel said to her, 'The Holy Spirit will come upon you, and the power of the Most High will overshadow you; therefore the child to be born will be holy; he will be called Son of God. ³⁶And now, your relative Elizabeth in her old age has also conceived a son; and this is the sixth month for her who was said to be barren. ³⁷For nothing will be impossible with God.' ³⁸Then Mary said, 'Here am I, the servant of the Lord; let it be with me according to your word.' Then the angel departed from her.

Context

The opening two chapters of Luke's gospel set the story about Jesus clearly within the context, language and theology of God's activity among the Jewish people. In this world angels act as the messengers of God.

Sensing

Here before you stands the angel Gabriel. Open your eyes and see his form. See radiance in the face of one who lives in the presence of the living God. See strength in the limbs of one who carries messages from God to God's chosen people. See power in the wings of one who spans the distance from the divine throne to communicate with frail human beings. See compassion in the eyes of one who comforts, as well as disturbs, in the name of the almighty creator. Here before you stands the angel Gabriel. Open your eyes and see his form.

Here before you stands the angel Gabriel. Prick up your ears and hear his voice. Hear the voice of greeting as God's messenger bridges heaven and earth,

> Greetings, favoured one! The Lord is with you!

Hear the voice of comfort as God's messenger responds to Mary's concern,

> Do not be afraid, Mary, for you have found favour with God.

Hear the voice of authority as God's messenger spells out his commission,

> You will conceive in your womb and bear a son, and you will name him Jesus.

Hear the voice of prophecy as God's messenger looks into the future,

> He will be great, and will be called the Son of the Most High.

Here before you stands the angel Gabriel. Prick up your ears and hear his voice.

Here before you stands the angel Gabriel. Be still and feel his presence. Feel your heartbeat quicken as you sense the closeness to God. Feel your eyes widen as you see the bright light of God's messenger. Feel your mind buzz as you understand the message proclaimed. Feel your spirits lift as you realize the age of the Messiah is about to dawn. Here before you stands the angel Gabriel. Be still and feel his presence.

Here before you stands the angel Gabriel. Know that he stands there as the messenger of God. Know that he brings God's good news to Mary the Virgin. Here before you stands the angel Gabriel.

Intuition

Here is a story about God's total demand and about Mary's total response. What ideas does that spark in your mind?

We do not know what plans Mary was making for her future.

But we do know that she had plans. She was engaged to Joseph. While Mary was busy making her plans for the future, God was making alternative plans for her. God's plans disturbed Mary's plans. What ideas does that spark in your mind?

We do not know what plans Joseph was making for his future. But we do know that he had plans. He was engaged to Mary. While Joseph was busy making his plans for the future, God was making alternative plans for him. God's plans disturbed Joseph's plans. What ideas does that spark in your mind?

As responsible human beings, we must make plans for the future. We need to anticipate, to shape, and to prepare for the future. But while we are busy making our plans for the future, God may be making alternative plans for us. God's plans may disturb our plans. What ideas does that spark in your mind?

When Mary came face to face with God's plans, she had a choice: a choice between backing God's plans and backing her own plans. Mary said, 'Here am I, the servant of the Lord, let it be with me according to your word.'

When Joseph came face to face with God's plans, he had a choice: a choice between backing God's plans and backing his own plans. Joseph's actions spoke out the response, 'Here am I, the servant of the Lord, let it be with me according to your word.'

When we come face to face with God's plans, we, too, have a choice: a choice between backing God's plans and backing our own plans. When you have come face to face with God's plans, what have you said in the past? When you come face to face with God's plans, what will you say in the future?

Here is a story about God's total demand and about Mary's total response. What ideas does this spark in your mind?

Feeling

Here is a story about human fear; a story about how fear can be either exploited or expelled.

Gabriel must have been used to generating fear wherever he went. Gabriel was known to be the angel of the Lord and in his world the angel of the Lord carried power. Confronted with Gabriel, Mary's reaction was totally predictable. She was afraid. Gabriel could either exploit or expel her fear.

Mary must have been used to experiencing fear wherever she went. Mary was young, and in her world young people were

generally powerless. Mary was female, and in her world women
were generally powerless. Confronted with Gabriel, Mary's reaction was totally predictable. She was afraid. Mary's fear could
have been either exploited or expelled.

Here is a story about human fear; a story about how fear can
be either exploited or expelled.

For Gabriel, so used to generating fear, it would have been
all too easy to forget the impact of fear on others. Gabriel could
have interpreted Mary's acquiesence as proper respect and grateful thanks. Gabriel could have exploited Mary's fear and
imposed the divine will. But Gabriel put himself in Mary's
shoes, saw the encounter from her perspective and said, 'Mary,
do not be afraid.'

For Mary, so used to experiencing fear, it would have been
all too easy to go on living under the shadow of fear. Mary
could have dismissed Gabriel's injunction not to be afraid as
but one more sign of exploitation. Mary could have gone on
living under the shadow of fear. But Mary put herself in
Gabriel's shoes, saw the encounter from his perspective, and
accepted the divinely inspired message, 'Mary do not be afraid.'

Here is a story about human fear, and about the God who
drives out all fear.

Thinking

Luke, theologian and apologist, anticipates the questions in his
readers' minds. Who is Jesus of Nazareth? How does this Jesus
fit into God's scheme of things? How do we know that the
'new' religion founded on Jesus is the proper continuation of
the 'old' Jewish religion already securely accepted in the Roman
Empire? Luke addresses these questions through the authorita-
tive voice of the divine messenger, the angel Gabriel himself.

The angel Gabriel announces that this Jesus will be called
the Son of the Most High. For those who have ears to hear,
connection is made with messianic prophecy like 2 Samuel
7:14,

I will be a father to him, and he shall be a son to me.

Here is the first clear link to the Davidic Messiah.

The angel Gabriel announces that to this Jesus will be given
the throne of his ancestor David. For those who have ears to

hear, connection is made with messianic prophecy like Isaiah 9:6–7,

> For a child has been born for us, a son given to us . . . and there shall be endless peace for the throne of David . . .

Here is the second clear link to the Davidic Messiah.

The angel Gabriel announces that Jesus will reign over the house of Jacob for ever, and of his kingdom there will be no end. For those who have ears to hear, connection is made with messianic prophecy like Psalm 89:29,

> I will establish his line for ever, and his throne as long as the heavens endure.

Here is the third clear link to the Davidic Messiah.

The angel Gabriel announces that this Jesus will be called the Son of God. For those who have ears to hear, connection is made with messianic prophecy like Psalm 2:7,

> You are my son; today I have begotten you.

Here is the fourth clear link to the Davidic Messiah.

Luke, theologian and apologist, is clear that this Jesus has inherited God's promises made to the Jewish people.

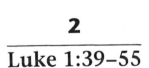

2

Luke 1:39–55

39In those days Mary set out and went with haste to a Judean town in the hill country, 40where she entered the house of Zechariah and greeted Elizabeth. 41When Elizabeth heard Mary's greeting, the child leapt in her womb. And Elizabeth was filled with the Holy Spirit 42and exclaimed with a loud cry, 'Blessed are you among women, and blessed is the fruit of your womb. 43And why has this happened to me, that the mother of my Lord comes to me? 44For as soon as I heard the sound of your greeting, the child in my womb leapt for joy. 45And blessed is

she who believed that there would be a fulfilment of what was
spoken to her by the Lord.'
      ⁴⁶And Mary said,
      'My soul magnifies the Lord,
            ⁴⁷and my spirit rejoices in God my Saviour,
      ⁴⁸for he has looked with favour on the lowliness of his
            servant.
            Surely, from now on all generations will call me blessed;
      ⁴⁹for the Mighty One has done great things for me,
            and holy is his name.
      ⁵⁰His mercy is for those who fear him
            from generation to generation.
      ⁵¹He has shown strength with his arm;
            he has scattered the proud in the thoughts of their
            hearts.
      ⁵²He has brought down the powerful from their thrones,
            and lifted up the lowly;
      ⁵³he has filled the hungry with good things,
            and sent the rich away empty.
      ⁵⁴He has helped his servant Israel,
            in remembrance of his mercy,
      ⁵⁵according to the promise he made to our ancestors,
            to Abraham and to his descendants for ever.'

Context

The opening two chapters of Luke's gospel present the three
songs of Mary, Zechariah and Simeon, known respectively as
Magnificat, *Benedictus* and *Nunc Dimittis* from the Latin Vulgate
translation. All three songs are a mosaic of Old Testament texts
which connect the story of Jesus with the established tradition
of the Jewish people.

Sensing

The song of Mary speaks to all four functions of the human
psyche. Here is a song of continuity with the past, a song of
stability and consistency. Here is a song that speaks to the
sensing person.

      The song of Mary is rooted in the promises made to our
ancestors, to Abraham and to his descendants for ever. Picture
in your mind the aged patriarch Abraham himself, and Sarah

his barren wife. Hear the promise proclaimed by God that Abraham would become the ancestor of a multitude of nations. Feel their joy as their son Isaac is born. Can you not hear them sing in unison with Mary, 'God's mercy is for those who fear him . . .'?

The song of Mary is rooted in the promises made to our ancestors, to Abraham and to his descendants for ever. Picture the Israelite people standing at the edge of the Red Sea. Feel the strong east wind drive back the sea to make a dry path. Join the pilgrim people as they cross to safety. Can you not hear them sing in unison with Mary, 'God has shown strength with his arm'?

The song of Mary is rooted in the promises made to our ancestors, to Abraham and to his descendants for ever. Picture the Egyptian chariots pursuing the Israelite people into the Red Sea. Hear the clatter of the chariots and the cries of the Egyptian soldiers as the sea rushes back across their path. Can you not hear the Israelite people sing in unison with Mary, 'God has brought down the powerful and lifted up the lowly'?

The song of Mary is rooted in the promises made to our ancestors, to Abraham and to his descendants for ever. Picture the Israelite people, pilgrims in the desert for forty years. Feel the hunger in their stomachs and join their cry as they appeal to the Lord for food. See their amazement as manna drops from the sky. Can you not hear them sing in unison with Mary, 'God has filled the hungry with good things'?

Mary's song is a song of continuity with the past; a song of stability and consistency.

Intuition

The song of Mary speaks to all four functions of the human psyche. Here is a song of vision which stretches our hearing and opens our eyes to the signs of God's activity in our own lives. Here is a song that speaks to the intuitive person.

Mary said, 'My soul magnifies the Lord.' Let Mary's song lead you out into the great open spaces of the world. Let Mary's song open your heart to the mystery of nature, to the magnitude of the night sky, to the depths of the deepest oceans. With Mary, let your spirit rejoice in the God who created you.

Mary said, 'My soul magnifies the Lord.' Let Mary's song lead you deep into the mysteries of the Christian faith. Let Mary's song open your heart to the profound love of Christ who died on the cross for the salvation of the whole world. Let Mary's song remind you of your own moment of salvation through the cross of Christ. With Mary, let your spirit rejoice in the saviour who redeemed you.

Mary said, 'My soul magnifies the Lord.' Let Mary's song lead you to experience anew the presence of the Holy Spirit working in the hearts of men and women. Let Mary's song open your eyes to the ways in which lives are transformed, new hope is given and old wounds are healed by the Spirit of the living God moving through our world. With Mary, let your spirit rejoice in the Holy Spirit who sustains you.

Mary's song is a song of vision which stretches our hearing and opens our eyes to the signs of God's activity in our own lives.

Feeling

The song of Mary speaks to all four functions of the human psyche. Here is a song of compassion, a song of concern for the poor and the oppressed. Here is a song that speaks to the feeling person.

The song of Mary proclaims good news to the homeless. The church of the Magnificat is a church concerned with the homeless in our own society; a church concerned with providing shelter, clothes and hot food for those who live rough on the streets of our cities. The God of the Magnificat fills the hungry with good things.

The song of Mary proclaims good news to the unemployed. The church of the Magnificat is a church concerned with the unemployed in our own society; a church concerned with creating jobs, with providing recreational centres, with restoring self-esteem. The God of the Magnificat lifts up the lowly.

The song of Mary proclaims good news to the elderly and the infirm. The church of the Magnificat is a church concerned with the elderly and infirm in our own society; a church concerned with creating sheltered accommodation, with organizing care schemes, with the practical provision of lunch clubs. The God of the Magnificat remembers such people in his mercy.

The song of Mary proclaims good news to the refugees and exiles. The church of the Magnificat is a church concerned with the displaced people who seek refuge in our own society; a church concerned with welcoming strangers into our community, with offering strangers the basic necessities of life. The God of the Magnificat fills the hungry with good things.

Mary's song is a song of compassion; a song of concern for the poor and for the oppressed.

Thinking

The song of Mary speaks to all four functions of the human psyche. Here is a song of justice, a song of concern for establishing truth and for seeing that right prevails. Here is a song that speaks to the thinking person.

The song of Mary issues the challenge of economic justice. Mary's voice makes us think seriously about the inequality in the distribution of resources. There is economic inequality between the rich and the poor in our society. There is economic inequality between the rich nations and the poor nations. There is economic inequality between those who have and the have-nots. What do you make of Mary's warning about the God who fills the hungry with good things and who sends the rich away empty?

The song of Mary issues the challenge of political justice. Mary's voice makes us think seriously about the imbalance between the powerful and the powerless. There is political inequality between the employee and the employer in our own society. There is political inequality between the strong dictator and the oppressed people in other places. There is political inequality between the developed world and the developing world. What do you make of Mary's warning about the God who brings down the powerful from their thrones and who lifts up the lowly?

The song of Mary issues the challenge of social justice. Mary's voice makes us think seriously about the unfairness with which human beings treat one another. There is social unfairness between the bully in the playground and the oppressed victim. There is social unfairness between the posh suburb and the inner city. There is social unfairness between the accepted and the despised. What do you make of Mary's warning about the God who scatters the proud in the thoughts of their hearts?

Mary's song is a song of justice; a song of concern for establishing truth and for seeing that right prevails.

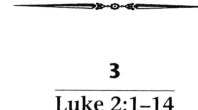

3
Luke 2:1–14

[1]In those days a decree went out from Emperor Augustus that
all the world should be registered. [2]This was the first registration
and was taken while Quirinius was governor of Syria. [3]All went
to their own towns to be registered. [4]Joseph also went from the
town of Nazareth in Galilee to Judea, to the city of David called
Bethlehem, because he was descended from the house and
family of David. [5]He went to be registered with Mary, to whom
he was engaged and who was expecting a child. [6]While they
were there, the time came for her to deliver her child. [7]And she
gave birth to her firstborn son and wrapped him in bands of
cloth, and laid him in a manger, because there was no place for
them in the inn.

[8]In that region there were shepherds living in the fields,
keeping watch over their flock by night. [9]Then an angel of
the Lord stood before them, and the glory of the Lord shone
around them, and they were terrified. [10]But the angel said
to them, 'Do not be afraid; for see – I am bringing you good
news of great joy for all the people: [11]to you is born this day
in the city of David a Saviour, who is the Messiah, the Lord.
[12]This will be a sign for you: you will find a child wrapped in
bands of cloth and lying in a manger.' [13]And suddenly there was
with the angel a multitude of the heavenly host, praising God
and saying,

[14]'Glory to God in the highest heaven,
    and on earth peace among those whom he favours!'

Context

In chapter one Luke has clearly anchored the story of Jesus
within the context, theology and language of God's activity in

the Old Testament. Now, in chapter two, God's activity is clearly located within the Roman Empire.

Sensing

Suspend your disbelief and allow the rich imagery of the Lucan Christmas story to feed your senses.

Suspend your disbelief and open wide your eyes. See two distant figures, weary figures, walking the dusty road from Nazareth to Bethlehem. See Joseph the young journeyman-carpenter. See Mary the young woman heavily pregnant. See the busy, bustling, overcrowded town of Bethlehem. See the inns and the lodging houses filled to capacity. See the humble cattle shed, the manger filled deep with hay. See the newborn baby who entered a world so unprepared for his birth. See the weary mother. See the anxious father. See the confused animals displaced from their eating place.

Suspend your disbelief and open wide your eyes. See many distant sheep scattered over the hillside. See their thick white fleeces reflecting the pale light of the shimmering moon. See the shabby tired shepherds wander through the night, committed to protecting their flocks from bandits and from wild beasts. See the lack of expectation, the lack of hope, the lack of promise in their world-weary eyes.

Suspend your disbelief and open wide your ears. Hear the first cries of the newborn infant. Hear the anguish of the mother. Hear the worry and concern of the father. Hear the steady munching of the beasts.

Suspend your disbelief and open wide your ears. Hear the voice of the angel ringing out across the pastures. Hear the message of the angel bringing good news of great joy. Hear the good news that today is born in the city of David a Saviour, who is the Messiah, the Lord. Hear the multitude of the heavenly host, praising God and saying,

Glory to God in the highest heaven,
and on earth peace among those whom he favours.

Suspend your disbelief, stir from your seat and follow those shepherds on their pilgrimage to the Christ-child.

Intuition

Allow your imagination full reign and let the rich imagery of the Lucan Christmas story nourish your faith.

Allow your imagination full reign and contemplate the mystery of Bethlehem. Translate the Hebrew name into 'House of Bread' and draw the connection with your Christian faith. There in the House of Bread is born the Christ who feeds you in the sacrament of the Eucharist under the guise of bread.

Allow your imagination full reign and contemplate the mystery of the manger. Translate the rough-hewn wood of the animal feeding trough now containing him who is the bread of life into the precious Eucharistic paten. There on the paten rests the body of Christ as you kneel to receive him at the altar rail.

Allow your imagination full reign and contemplate the mystery of the firstborn son. Recall how in the Old Testament Abraham was called by God to sacrifice his firstborn son, redeemed by the life of a ram. But there in the manger is the firstborn son whose life was given on the cross to redeem us all.

Allow your imagination full reign and contemplate the mystery of the shepherds watching over their flock by night. Recall how the prophet Micah foresaw a mother in labour giving birth in Bethlehem to one who will be shepherd to the scattered flock of Israel. There the shepherds come to the chief shepherd of them all.

Allow your imagination full reign and contemplate the mystery of the heavenly song. Then lift up your hearts and join in their eternal hymn of praise,

> Glory to God in the highest heaven,
>   and on earth peace among those whom he favours.

Feeling

Step aside from the romanticized view of Christmas and let the human story touch your heart.

Step aside from the romanticized view of Joseph. Step into his shoes and see the story through his eyes. According to the tradition Joseph had been living in Nazareth. Now he was being compelled to make the journey to Bethlehem to be registered by the Roman census. Joseph was living in an occupied land

and his life was disrupted by the occupying forces. How would you feel living in that situation?

Step aside from the romanticized view of Joseph. Step into his shoes and see the story through his eyes. According to the tradition the order to go to Bethlehem could not have come at a worse time. Joseph's wife was heavily pregnant, her first child due at any time. The journey was not good for a woman in her condition. The rooms in the inn were already fully booked. There was no maternity hospital in Bethlehem. Only the animals' feeding shed was available for the imminent birth. Joseph was a man living under pressure and on the edge of his reserves. How would you feel living in that situation?

Step aside from the romanticised view of Mary. Step into her shoes and see the story through her eyes. According to the tradition Jesus was Mary's first child. Now she is to experience the process of birth for the very first time. Now she longs for the support of her family and the security of her home. Instead she is in a strange place. Now she longs for the support of the women she knows so well. Instead she is surrounded by strangers. Mary was a woman whose time had come at the wrong time and in the wrong place. How would you feel living in that situation?

Step aside from the romanticised view of Mary. Step into her shoes and see the story through her eyes. According to the tradition, the angel Gabriel had promised Mary that she would give birth to the Son of the Most High. Yet she gave birth in the most lowly of places. The angel Gabriel had promised Mary that her son would reign over the house of David for ever. Yet she was visited by humble and confused shepherds. Mary was a woman confronted with paradox and contradiction. How would you feel living in that situation?

Step aside from the romanticized view of Christmas and let the human story touch your heart.

Thinking

The census is the key event on which the Lucan birth narrative hinges. Without the census Joseph's journey would never have been made from Nazareth to Bethlehem. Without the journey to Bethlehem the Messiah would not have been born in the city of David and the prophecy would not have been fulfilled. The question is whether Luke's interest in the census was primarily historical or theological. What do you think?

For centuries Luke was regarded as the *historian* among the gospel writers. After all, it is Luke who begins his gospel by offering a clear statement of historical method.

> I . . . decided, after investigating everything carefully from the very first, to write an orderly account.

What do you think?

Luke's account of the census, however, provides its own historical problems. Luke claims that a decree went out from the Emperor Augustus that all the world should be registered. Roman censuses tended to be conducted in different provinces at different times, and were usually conducted on the authority of the provincial governor. What do you think?

Luke's account of the census provides its own historical problems. Luke claims that the censuses took place while Quirinius was governor of Syria, and that the conception of John the Baptist and Jesus took place in the days of King Herod of Judea. Quirinius' census took place in AD 6–7 while Herod died in 4 BC. What do you think?

Luke's account of the census, however, provides its own clear theological rationale. In the Old Testament the prophet Isaiah had seen the foreign ruler Cyrus as the Lord's anointed one, empowered to restore God's people. The theological story of salvation employed the potential oppressors to work God's will. What do you think?

Luke's account of the census provides its own clear theological rationale. The fulfilment of God's prophecy to raise up a new Messiah from Bethlehem was brought about at the direct hand of the Roman Empire. In the light of such extraordinary divine guidance how on earth could the Roman Empire refuse to accept the faith founded on this new Messiah as the true heir to the Jewish tradition? What do you think?

The question is whether Luke's interest in the census was primarily historical or theological.

4

Luke 2:8–20

[8]In that region there were shepherds living in the fields, keeping watch over their flock by night. [9]Then an angel of the Lord stood before them, and the glory of the Lord shone around them, and they were terrified. [10]But the angel said to them, 'Do not be afraid; for see – I am bringing you good news of great joy for all the people: [11]to you is born this day in the city of David a Saviour, who is the Messiah, the Lord. [12]This will be a sign for you: you will find a child wrapped in bands of cloth and lying in a manger.' [13]And suddenly there was with the angel a multitude of the heavenly host, praising God and saying,

[14]'Glory to God in the highest heaven,
        and on earth peace among those whom he favours!'

[15]When the angels had left them and gone into heaven, the shepherds said to one another, 'Let us go now to Bethlehem and see this thing that has taken place, which the Lord has made known to us.' [16]So they went with haste and found Mary and Joseph, and the child lying in the manger. [17]When they saw this, they made known what had been told them about this child; [18]and all who heard it were amazed at what the shepherds told them. [19]But Mary treasured all these words and pondered them in her heart. [20]The shepherds returned, glorifying and praising God for all they had heard and seen, as it had been told them.

Context

In chapter one Luke already established the divine authority underpinning the story of Jesus through the voice of the angelic messenger. Now, in chapter two, the angel of the Lord announces the birth of Jesus to the shepherds.

Sensing

The angel who stood before the shepherds of Bethlehem brought a powerful message for those whose faith is nurtured by sensing. Here is an angel who understood the needs of men and women whose faith is rooted in the tangible and concrete world of everyday experience. This angel pointed to no distant ethereal mystery but to a small, living, newborn baby.

Shepherds, who lived by their senses, were called away from their night-time watch to go to Bethlehem and to see for themselves. There they saw the promised sign. They saw the child wrapped in bands of cloth and lying in a manger. The sense of sight called these shepherds to faith in the living God. Open your eyes and follow their gaze. Let your sense of sight lead you to the same faith in the living God.

Shepherds, who lived by their senses, were called away from their night-time vigil to go to Bethlehem and to hear for themselves. There they heard the promised sounds. They heard God's gift drawing breath as a human child, crying as a newborn babe. The sense of sound called these shepherds to faith in the living God. Open your ears and follow those sounds. Let your sense of sound lead you to the same faith in the living God.

Shepherds, who lived by their senses, were called away from their night-time fires to go to Bethlehem and to touch for themselves. There they held out their hands to the promised life. They touched the straw in the manger and held the hand that sustained their world. The sense of touch called these shepherds to faith in the living God. Open your hands and feel there the Body of Christ. Let your sense of touch lead you to the same faith in the living God.

Shepherds, who lived by their senses, were called away from their night-time duty to go to Bethlehem and to smell for themselves. There they breathed in the familiar smells of straw, animals and human life. The sense of smell called these shepherds to know that the living God was there in the middle of the world they knew so well. Breathe in and share these aromas. Let your sense of smell lead you to the same faith in the living God.

And so the shepherds returned, glorifying and praising God for the message that had spoken so powerfully to their senses,

Glory to God in the highest heaven.

Let your senses join in their song.

Intuition

The angel who stood before the shepherds of Bethlehem brought a powerful message for those whose faith is nurtured by intuition. Here is an angel who understood the needs of men and women whose faith is rooted in the intangible and intuitive world of their imagination. This angel did not rest content with the baby lying in the manger but pointed to good news of great joy for all the people.

The imagination of these shepherds was fired when the angel stood before them. The veil between heaven and earth was pulled back. In that moment the shepherds began to glimpse new hopes for the future, new possibilities for the days to come. Good news began to penetrate their consciousness. Can you, too, catch the vision?

The imagination of these shepherds was fired when the glory of the Lord shone around them. Their eyes were lifted from the earth to heaven. In that moment the shepherds began to glimpse new hope for the future, new possibilities for their lives. Good news began to flood through their souls. Can you, too, grasp the hope?

The imagination of these shepherds was fired when the angelic voices rang through the air. The sounds they heard were of this world but rooted in the world to come. In that moment the shepherds began to glimpse new hopes for the future, new possibilities for the world around them. Good news began to take over their way of seeing things. Can you, too, see the possibilities?

The imagination of these shepherds was fired when they set out on the pilgrim's path to Bethlehem. The journey they initiated was started in time but led into eternity. In that moment the shepherds began to glimpse new hopes for the future, new destinations hidden from human sight. Good news began to direct their path. Can you, too, step out in faith?

And so the shepherds returned, glorifying and praising God for the message that had spoken so powerfully to their imagination,

Glory to God in the highest heaven.

Let your imagination join in their song.

Feeling

The angel who stood before the shepherds at Bethlehem brought a powerful message for those whose faith is nurtured by feeling. Here is an angel who understood the needs of men and women whose faith is rooted in the subjective realm of human values and in interpersonal relationships. This angel pointed to no abstract theological principles, but to the lived-out faith of those touched by the hand of God.

The hearts of these shepherds were touched by the message, 'Do not be afraid.' Herein is a fundamental principle of life lived in the presence of God. Fear keeps one locked away in personal oppression. Fear keeps people apart, distanced by deep suspicion. Fear keeps God out, banished from seeing me for who I am. Life lived in the presence of God makes no room for fear. Has your heart been touched by that profound message of the angel, 'Do not be afraid'?

The hearts of these shepherds were touched by the message concerning 'news of great joy'. Herein is a fundamental principle of life lived in the presence of God. Joy lifts my spirits and brings me contentment with my own company. Joy brings people together and generates human fellowship and society. Joy sings the praises of God deep in my heart. Life lived in the presence of God makes room for joy. Has your heart been touched by that profound message of the angel concerning 'news of great joy'?

The hearts of the shepherds were touched by the message proclaiming 'on earth peace'. Herein is a fundamental principle of life lived in the presence of God. Peace enables me to sleep sound in my bed at night. Peace enables me to look others in the eyes. Peace welcomes the company and the scrutiny of God. Life lived in the presence of God makes room for peace. Has your life been touched by that profound message of the angels proclaiming 'on earth peace'?

And so the shepherds returned, glorifying and praising God for the message that had spoken so powerfully to their concern for human values,

Glory to God in the highest heaven.

Let your feeling join in their song.

Thinking

The angel who stood before the shepherds at Bethlehem brought a powerful message to those whose faith is nurtured by thinking. Here is an angel who understood the needs of men and women whose faith is rooted in the direct analysis of evidence, truth and logic. This angel did not rest content with the theatre of human activity but drew on the timeless realities of God's own revelation.

The minds of the shepherds were engaged by the title 'Saviour' so carefully given to the child by the angelic messenger. So how do you understand the term 'Saviour'? In days of old Moses had saved the people of God by leading them through the Red Sea to the promised land. Is Jesus a saviour like that? From what does Jesus save?

The minds of the shepherds were engaged by the title 'Messiah' so carefully given to the child by the angelic messenger. So how do you understand the term 'Messiah'? Literally the term refers to a person anointed by God. In days of old, David had been anointed king to lead and to rule over God's people. Is Jesus a Messiah like David? How was Jesus anointed?

The minds of the shepherds were engaged by the title 'Lord' so carefully given to the child by the angelic messenger. So how do you understand the term 'Lord'? The Greek word *Kurios* (translated Lord) was routinely used in the Greek Old Testament to translate the Hebrew name for God. In days of old, *Kurios* was reserved for God's own name. Was Jesus already to be affirmed as Lord and God?

And so the shepherds returned, glorifying and praising God for the message that had spoken so powerfully to their concern for truth,

Glory to God in the highest heaven.

Let your thinking join in their song.

5

Luke 2:22–40

²²When the time came for their purification according to the law of Moses, they brought him up to Jerusalem to present him to the Lord ²³(as it is written in the law of the Lord, 'Every firstborn male shall be designated as holy to the Lord'), ⁴and they offered a sacrifice according to what is stated in the law of the Lord, 'a pair of turtle-doves or two young pigeons'.

²⁵Now there was a man in Jerusalem whose name was Simeon; this man was righteous and devout, looking forward to the consolation of Israel, and the Holy Spirit rested on him. ²⁶It had been revealed to him by the Holy Spirit that he would not see death before he had seen the Lord's Messiah. ²⁷Guided by the Spirit, Simeon came into the temple; and when the parents brought in the child Jesus, to do for him what was customary under the law, ²⁸Simeon took him in his arms and praised God, saying,

²⁹'Master, now you are dismissing your servant in peace,
    according to your word;
for my eyes have seen your salvation,
    which you have prepared in the presence of all peoples,
a light for revelation to the Gentiles
    and for glory to your people Israel.'

³³And the child's father and mother were amazed at what was being said about him. ³⁴Then Simeon blessed them and said to his mother Mary, 'This child is destined for the falling and the rising of many in Israel, and to be a sign that will be opposed ³⁵so that the inner thoughts of many will be revealed – and a sword will pierce your own soul too.'

³⁶There was also a prophet, Anna the daughter of Phanuel, of the tribe of Asher. She was of a great age, having lived with her husband for seven years after her marriage, ³⁷then as a widow to the age of eighty-four. She never left the temple but worshipped there with fasting and prayer night and day. ³⁸At that moment she came, and began to praise God and to speak about the child to all who were looking for the redemption of Jerusalem.

³⁹When they had finished everything required by the law of

the Lord, they returned to Galilee, to their own town of Nazareth. ⁴⁰The child grew and became strong, filled with wisdom;
and the favour of God was upon him.

Context

The first two chapters of Luke's gospel locate the Christian story
firmly within the traditions of the Jewish people. This passage
shows how Jesus was nurtured in these traditions, and how they
point to Jesus' own transforming importance.

Sensing

Sometimes we only get hold of half the picture. Sometimes we
only get hold of half the picture because we stop listening
before the story is fully told. Stay and hear the story through.

Stay and listen to the story about Zechariah, the pious priest
serving in the temple. Listen to Zechariah lift up his voice and
prophesy,

> Blessed be the Lord God of Israel
> for he has looked favourably on his people.

Zechariah looks to a new future which will bring the knowledge
of salvation to God's people. Zechariah looks to a new future
which will bring light to those who sit in darkness. Picture
Zechariah's beard in your mind and give thanks for the way
God speaks through men. Sometimes we only get hold of half
the picture.

Stay and listen to the second half of the story, the story
about the pious maiden. This time listen to Mary lift up her
voice and prophesy,

> My soul magnifies the Lord
> and my spirit rejoices in God my saviour.

Mary looks to a new future which will fulfil the promises made
to her ancestors. Mary looks to a new future in which the lonely
will be lifted high and the hungry filled with good things. Now
picture Mary's flowing locks in your mind and give thanks for
the way God speaks through women. Sometimes we need to get
hold of the second half of the picture.

Stay and listen to the story about Simeon, the aged and

devout man serving in the temple. Listen to Simeon lift up his voice and prophesy,

Master, now you are dismissing your servant in peace.

Simeon looks to a new future which brings salvation to all people. Simeon looks to a new future which will bring light to the Gentiles. Picture Simeon's grey beard in your mind and give thanks again for the way God speaks through men. Sometimes we only get hold of half the picture.

Stay and listen to the second half of the story, the story about the pious widow serving in the temple. This time listen to Anna prophesying about the child to all who are looking for the redemption of Jerusalem. Now picture Anna's greying locks in your mind and give thanks again for the way God speaks through women. Sometimes we need to get hold of the second half of the picture.

Intuition

Letting go can be a problem. When we have worked really hard to build up a way of life, a way of doing things, it can be painful to see it pass away and something new stand in its place. The aged Simeon had invested all his years in the Jewish way of life, and yet now he welcomed its passing. Could you do the same?

Letting go can be a problem. When we have worked hard to build a church, to establish a style of worship, to create a fellowship, it can be painful to consider that God may be wishing to plant something new in its place. The aged Simeon had invested all his years in witnessing to the ritual of the temple, and yet now he welcomed its passing. Could you do the same?

Letting go can be a problem. When we have worked hard to establish *our* generation and our generation's way of looking at life, it can be painful to see young faces oust us from our position and stand where we had stood. The aged Simeon had invested all his years in looking for a better world, and yet now he welcomed the youngest of faces to stand where he had stood. Could you do the same?

Letting go can be a problem. When we have struggled all our lives to grow into the maturity into which God calls us, it can be painful to face the finite nature of our bodies and the decay

that awaits us. The aged Simeon had grown old in the service of
his Lord, and now embraced with joy the accomplishing of his
earthly service. Could you do the same?

Letting go can be a problem. Pray that God may give us
grace to outgrow that problem and to embrace change with that
quiet confidence which characterized the righteous and devout
prayer of Simeon,

> Master, now you are dismissing your servant in peace,
>   according to your word.

Feeling

Surely Mary must have become accustomed to facing the God
of surprises. Put yourself in her shoes and experience it all on
the inside.

It all began when the angel Gabriel announced that the
power of the Most High would overshadow her, that she would
conceive and bear a son, and that the child to be born would
be called the Son of God. Put yourself in Mary's shoes and
experience it all on the inside. Her world was turned upside
down. She had come face to face with the God of surprises.

It all continued when the shepherds made their way to
Bethlehem and greeted the weary mother and the newborn
child. It all continued when the shepherds unfolded the message, revealed to' them by the angel, that there is news of great
joy for all the people, that here is born in the city of David a
Saviour, who is the Messiah, the Lord. Put yourself in Mary's
shoes and experience it all on the inside. Mary had much to
treasure and to ponder in her heart. She had come face to face
with the God of surprises.

It all continued when the righteous and devout Simeon was
led by the Spirit into the temple. It all continued when Simeon
took the child in his arms and proclaimed that his eyes now
saw the salvation which God had prepared in the presence of
all peoples, that here is a child destined for the falling and
the rising of many in Israel, and that a sword would pierce
Mary's own soul too. Put yourself in Mary's shoes and experience it all on the inside. Mary had much to treasure and ponder
in her heart. She had come face to face with the God of
surprises.

It all continued when the holy and devout Anna was led by

the Spirit into the temple. It all continued when Anna began to praise God and speak about the child to all who were looking for the redemption of Jerusalem. Put yourself in Mary's shoes and experience it all on the inside. Her world was turned upside down. She had come face to face with the God of surprises.

Thinking

Simeon's song raised profound theological questions for his generation. What do you see to be the implications for our theology today?

Simeon had grown up with an exclusivist world-view. The theology of his generation encouraged nothing less. For his generation the world was clearly divided into God's people Israel and the Gentile nations of the world. Surely salvation was for the people of God, not for the nations of the world. What do you see to be the implications for our theology today?

Simeon shattered the exclusivist world-view with which he had grown up. The promptings of his God encouraged nothing less. For his God the salvation offered by Jesus had been prepared in the presence of all peoples. Here was a light for making God known to the nations of the world as well as for the glory of God's people Israel. What do you see to be the implications for our theology today?

Simeon proclaims an inclusivist world-view. The theology of the early Christian church rejoiced to know that in the eyes of the God of the Lord Jesus Christ there was neither Jew nor Gentile, but one salvation and one people. Now the good news once proclaimed in Jerusalem could travel to Rome and to the ends of the earth. What do you see to be the implications for our theology today?

Simeon proclaimed an inclusivist world-view. His song raised profound theological questions for his generation. Pray that today we may never lose sight of his vision.

6

Luke 2:41–52

⁴¹Now every year his parents went to Jerusalem for the festival of the Passover. ⁴²And when he was twelve years old, they went up as usual for the festival. ⁴³When the festival was ended and they started to return, the boy Jesus stayed behind in Jerusalem, but his parents did not know it. ⁴⁴Assuming that he was in the group of travellers, they went a day's journey. Then they started to look for him among their relatives and friends. ⁴⁵When they did not find him, they returned to Jerusalem to search for him. ⁴⁶After three days they found him in the temple, sitting among the teachers, listening to them and asking them questions. ⁴⁷And all who heard him were amazed at his understanding and his answers. ⁴⁸When his parents saw him they were astonished; and his mother said to him, 'Child, why have you treated us like this? Look, your father and I have been searching for you in great anxiety.' ⁴⁹He said to them, 'Why were you searching for me? Did you not know that I must be in my Father's house?' ⁵⁰But they did not understand what he said to them. ⁵¹Then he went down with them and came to Nazareth, and was obedient to them. His mother treasured all these things in her heart.

⁵²And Jesus increased in wisdom and in years, and in divine and human favour.

Context

This is the last part of the prologue foreshadowing the themes of the gospel. It relates a story from Jesus' boyhood. Luke shows us that 'from the boy comes the man'. As a boy, Jesus already possesses divine understanding and a relationship of obedience with God as his Father.

Sensing

Remember the time when you were twelve, a wonderful age of adventure and new thinking. At twelve you understood how things worked, your childhood horizons widened and the world, not the home, became the sphere of knowledge. Be a cousin and go with Jesus as a twelve-year-old. Leave behind your home village for your first trip to the big city at Jerusalem. There, leaders of the nation and the leaders of religion live. Feel the excitement as he shouts to you, 'This year in Jerusalem for Passover!'

On the road with Jesus rush backwards and forwards to greet other members of the family. You are all full of energy. Bring back the news of new sights and new learning. Let your eyes sparkle at the vista of the city and the vision of the temple in the heart of it. It is a marvel of architecture and a revelation of God. You will find the wise and the faithful there. It is God's dwelling. Sense the excitement of being twelve. Discover all the new places in the city.

Hear the anxious shouts of Mary and Joseph, 'Has anyone seen our son, Jesus? Oh, you twelve-year-olds, running off on your own as if there was no one else in the world. You think and act as if you were grown-up and you haven't any wisdom at all. Jesus is acting as if he doesn't belong to us.' Share their rising alarm on the second day of searching, and more again after a third day has passed. 'What could have happened to him?' Go searching with them.

Over there! See your cousin sitting with the rabbis, listening, arguing, questioning. Watch the learned men nodding in affirmation. Listen to their comments as Mary and Joseph approach. 'Your boy is a wonder. You should be proud of him. He's got the answers, and at such an early age. What does the future hold for him?'

Sense the strain in the mother's smile, proud and then angry. See the family take their leave with politeness and hurry off across the courtyard. Catch the fragments of the conversation, 'Your father and I . . . how could you do it?' . . . 'You must have known where I would be . . . Father's house' . . . 'Who do you think you are?' . . . 'Who am I?'

Every twelve-year-old has to work out who they are and form a vision of who they will be when they are grown-up. These are the questions of youth. Remember the time when you were twelve.

Intuition

Youth is the age of questioning. At twelve you know enough and are articulate enough to want to enter into the debate with adults about life and its meaning. It is a time for parents and children to sit down together to talk things through.

Growing up is a difficult process in any society. Each generation sees things in a different light. Young people see life as an adventure and throw caution to the winds. They reach for new boundaries. They debate every issue as if there was a clean slate and endless possibilities, never tried before. They question everything except their own limitations. Older people are protective of the young. Experience tells them life is hard. Realism has tempered their dreams. They have learnt the value of caution as well as courage. Youth and age approach the questions from different ends.

Dialogue is important for both generations. Asking questions is better than making statements. Luke records lots of questions. He tells us that Jesus sat with the elders, listening and asking them questions. The dialogue with his parents is a series of questions – one 'why?' is answered with another 'why?'. Questions sustain a dialogue. Questions are a gift from the young and gifts from the young at heart.

The festivals of a society are markers for young people in their growth to maturity. Festivals are times of family gathering and of heightened awareness. Christmas, Good Friday, Easter, Ascension, Pentecost, are not only opportunities for worship but also for dialogue about the life and teaching of Jesus and our reactions to them. For a Jewish boy the festival of Passover raises questions: Who am I? What is my relationship with God? What is my relationship with my community? Every twelve-year-old searches to find answers to such questions. These are the questions of youth. What is the response of the mature?

Feeling

There is a lot in this passage about interpersonal feelings. Put yourself in the place of Mary and Joseph and feel their pride, anxiety, bewilderment. Feel some of the excitement, assurance, commitment of Jesus. Feel the tension between them and the willingness of both sides to learn and to listen in love.

What feelings did Jesus have towards his parents? Surely he

was happy to be able to accompany them on their annual visit to Jerusalem. He would have felt supported by being trusted enough to be left in the care of the wider family for some of the time. He would have been thrilled to be able to debate issues with some of the men of learning. He would be puzzled at the lack of understanding by his parents about his relationship with God. He would be contented to be back in the family circle, showing and receiving affection and affirmation after forgiveness.

What feelings did Mary and Joseph have towards Jesus? Surely they were rightly protective of their son on his first visit to the big city. They were willing to take some risks now that he was twelve years of age. They would be proud to see their son take his place in the group of relatives and friends. They would be amazed to discover his level of wisdom and maturity. They would be annoyed at his disregard of time which cost them three days of extreme anxiety. They would be assertive of their role of being the true parent of such a child. They would love him dearly for his own good and for their later support.

This passage is full of feelings about interpersonal relation-ships. What would our feelings and reactions be in similar circumstances? These are the questions of youth and age.

Thinking

Why do you think that Luke included this little interlude about boyhood in his gospel? Was it simply a bridge between the birth narratives and the entry of John the Baptist with his call to repentance? Should we take this passage about Jesus' youth seriously? Surely it is possible to say that most young people 'increase in wisdom and in years, and in divine and human favour'.

We know that Luke is a craftsman of story and proclamation. Everything for Luke has a purpose and a plan. This reflects his conviction that the coming of Jesus and all that happened to him was in accordance with divine purpose. The coming of the Holy Spirit and the spread of the church was also in accordance with the divine plan. By including this passage Luke makes it clear that he believed such a plan was there from the beginning, right from the birth and boyhood of Jesus. The relationship between Jesus and God was also there from the beginning, not just in the circumstances of his birth but also in his growing up.

The passage shows Luke's belief that Jesus always knew that he was both son of Mary and Son of God. This will be affirmed by the voice at his baptism, but his knowledge of the relationship with God did not begin there. The ability of Jesus to understand the mind of God and reveal it through his life and teaching was not something that occurred when he began his public ministry. It was there even in his youth.

For Luke this incident foreshadows some of the great themes of the gospel which follow. These are the themes of sonship, of taking risks to accept new teaching, of searching for the truth, of being lost and found, of bewilderment and understanding. The ways of God do not change. They are there from our youth to our resurrection.

What do you think about the plan that God has for your life? Has it been at work through your birth and youth as well as your maturity? Has the potential of your youth been fulfilled in adulthood? These are the questions of youth that we weigh up when we are older.

———————◦◦◦——————

7
Luke 3:1–6

¹In the fifteenth year of the reign of Emperor Tiberius, when Pontius Pilate was governor of Judea, and Herod was ruler of Galilee, and his brother Philip ruler of the region of Ituraea and Trachonitis, and Lysanias ruler of Abilene, ²during the high-priesthood of Annas and Caiaphas, the word of God came to John son of Zechariah in the wilderness. ³He went into all the region around the Jordan, proclaiming a baptism of repentance for the forgiveness of sins, ⁴as it is written in the book of the words of the prophet Isaiah,

'The voice of one crying out in the wilderness:
"Prepare the way of the Lord,
    make his paths straight.
⁵Every valley shall be filled,
    and every mountain and hill shall be made low,

and the crooked shall be made straight,
and the rough ways made smooth;
⁶and all flesh shall see the salvation of God." '

Context

A new style of writing marks the opening of the proclamation of the Good News about Jesus Christ. The stage is set for Jesus by the work of John the Baptist. He is the forerunner who calls for repentance through baptism. The passage is set in history by reference to the various rulers who exercised authority in the area. The year is AD 26 or 27.

Sensing

Go out into the rough country of rock and heat near the River Jordan. Take a look at this strange character whom you have journeyed to see. Note his tall figure and straight back. Look into his eyes. They are sharp and bright and far-seeing. See in John the successor of the prophets of earlier times – Amos, Isaiah, Jeremiah. He has the same challenging stance. He seems to look straight at you when he calls for repentance. His salvation challenge rings out, 'Build a new road.' My ears catch the sound but I do not yet grasp the message.

Feel the heat of the deserted wild place, this earthquake rift at the bottom of which flows the cooling stream of river water. His message is like an earthquake shattering our complacency. Feel the burning heat of the sun. Feel the searing words of the prophet. The glare of the sun reflects off the stones and dazzles our eyes. Down below, the green water is enticing with its coolness and shade. Water will cool the body and refresh the soul. We must strip off our old dirty clothes and dip in the waters to find renewed life and salvation.

Hear the challenge in the prophet's voice,

The crooked shall be made straight,
and the rough ways made smooth.

There must not only be a change of heart but also a change in society. The conditions of life for others must be straightened out and smoothed with sympathy.

Smell the people around you. They are a curious mixture of those who have walked out of their current lives to follow the scent of something new. A dip in the water will cleanse them as well as renew their vigour.

Walk on down with the crowd to the river with the sense of anticipation of a great event. Be ready to follow. Be ready for what is to come. Be ready to do what is asked of you. Be ready to see the salvation of God.

Intuition

What is Advent? Is it not the season of preparation when we can examine our lives after the travel of another year? Advent takes us to the desert where we must focus on the harsh realities of life. The wilderness is no place for soft excuses.

Is not Advent a new period of time, the start of a new historical moment in our living? We live in history and we make history. History shapes us and by our actions we shape what is yet to be. Our actions do matter, not for ourselves alone but for our whole communities. Advent is a time to take stock and to take action.

Is not Advent a time for prophecy? Where are the prophets for our times? The word of God came to John and the prophet was filled with a message from God. It was God's word that touched his lips. His voice made it heard. Do we listen and respect the words of the prophets in our generation?

Is not Advent a time to seek forgiveness? Do we seek to avoid the opportunity and say, 'Can't I just enjoy the Christmas festival of love and hope without bringing sin into it? Surely there are enough deserts in life without reminding me of my own just before Christmas. What I want is a message of refreshment, not of repentance.' You cannot have one without the other!

Is not Advent a time of corporate responsibility? John's words about new roads imply the need for heavy earth-moving machinery. We do not have that type of resources as individuals. A corporate effort is required. The call implies radical restructuring, one level brought up and another level brought down to make it a level playing field. That is a society matter. How can we help society to be ready for Christmas?

Is not Advent a time to listen and a time to act?

Feeling

It is easier to take a look at interpersonal relationships at a distance. No wonder John went into the desert to work things out. I wonder what he felt about the society in which he lived and his relationships with people.

Imagine how John felt about the religious institutions of his day. His father Zechariah was a priest of the temple. I wonder how John related to the high priests of the past and the present. Surely it was their job to make God's presence real for people. They would have had strong feelings about John challenging and baptizing. What do we feel about the religious establishment of our day? How do we react to the tension when our hearts want to feel close to God in the liturgy of the church, and our ears must pay attention to the words of God spoken by the prophets?

Imagine how John felt about the civil authorities. The Roman Empire had brought the benefits of international communication, law and order, the protection of the rights of individuals through accountability to a power greater than the local dictator, better administration, respect for different religions, a kind of peace even if enforced by military power. Surely such advantages should be preserved by keeping on the right side of the civil authorities. What do we feel about our relationship with the state? It is hard to voice criticisms when so much is provided for us by the state.

Imagine how John felt about his father. Zechariah was an old faithful priest of a former generation. His faithfulness to the routine was remarkable. His God was fixed and sure. What did this rebel son feel about his father? Would they understand one another and if so how would they communicate? How do we feel about our parents? What is our relationship with them as we get ready for Christmas, the family festival which tests all relationships against the measure of love?

In our relationships, how can we achieve reconciliation with church, with government and with our family this Christmas?

Thinking

There is no doubt that Luke intends to root John the Baptist in the reality of the history of the time. John's voice speaks to a given situation. He speaks with power among the voices of power. His words are spoken in the context of the Roman Empire, not in the localized context of the tiny community in southern Galilee. When we think about it Luke is explaining that this is a worldwide message about salvation for every person, of every generation and place. His message is for the members of the early church as much as for the first hearers in the desert. It is a message for me. This is a wake-up call for all of humanity.

The message of this prophet is more powerful than the words of any emperor, governor, local prince or even religious authority. They are the backdrop. The prophet takes the foreground. God has spoken and the word must be proclaimed. Do we take notice of the message in such a context? Have we sat up and put our minds to its meaning for our lives?

What do we think about using the words of one prophet as a commentary on another? They stood generations apart, yet Luke uses Isaiah's words to define the role of John. Does God speak from generation to generation, ever making new in different contexts the eternal truths about life and our relationship with God? If our answer is 'Yes', then how do we hear the word of God for our context?

How does our intellect 'translate' prophetic pictures into practical outcomes? We know that the prophet is not talking about physical road-making but about practical proposals for our own readiness to receive Christ at Christmas (or at other times of incarnation in our world).

Luke's theme in the gospel is about the proclamation of Jesus Christ as Saviour of the whole world. His quotation from Isaiah makes this point by his inclusion of the words, 'All flesh shall see the salvation of God.' Mark only includes one verse about preparation and Matthew follows this pattern. Let Luke's vision shape our message during Advent. Do we concentrate on amendment of life or do we also think of ways to proclaim Jesus as Saviour of the world at Christmas? Luke would have us do both. Let us put our minds to it.

8
Luke 3:7–18

[7]John said to the crowds that came out to be baptized by him, 'You brood of vipers! Who warned you to flee from the wrath to come? [8]Bear fruits worthy of repentance. Do not begin to say to yourselves, "We have Abraham as our ancestor"; for I tell you, God is able from these stones to raise up children of Abraham. [9]Even now the axe is lying at the root of the trees; every tree therefore that does not bear good fruit is cut down and thrown into the fire.'

[10]And the crowds asked him, 'What then should we do?' [11]In reply he said to them, 'Whoever has two coats must share with anyone who has none; and whoever has food must do likewise.' [12]Even tax-collectors came to be baptized, and they asked him, 'Teacher, what should we do?' [13]He said to them, 'Collect no more than the amount prescribed for you.' [14]Soldiers also asked him, 'And we, what should we do?' He said to them, 'Do not extort money from anyone by threats or false accusation, and be satisfied with your wages.'

[15]As the people were filled with expectation, and all were questioning in their hearts concerning John, whether he might be the Messiah, [16]John answered them all by saying, 'I baptize you with water; but one who is more powerful than I is coming; I am not worthy to untie the thong of his sandals. He will baptize you with the Holy Spirit and fire. [17]His winnowing-fork is in his hand, to clear his threshing-floor and to gather the wheat into his granary; but the chaff he will burn with unquenchable fire.'

[18]So, with many other exhortations, he proclaimed the good news to the people.

Context

This passage is one of explanation which leads to expectation. John the Baptist explains how the call to repentance applies to particular groups in society. Then he builds up the expectation of the coming of the Messiah, pointing to Jesus whose baptism brings salvation (God's Spirit) and judgement (God's fire).

Sensing

Feel your heart beating as the preacher calls you a 'brood of vipers'. Your blood is boiling at such an insult. This preacher's message is startling in its bluntness. No one is allowed to escape from facing this challenge to repentance. It applies to all, you included.

Feel your ears tingle as the words strike home to you. Feel the embarrassment at not being able to hide behind the cloak of respectability. The words cut to your heart as surely as an orchard-owner cuts out a tree that fails to bear fruit. It may look like a fruit tree, but without fruit it is only good for burning.

Take your place in the crowd. Look into the piercing eyes of the prophet as he identifies your role in society: 'Change the way you do what you do. There is no need to change your occupation. Your job may be difficult, but still do it differently with a spirit of honesty, love and respect.'

Feel your heart thumping as you face the challenge and apply the call to your own work and witness. With the coming of the Messiah, God's rule is being revealed with salvation and with judgement. When God is at hand things must happen now.

Hear yourself say, 'That's it' when the word of God identifies what things must be done. Feel the excitement of a new way of life for yourself and those around you. Sense the anticipation that Christmas will be different as we all change the way we act towards one another.

Smell the roast of meat that you will share with your neighbours. Feel the joy of generosity as you pay your taxes gladly. Touch the hand of the desperate and see the smile of restored dignity. Kneel in humble expectation to receive the Messiah's blessing, bringing salvation and judgement, hand in hand.

Intuition

What are the issues about baptism that this passage raises for you? John restricts his baptism to water for cleansing. Jesus' baptism is different. It will be with the Holy Spirit and with fire. Do you question the adequacy of your own baptism in water? Do you claim baptism in the Holy Spirit is superior to baptism in water? What does the image of baptism say to you?

What are the issues about fire that this passage raises for

you? Does the thought of fire disturb you with memories of threats that God will commit the sinful to the fires of hell? Where is God's judgement when we see such evil persisting all around us in society? We rejoice at Christmas because we hear of the birth of the Saviour. How does the Saviour judge us as well as save us? The image of fire on the Christmas card is the fire burning in the hearth to bring warmth and joy, not of fire burning in the heart to destroy evil. What does the image of fire say to you?

What are the issues that the picture of the slave and the sandals raises for you?

Untying sandals that had trodden through dust and dung was a smelly job to be carried out by a captured slave. If the slave was a Jew it would not be their task; their race was too dignified for that. Why then does John cast himself with the foreigner and the lowest of the low? After all, he is Jesus' cousin. Both of them were honoured with the title of teacher. John had been first on the scene and had won popular support. Why does he seem to grovel so low before Jesus? What does the image of the slave and the sandals say to you?

What are the issues that the reference to money raises for you? Are you obliged to go through your wardrobe and give away half of it to the poor? Can you have a feast without feeling guilty that some will have so little? What level of sharing are you to reach – 10 per cent or 50 per cent? When is enough, enough? What does the image of money say to you?

This passage raises a number of issues. What is your response?

Feeling

As we read the message of John the Baptist we are challenged to reconsider our feelings towards others. Our duty to God is worked out in the fulfilment of God's command to care for our neighbours. Each of the groups who came to John asked him to tell them how they should act in their social dealings with others. As we listen to John's answers we can feel ourselves standing in the shoes of the various groups. John did not tell them to pray more or to believe differently but to act more fairly towards those they encountered in their daily occupations.

What do you feel about relationships in the workplace? Do

you treat those you meet as an opportunity for self-aggrandizement, or generators of income, or fellow-workers for the good of all? Your actions towards them will demonstrate the salvation and judgement of the Messiah among them.

What do you feel about relationships in the shops this Christmas? Be a shopkeeper who tries to make a fair living from the trade and not one who makes a killing from the profit on things people neither need nor can afford. Be a customer who respects the shop assistants and treats them as people rather than servants or sharks.

What do you feel about your relationship to God? Do you feel you have a privileged position as a 'descendant of Abraham', part of the known family of God? Or do you see yourself as an outsider like a tax collector, as a traitor to the cause? Be humble but do not feel overawed by God. Allow yourself to be embraced as God welcomes you back as a repentant child.

How do you feel about the law-and-order agencies: the armed forces personnel, police and traffic officers? Put yourself in their position. Many see them as tainted by violence. Others welcome them as fighters for peace. At worst they are enemies to be loved; at best protectors of our lives at risk to their own. Feel for them this Christmas as they try to prevent goodwill becoming evil deeds.

Christmas brings us close to so many people. In your relationships share the hope of salvation and the necessity of judgement with those you meet.

Thinking

The debate about good and evil has dominated both theology and philosophy. The difficulty is to hold together the need to promote the good and to restrain the evil. It is impossible for good to flourish if evil is allowed to exist without being overcome.

Here, treasuring the wheat and burning the chaff is used to illustrate the debate about good and evil.

Think about this question: How can God promote the good without damaging those who do the evil? How can the bad be destroyed without the destruction of bad people? Is hell-fire a necessary principle in God's good world? We are obliged to live with the consequences of our actions, and we leave their legacy to our children. What can save us from our own evil and from the evil of others? The answer needs to be as definite and practical as the answers that John the Baptist gave to those who put questions to him.

Consider our prison system. How can society uphold both the promise of salvation and the reality of judgement? What is redemptive judgement and restorative justice in prisons? Punishment is often destructive as the number of suicides shows. What alternatives can we find to express the judgement of society and the salvation of sinners? We must collectively put our minds to such issues and not just leave them to the 'authorities'. We cannot claim that the kingdom of God has come in Christ, without facing up to the fact that our prisons are full to overflowing and many are repeat-offenders.

The final verse is one of hope, proclaiming good news to all people. That must include the prisoner as well as the perfect. No one is outside the circle of God's love, God's concern and God's promise to those who want to repent and begin a new life in the power of the Holy Spirit.

Think about Jesus as the Judge *and* the Saviour, and greet him with joy.

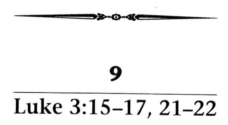

9
Luke 3:15–17, 21–22

¹⁵As the people were filled with expectation, and all were questioning in their hearts concerning John, whether he might be the Messiah, ¹⁶John answered them all by saying, 'I baptize you with water; but one who is more powerful than I is coming; I am not worthy to untie the thong of his sandals. He will baptize you with the Holy Spirit and fire. ¹⁷His winnowing-fork is in his hand, to clear his threshing-floor and to gather the wheat into his granary; but the chaff he will burn with unquenchable fire.'

²¹Now when all the people were baptized, and when Jesus also had been baptized and was praying, the heaven was opened, ²²and the Holy Spirit descended upon him in bodily

form like a dove. And a voice came from heaven, 'You are my Son, the Beloved; with you I am well pleased.'

Context

The baptism of Jesus is the final act of John's ministry in this gospel. He has prepared well for Jesus. The people have responded to his call to repent and be baptized. John's hopes are fulfilled as Jesus appears before him and receives baptism. In two final verses Luke describes for us the nature of Jesus, his relationship with God, and the presence of the Holy Spirit.

Sensing

Take your place in the swelling crowd of those who have gone out to hear this prophet and have fallen under his spell and accepted baptism. Stand in the cool waters of the River Jordan as it flows downstream carrying your sins away like the dust and dirt from off your tired feet. Feel yourself invigorated by the refreshing water and the expectancy in the crowd that something new is about to begin.

Watch as Jesus descends into the waters after you and John goes over to him. All the crowd follow John with their eyes as he moves over to where Jesus is standing in the waist-deep waters. Up to that point John has stood in the river and all the people have come to him. Now he moves towards Jesus as he steps down into the Jordan. Observe the two men look at one another with joy and expectation. Jesus looks up to the heavens in prayer. His lips move as if he is talking with one whom he knows well.

Let your eyes follow his and see the heavens open to let a shaft of new light come through and rest on Jesus' head. The light is bright but gentle. It reaches like a rainbow from heaven to earth. At the end of the radiance there seems to be a physical form. It looks like a dove. In the story of Israel the dove is the servant of God. In the story of the Ark the dove is the symbol of promise and the hope of new life.

Open your ears to hear the sound from heaven. Someone in the crowd interprets it from the scriptures, repeating the words of the Messianic Psalm (2:7) 'You are my son.' Another adds a verse from Isaiah (42:1) describing God's servant as 'my chosen one with whom I am well pleased'. Feel the intense excitement. We have all experienced something of the wonder of the presence of God and the joy of a new era. We have seen the dove. We have witnessed the Son.

Intuition

Baptism is a powerful experience for us all. We may have been baptized as a young child or at an age when we were conscious of our response to God and the feel of the water. Whatever our age at baptism we are now aware of what God has done for us. In our baptism it is not our worthiness or even our faith that is dominant. It is God's amazing grace that names us as a child of God. It is God's amazing goodness that allows us to share in the life and witness of the Holy Spirit. It is God's faith in us that we can fulfil our role as servant of God.

Baptism is an affirmation from God. Affirmation is essential for human beings to feel valued and esteemed, not for what they do but for what they are. Affirmation is part of being loved. At his baptism Jesus hears this affirmation from God: 'You are my child. You are my loved one. You bring me only pleasure.' Our own baptism gives us similar affirmation.

Divine affirmation needs human confirmation to embody it. When did we last affirm another human being? If we are a parent, when did we last affirm our child of whatever age? When did we affirm others in our workplace or home setting? Affirmation builds up the relationship of love and gives hope and confidence. Affirmation does not deceive with false words of praise. It speaks of the value of the person and the relationship rather than the work or the worthiness of the other.

For Jesus the Holy Spirit is embodied as a dove. How do we experience the Holy Spirit? Jesus relates to the Spirit as part of the intimate and personal relationship within the Godhead. We can experience the Spirit in Christ and through Christ. We can experience the Spirit in its own right as the way that we are in touch with the divine. From our baptism we can explore that relationship and find something of the gentleness, the patience, the warmth and the richness of God. Is not the dove a suitable embodiment of these qualities?

Feeling

Imagine how John the Baptist must have felt about his relationship with Jesus. Up to that point John had been the prominent
person. People had streamed out into the wild to listen to the
prophet. He spoke with the challenge of justice like Amos; with
the hope and covenant love of Hosea; with the power and
majesty of Isaiah; with the promise and judgement of the
people of God like Jeremiah; and with the certainty of the
saving work of God like Elijah.

With Jesus taking centre stage, imagine how John felt. Put
yourself in his place. Are you able to step aside with pride
because you have done the task of preparation for which you
were chosen? Can you be sure that your cousin would faithfully
carry on your work and message? Do you feel anxious that you
will be forgotten in the years to come and that people will only
remember the Messiah? Can you handle your feelings in such a
situation?

It takes humility to work in a team. When the time is
right can you hand over to your successors in the task? Can
you affirm that you are not the one to take the key position
without feeling put down or without putting others down? It
is difficult to be one of a team, especially a less important
player.

Imagine what it would be like to be full of the Holy Spirit.
The Holy Spirit is claimed as a source of God's power, yet its
symbol is a dove. This is the symbol of gentleness and servanthood. It is the symbol of sacrifice. How does this shape your
feelings of being powerful? If the Spirit's power enables people
to be servants of God, how should we relate to others? The
Spirit is the Spirit of fellowship. It enables people to work as a
team. The gifts of the Spirit stimulate the power to create and
sustain the necessary fellowship for relationships.

Thinking

Luke introduces the concept of 'Messiah' early in his gospel.
The word is used in the Hebrew to focus the concept of a person
anointed by God to be the leader of God's people. It was used
of Samuel and David as the ideal leaders, those who were subject
to the law of God and who established God's rule. The Messiah
was to be the king who held power from God and on behalf of

God, but who did not hold power in his own right or for his own honour.

At the Exile the people of God prayed for a new leader who would faithfully carry out the will of God, not for his own benefit but for that of the people of God. When the country was taken over under the power of the Roman Empire, the Jewish people began to formulate an idealism that a Messiah would arise who would restore the power to God and would rule over a kingdom where justice and truth would be established. The dilemma which faced such a Messiah was to choose an acceptable method by which to establish such a rule. Could force be used to overcome force? Could guile be used to out-manoeuvre the opposition? Could flattery be used to win over influential people?

Luke avoids the word 'anointed' in his description of the baptism of Jesus. The Holy Spirit 'descends' upon Jesus at prayer. The voice from heaven declares Jesus to be 'Son' and 'the Beloved'. There are close associations here with anointing and kingship, but the words are not used as such. The reader is left to puzzle out the connections. Is Jesus the Messiah, or is his role of leadership to be exercised in a different way? Does his power lie in force or in servanthood? The Son is indeed different from the servant, but how?

The same challenge faces us as we think about Jesus. Who is he in relationship to our understanding about God? How does he exercise power on our behalf? What do we expect from the announcement that the Holy Spirit has descended upon Jesus?

10

Luke 4:1–13

¹Jesus, full of the Holy Spirit, returned from the Jordan and was led by the Spirit in the wilderness, ²where for forty days he was tempted by the devil. He ate nothing at all during those days, and when they were over, he was famished. ³The devil said to

him, 'If you are the Son of God, command this stone to become a loaf of bread.' ⁴Jesus answered him, 'It is written, "One does not live by bread alone."'

⁵Then the devil led him up and showed him in an instant all the kingdoms of the world. ⁶And the devil said to him, 'To you I will give their glory and all this authority; for it has been given over to me, and I give it to anyone I please. ⁷If you, then, will worship me, it will all be yours.' ⁸Jesus answered him, 'It is written,

> "Worship the Lord your God,
> and serve only him."'

⁹Then the devil took him to Jerusalem, and placed him on the pinnacle of the temple, saying to him, 'If you are the Son of God, throw yourself down from here, ¹⁰for it is written,

> "He will command his angels concerning you,
> to protect you,"

¹¹and

> "On their hands they will bear you up,
> so that you will not dash your foot against a stone."'

¹²Jesus answered him, 'It is said, "Do not put your God to the test."'

¹³When the devil had finished every test, he departed from him until an opportune time.

Context

Before describing the opening of Jesus' ministry in Galilee, Luke sets out a time of testing which Jesus experienced. Empowered by God through baptism to fulfil the role of leadership, Jesus had to decide how he could achieve his goals and how to use the power he had been given. This time of trial was but the beginning of a continual testing of the appropriate methods to combat the stubborn evil within humanity.

Sensing

Stand there in the heat of the deep rift through which the River Jordan flows. Experience the solitude of this deserted place providing space for thought, but in the darkness lions may hunt; in the shadows images of demons may hide. Look about you; here life is raw and is reduced to the basics. The outward wilderness reflects the struggle within the human heart and soul.

Feel the flat stones shimmering in the heat. In your hunger touch them. They feel like loaves of hot bread that have just come from the oven. Should we not use the power of God to provide for our own needs? Should we not feed the hungry with the power that God has given us? Then all the world will believe in God. Is not this a proper use of power?

Hear the inner voice that whispers, 'Do it my way. Everything will be alright. The ends will justify the means!' Listen to the subtle words, 'Just acknowledge my power and I can make things go right for you. A little cunning, a little manipulation of the truth, a little ingratiating yourself with the right people, a little false humility, a few secret deals – it could all work well for you in the end.' What is wrong with using all the different ways possible to achieve your goal?

See the crowd that John attracted. You can do anything with crowds if you are clever enough. They only ask for a miracle or two. They will hail you as Messiah if you demonstrate your power in some sparkling spectacle. Jumping from the temple parapet would do the trick.

Hear Jesus say, 'Only God's way is right.' People in the end will not believe in God because they are fed or manipulated or stunned. Do not fool yourself. There is only one way into the kingdom of God; the entrance is narrow though many wide paths lead down the slippery road to destruction.

Intuition

What are the modern equivalents of the temptations of Christ? How do we work through our own struggle for power?

Evangelism through social justice: is not that the best method to use to bring in God's kingdom? Feed the hungry and that will restore their dignity as human beings. Food aid is the best way to spread the gospel; it is so tangible and practical. Nice words were never a good substitute for a good dinner on an empty stomach. Once people see Christians caring for them, then they will believe in God – or will they? Jesus said, 'One does not live by bread alone.'

Power evangelism is popular. What methods are appropriate to persuade people of the truth of the gospel? Why not simplify things down to a few basics, even if that means distorting matters a bit? For the purposes of evangelism why not extract out of Jesus' message the parts that will have popular appeal?

You can always find some good in the opposition's way of doing things. You can use scientific method to explain away all the difficulties in the Christian message: creation can become evolution; prayer can be explained as technical communication with God; the feeding of the five thousand can be interpreted in terms of each social group sharing their food. There is no need for mystery if you follow other methods of explanation.

Signs and wonders are the key to conversion. Just wait upon God's Spirit and you can be sure of something spectacular. Speaking in tongues is essential for evangelism. Divine healing gives proof of the existence of God. All this study of the scriptures is a waste of time. Just believe it all with open trust and God will bless you with abundant prosperity.

What other examples test Christians' use of power today?

Feeling

Put yourself in the place of Jesus as he has a great religious experience. Feel yourself being 'filled with the Spirit', on top of the world and ready for anything.

Sense a new relationship with God and with your fellow human beings. Feel that God has given you great power and authority.

Put yourself in Jesus' sandals after his baptism and the experience of the Spirit. Now you must be ready to provide leadership and miracles of grace: healing the sick, feeding the hungry, declaring God's truth, convincing people of your authority. Remember your own experience of God at baptism, commitment, conversion or confirmation. What values have you used to change the world with the power of God?

Put yourself in Jesus' sandals in the wilderness. God's Spirit said 'Wait' and asked difficult questions about *how* things might be achieved. There is this inner struggle before we are fit to serve. Now recall your own experience of doubt after everything seemed so certain. You probably had doubts about the meaning of scripture. You probably had doubts about the best method to share the good news that you had discovered. You probably had doubts about God's ability to confirm your words with deeds of power. Your doubts kept you in the wilderness of uncertainty, hungry to get on with the task but confused as to the best way to take the gospel to those around you. This struggle was important to clarify your principles of service.

Put yourself in Jesus' sandals. Ask yourself, 'Was the voice you heard from God or from the tempter?' Sometimes it is difficult to tell the difference. When you relate to God and then have to relate to evil does talk of the devil send shivers up your spine or can you face up to evil as part of your growth to maturity?

How comfortable do you feel in Jesus' sandals?

Thinking

When you think about it, all our thinking puts God to the test. We are called upon to work things out in our minds. We are not robots who accept everything in blind faith.

This passage proves that Jesus had to test out the methods appropriate for his ministry. He had to apply his mind to the problems of textual criticism. The bible could not be taken literally without clashes between the meaning of different verses. There had to be interpretation and application. How do you use your judgement in interpreting scripture? Does God's protection mean that you can take any risk and God will keep you safe? Does Luke imply that the old idea of protection is superseded because of the experience of the cross?

Luke indicates that these temptations were part of a continual struggle within the mind of Jesus about power and the methods of ministry. Is this a 'summary' scene rather than an actual experience of Jesus? Does your response to this question make a difference to your understanding of Jesus' ministry?

Luke alone puts the testing in the temple as the conclusion. How does this link the temptations to the Passion narratives? Should we consider the Passion events as another part of the testing of Jesus' ministry? Was the resurrection a miracle to enforce belief? What do you think?

When you think about it should the 'devil' have a small 'd' or a capital 'D'? Luke depicts the Evil One talking, debating, claiming authority. Is this symbolic language or does it refer to a real event? What is your attitude to the D/d-evil? What do you think?

This passage sets the scene as the framework for the ministry of Jesus in Galilee and Jerusalem in the gospel of Luke. Does the gospel record keep faith with the principles expressed here? In the light of the temptations, what do we make of the feeding of the five thousand and the miracles of healing? Would it be more rational to think that Jesus had to work out his ministry methods in the light of ongoing experience rather than have a plan formulated at the beginning? Maybe this is what Luke means by indicating in the last verse that the testing went on throughout the whole of Jesus' ministry. Does it help you to understand the gospel as a whole to have this summary at the beginning?

This is a key passage to understand better the place of power in the ministry of Christ.

11

Luke 4:14–21

¹⁴Then Jesus, filled with the power of the Spirit, returned to Galilee, and a report about him spread through all the surrounding country. ¹⁵He began to teach in their synagogues and was praised by everyone.

¹⁶When he came to Nazareth, where he had been brought up, he went to the synagogue on the sabbath day, as was his custom. He stood up to read, ¹⁷and the scroll of the prophet Isaiah was given to him. He unrolled the scroll and found the place where it was written:
¹⁸'The Spirit of the Lord is upon me,
   because he has anointed me to bring good news to the
      poor.
He has sent me to proclaim release to the captives
   and recovery of sight to the blind,
      to let the oppressed go free,
¹⁹to proclaim the year of the Lord's favour.'
²⁰And he rolled up the scroll, gave it back to the attendant, and sat down. The eyes of all in the synagogue were fixed on him. ²¹Then he began to say to them, 'Today this scripture has been fulfilled in your hearing.'

Context

At Jesus' baptism, according to Luke in chapter three, the Holy Spirit descended upon him in bodily form. In chapter four the Holy Spirit led Jesus in the wilderness. Then 'filled with the power of the Spirit' Jesus returned to Galilee. Now the scripture from Isaiah interprets what is taking place.

Sensing

Jesus grew up in quite a different world from the world in which we grow up today. In our world the accent is on the global. In Jesus' world the accent was on the local. To grasp the power of Nazareth in Jesus' life, we must first recapture the power of the local.

Picture the local world that Jesus knew so well. Picture Nazareth where Jesus had grown up. Picture the houses: the houses are so so familiar. Picture the streets: the streets are so so familiar. Picture the faces of the people: the faces of the people are so so familiar. Jesus knew everyone by sight. Everyone knew Jesus by sight. In Jesus' world the accent was on the local.

Listen to the local world that Jesus knew so well. Listen to the sounds of Nazareth where Jesus had grown up. Listen to the hammering in the carpenter's shop: the sound of the hammer is so so familiar. Listen to the sheep in the fields: the sound of the animals is so so familiar. Listen to the sounds of the people: the voices of the people are so so familiar. Jesus knew everyone by the sound of his or her voice. Everyone knew Jesus by the sound of his voice. In Jesus' world the accent was on the local.

Smell the local world that Jesus knew so well. Sniff the smells of Nazareth where Jesus had grown up: the rich aroma of baking bread: the aroma of fresh bread is so so familiar. Smell the pungent fish in the market place: the smell of fish is so so familiar. Smell the distinct scent of every house: the scents of the houses are so so familiar. Jesus recognized every home by its scent. Everyone recognized the scent of Jesus' home. In Jesus' world the accent was on the local.

Jesus grew up in a quite different world from the world in which we grow up today. In our world the accent is on the global, in Jesus' world the accent was on the local. To grasp the power of Nazareth in Jesus' life, we must first restore the power of the local.

Intuition

Here is a story about changing expectations. How able are you to accept such changes?

As a child Jesus lived with his parents in Nazareth. He had grown accustomed to being taught in Nazareth's synagogue. Was he always to remain a child? Was he always to remain the one taught by others? And what about you? Are there parts of you that want always to remain a child, that want always to defer to the wisdom of others? Today Jesus outgrew his childhood. Today Jesus outgrew Nazareth. Here is a story about changing expectations. How able are you to accept such changes?

The people of Nazareth had watched Jesus as a child in their community, living with his parents. They had grown accustomed to seeing him being taught in Nazareth's synagogue. Were they always to treat him as a child? Were they always to feel that he needed teaching by others? And what about you? Are there parts of you that want always to keep others from growing up, that want always to keep your superiority over them? Today the people of Nazareth saw Jesus outgrow his childhood. Today the people of Nazareth saw Jesus preside in Nazareth's synagogue. Here is a story about changing expectations. How able are you to accept such changes?

The people of Nazareth had grown up with the prophecies of Isaiah ringing in their ears. They had grown accustomed to setting their eyes on the future and setting their hearts on the days to come. Were they always to wait for God to act in the future? Were they always to feel that the kingdom was just beyond reach? And what about you? Are there parts of you that want always to keep God's promises in the future, that want always to plan for your future commitment? Today the people of Nazareth saw prophecy fulfilled. Today the people of Nazareth were confronted with the reality of the kingdom.

Here is a story about changing expectations. How able are you to accept such changes?

Feeling

In Nazareth's synagogue Jesus proclaimed the gospel of good news to the people whose lives cried out for hope, for comfort and for salvation.

In Nazareth's synagogue Jesus proclaimed the gospel of good news to the poor. Feel what life is like with the empty belly, with the empty purse. Put yourself in the leaky shelter and the unsanitary hovel of the poor. Feel what life is like with few possessions, with few claims on the world. Then feel your spirits lift as God's promise of good news is proclaimed to the poor.

In Nazareth's synagogue Jesus proclaimed the gospel of good news to the captives. Put yourself in the prison cell and within the confined space of the captive. Feel what life is like with your freedom taken away, with your autonomy in tatters. Put yourself in the prison camp and within the guarded compound of the captive. Feel what life is like with your every movement watched and your liberty forgotten. Then feel your spirits lift as God's promise of good news is proclaimed to the captive.

In Nazareth's synagogue Jesus proclaimed the gospel of good news to the blind. Put yourself in the world of darkness and within the sight deprivation of the blind. Feel what life is like with your vision taken away, with your sight darkened. Put yourself in a world which sees only by touch and by sound. Feel what life is like not seeing the sunset, not seeing the faces of your loved ones. Then feel your spirit lift as God's promise of good news is proclaimed to the blind.

In Nazareth's synagogue Jesus proclaimed the gospel of good news to the oppressed. Put yourself in the shoes of the child who is bullied at school, in the shoes of young women battered at home, in the shoes of the middle manager who is intimidated at work, in the shoes of the infirm elder who is abused in the very place which should offer care. Feel what life is like when others have destroyed your self-respect. Then feel your spirits lift as God's promise of good news is proclaimed to the oppressed.

In Nazareth's synagogue Jesus proclaimed the gospel of good news to the people whose lives cried out for hope, for comfort and for salvation.

Thinking

Have you noticed how interested Luke is in the theology of the Holy Spirit?

Luke's gospel opens with the angel announcing to Zechariah the birth of John the Baptist. According to the angel, even before his birth John will be filled with the Holy Spirit. Have

you wondered why Luke is so interested in the theology of the
Holy Spirit?

According to Luke, when the angel Gabriel announced to
Mary the birth of Jesus himself, the angel said,

The Holy Spirit will come upon you . . .
therefore the child to be born will be holy.

Have you wondered why Luke is so interested in the theology
of the Holy Spirit?

According to Luke, when John the Baptist was born, his
father Zechariah was filled with the Holy Spirit and spoke the
prophecy,

Blessed be the Lord God of Israel.

Have you wondered why Luke is so interested in the theology
of the Holy Spirit?

According to Luke, when Jesus was brought to Jerusalem for
the rite of purification, the aged Simeon was guided by the Holy
Spirit to come into the temple to proclaim Jesus,

a light for revelation to the Gentiles.

Have you wondered why Luke is so interested in the theology
of the Holy Spirit?

According to Luke, when Jesus was baptized by John the
Baptist, the Holy Spirit descended on him in bodily form like a
dove and immediately afterwards, full of the Holy Spirit, Jesus
was led by the Spirit in the wilderness, where for forty days he
was tempted by the devil. Have you wondered why Luke is so
interested in the theology of the Holy Spirit?

According to Luke, when Jesus returned from the wilderness
to Galilee, he was filled with the power of the Spirit. In the
power of the Holy Spirit Jesus came to Nazareth, stood to read
in the synagogue, and turned to the prophet Isaiah. Have you
wondered why Luke is so interested in the theology of the Holy
Spirit?

Turning to the prophet Isaiah, Luke at last reveals the key to
his theology of the Holy Spirit. Here in Jesus the work of the
Holy Spirit, prophesied of old, has reached fulfilment. Now we

know why Luke is so interested in the theology of the Holy
Spirit.

12

Luke 5:1–11

[1]Once while Jesus was standing beside the lake of Gennesaret,
and the crowd was pressing in on him to hear the word of God,
[2]he saw two boats there at the shore of the lake; the fishermen
had gone out of them and were washing their nets. [3]He got into
one of the boats, the one belonging to Simon, and asked him to
put out a little way from the shore. Then he sat down and
taught the crowds from the boat. [4]When he had finished speaking, he said to Simon, 'Put out into the deep water and let down
your nets for a catch.' [5]Simon answered, 'Master, we have
worked all night long but have caught nothing. Yet if you say
so, I will let down the nets.' [6]When they had done this, they
caught so many fish that their nets were beginning to break. [7]So
they signalled to their partners in the other boat to come and
help them. And they came and filled both boats, so that they
began to sink. [8]But when Simon Peter saw it, he fell down at
Jesus' knees, saying, 'Go away from me, Lord, for I am a sinful
man!' [9]For he and all who were with him were amazed at the
catch of fish that they had taken; [10]and so also were James and
John, sons of Zebedee, who were partners with Simon. Then
Jesus said to Simon, 'Do not be afraid; from now on you will be
catching people.' [11]When they had brought their boats to shore,
they left everything and followed him.

Context

In chapter four Jesus began his public ministry of teaching in
the synagogue, and he was thrown out of the town. Now, in
chapter five, Jesus takes his teaching outside the formal structures, and new disciples follow him.

Sensing

Visiting preachers can sometimes cause quite a stir.

Picture a day in the life of the synagogue at Nazareth. You are sitting in your usual seat. You are surrounded by your usual friends. You are expecting the usual form of service. You are waiting for the usual teacher.

Picture a day in the life of the synagogue at Nazareth. You are disturbed by the unexpected. You see an unexpected hand take the scroll of scripture. You hear an unexpected voice proclaim the prophecies from Isaiah. You see an unexpected face interpreting the scriptures. You hear an unexpected note of authority in the preacher's voice.

Picture a day in the life of the synagogue at Nazareth. You see your usual friends disturbed by the unexpected teacher. You hear your usual friends complain loudly that they no longer can sit still to listen to the words of the carpenter's son. You see your usual friends rise up and drive the carpenter's son out of town. You hear your usual friends filled with rage.

Visiting preachers can sometimes cause quite a stir. Certainly there was no room for Jesus of Nazareth in the synagogue.

Picture a day in the life of the fishing community by the lake of Gennesaret. You are washing your nets in the usual way. You are surrounded by your usual friends. You are expecting the usual end to the day. You are waiting for the usual call to go home.

Picture a day in the life of the fishing community by the lake of Gennesaret. You see an unexpected wandering preacher. You hear the clamour of an unexpected crowd pressing to hear the word of God. You see the preacher make an unexpected path to one of the boats. You hear an unexpected request to put out a little way from the shore.

Picture a day in the life of the fishing community by the lake of Gennesaret. You see your usual friends attracted by the unexpected teacher. You hear your usual friends proclaim loudly that they respect the preacher's wisdom and authority. You see your usual friends rise up and follow the preacher from the shore. You hear your usual friends filled with faith.

Visiting preachers can sometimes cause quite a stir. If there was no room for Jesus in the synagogue, certainly there was plenty of room for him in the hearts of honest men and women.

Intuition

Vision, faith and risk so often go hand in hand for those who catch the gospel of Christ. Do you grasp the vision?

Take the case of Simon's fishing expedition, for example. Simon would not have gone far without vision, would he? And even a whole night's labour catching nothing still failed to quench his vision. It was vision that made him try again. Simon would not have gone far without faith, would he? And at this point in time he had no evidence that there would be fish. It was faith that made him trust Jesus' command to let down the nets. Simon would not have gone far without risk, would he? And Jesus' command was quite clear to leave the shallows and to put out into deep water. It was that risk which landed the catch.

Vision, faith and risk so often go hand in hand for those who catch the gospel of Christ. Do you have the faith?

Take the case of Simon's call to discipleship, for another example. Simon would not have gone far without vision, would he? And even a whole life spent repairing boats, mending nets and catching fish still failed to quench his vision for a brand new start. It was vision that made him try something new. Simon would not have gone far without faith, would he? And at this point in time he had no evidence that there would be people who would respond to the call of the kingdom. It was faith that made him trust Jesus' command to catch people for God. Simon would not have gone far without risk, would he? And Jesus' command was quite clear to beach their boats, to leave everything behind and to follow him. It was risk that made Simon useful to God.

Vision, faith and risk so often go hand in hand for those who catch the gospel of Christ. Do you run the risk?

Feeling

Here is a story about dispirited people. Climb into their boat and grasp how things felt to them.

Here is a story about dispirited people. Here are tired men, weary from the long, long night shift, paddling oars, dragging nets, moving backwards and forwards across the lake. Here are tired men.

Here is a story about dispirited people. Here are frustrated men, frustrated from hours of unrewarded effort, spying shoals and yet missing the fish, pulling in the nets and yet catching nothing, moving backwards and forwards across the lake. Here are frustrated men.

Here is a story about dispirited people. Here are anxious men, anxious about the future of their industry, doing their best to preserve and protect their nets, useless as they have been, doing their best to patch the holes, doing their best still to keep working after the end of the night shift. Here are anxious men.

Here is a story about dispirited people. Here are hungry men, hungry after the long night of work, hungry for their breakfast of fresh-grilled fish, hungry to feast off their labours, but going home with empty stomachs. Here are hungry men.

Here is a story about dispirited people. Here are despondent men, despondent to return home to their wives and children with empty hands and with empty baskets, despondent to face the hunger of their families, despondent to face the demands of their creditors. Here are despondent men.

Here is a story about dispirited people. Climb into their boat and grasp how things felt to them. It was, of course, to these dispirited people that Jesus himself came. It was to these dispirited people that Jesus offered a new catch, a new hope, a new way of life. Here is a story about dispirited people transformed. Climb out from the boat with them and grasp the power of their transformation. Here is a story about dispirited people transformed.

Thinking

For Luke's Gentile readers in the Roman Empire, the story of Jesus presented one incredible puzzle. Why should a Gentile world follow a Jewish Messiah who was so clearly rejected by his own people? It is this question that Luke keeps firmly in mind from the very beginning of his gospel narrative.

It is no accident, then, that Luke begins his account of Jesus' public teaching in chapter four with Jesus clearly starting off close to his Jewish roots. Jesus goes to the synagogue to teach, for the Jewish faith is rooted in the synagogue. He chooses no other synagogue than the one in Nazareth, for Jesus' own personal story was rooted in Nazareth. Here in the synagogue in Nazareth Jesus was rejected and driven violently from that town.

Having been rejected in his own town, in chapter five Jesus steps a little way from home, as far as the lake of Gennesaret. Having been rejected in the synagogue, he creates his own meeting of the people by the lakeside. Jesus creates his own seat of teaching from the boat. Here, just a little distance from the structures, rejection is turned to welcome.

Then throughout the gospel Luke continues to develop the motif of rejection at home and acceptance beyond. The very story that leads to crucifixion in Jerusalem leads also to acceptance in Rome.

For Luke's Gentile readers in the Roman Empire, the story of Jesus presented one incredible puzzle. Why should a Gentile world follow a Jewish Messiah who was so clearly rejected by his own people? The answer to this key question is already there in essence when Jesus exchanged the *rejection* of the synagogue for the *acceptance* of the lakeside.

13
Luke 6:17–26

[17]He came down with them and stood on a level place, with a great crowd of his disciples and a great multitude of people from all Judea, Jerusalem, and the coast of Tyre and Sidon. [18]They had come to hear him and to be healed of their diseases; and those who were troubled with unclean spirits were cured. [19]And all in the crowd were trying to touch him, for power came out from him and healed all of them.

[20]Then he looked up at his disciples and said:

'Blessed are you who are poor,
  for yours is the kingdom of God.
[21]'Blessed are you who are hungry now,
  for you will be filled.
'Blessed are you who weep now,

for you will laugh.

²²'Blessed are you when people hate you, and when they exclude you, revile you, and defame you on account of the Son of Man. ²³Rejoice on that day and leap for joy, for surely your reward is great in heaven; for that is what their ancestors did to the prophets.

²⁴'But woe to you who are rich,

for you have received your consolation.

²⁵'Woe to you who are full now,

for you will be hungry.

'Woe to you who are laughing now,

for you will mourn and weep.

²⁶'Woe to you when all speak well of you, for that is what their ancestors did to the false prophets.'

Context

This section of teaching in Luke's gospel is generally known as the sermon on the plain in contrast to the sermon on the mount reported by Matthew. In Luke this teaching about life in the kingdom follows immediately after the call of the twelve apostles.

Sensing

Over the last few days there has been a lot of coming and going around Jesus of Nazareth. You have been there in the thick of it and now you are feeling quite dazed.

To begin with you saw Jesus slip away to the mountain. You followed, at a safe distance, curious to see what Jesus had in mind. You saw Jesus fall to the ground in prayer. You hushed your footsteps. You quietened your breathing. You waited to see what would happen. You waited all night while Jesus stayed earnest in prayer.

Then you heard Jesus call his disciples to join him on the mountain. One by one they climbed the hilly path. Straining your ears you heard Jesus call twelve of them out by name, twelve men appointed to become his closest apostles. You count them and immediately recall how you have learnt about the twelve leaders of the twelve tribes of Israel.

Over the last few days there has been a lot of coming and

going around Jesus of Nazareth. You have been there in the thick of it.

You saw Jesus and the twelve coming down from the mountain. There at the mountain's base the plain was already crowded. You saw a multitude of people, people pressing in from all Judea, from Jerusalem, from the coast of Tyre and Sidon. You saw the healthy stand alongside the sick. You saw the sick made well and the possessed healed.

You heard Jesus lift up his voice. You heard Jesus begin to teach. You heard the regular rhythm and structure of the beatitudes.

Blessed are you who are poor . . .
Blessed are you who are hungry now . . .

You heard the regular rhythm and structure of the woes.

Woe to you who are rich . . .
Woe to you who are full now . . .

You heard the wisdom of the world set upside down.

Over the last few days there has been a lot of coming and going around Jesus of Nazareth. You have been in the thick of it and now you are feeling quite dazed.

Intuition

There, in the sermon on the plain, Jesus proclaims the most radical of gospels. How radical are you willing to be in following Jesus' lead?

In the sermon on the plain Jesus teaches about economics, and questions the wisdom of his age. For Jesus it is the poor who are blessed. So where do you stand on the economic principles of your generation? What are your views on lowering taxes? What are your views on reducing investment in education, in health services and in social support? What are your views on the economic engine of the market economy? What voice should the church raise today about matters of economics?

In the sermon on the plain Jesus teaches about hunger and the supply of food, and questions the wisdom of his age. For Jesus it is the hungry who are blessed. So where do you stand on the attitude to food resources promoted by your generation? What are your views on subsidizing the farming industry? What are your views on protecting the fish resources of the seas? What are your views on promoting genetically modified crops? What are your views on the distribution of the world's food? What voice should the church raise today about the food industry?

In the sermon on the plain Jesus teaches about leisure, pleasure and fun, and questions the wisdom of his age. For Jesus it is those who weep who are blessed. So where do you stand on the attitude to pleasure promoted by your generation? What are your views on the growth of the leisure industry? What are your views on contemporary emphases concerning the right to self-fulfilment? What are your views on the quest for fun without responsibility? What voice should the church raise today about leisure?

There, in the sermon on the plain, Jesus proclaims the most radical of gospels. How radical are you willing to be in following Jesus' lead?

Feeling

Optimists and pessimists live in the same world but they see the world in very different ways. Put on the pessimist's spectacles and see the world through pessimistic eyes.

Woe to the poor, says the pessimist, for they have nothing to live for. Their lot indeed is a pitiful one. Without money the poor have no clothes. Without money the poor have no shelter. Without money the poor have no food. Without money the poor have no self-respect. Without money the poor have nothing to live for. Woe to the poor, says the pessimist.

Woe to the hungry, says the pessimist, for they have nothing to live on. Their lot is indeed a pitiful one. Without food the hungry have nothing to sustain their bodies. Without food the hungry have nothing to sustain their minds. Without food the hungry have nothing to satisfy their souls. Without food the hungry have nothing to live on. Woe to the poor, says the pessimist.

Woe to those who weep, says the pessimist, for they have nothing to raise their spirits. Their lot is indeed a pitiful one. Woe to those who weep, says the pessimist.

Optimists and pessimists live in the same world but they see the world in very different ways. Now put on the optimist's spectacles and see the world through optimistic eyes.

Blessed are the poor, says the optimist, for theirs is the kingdom of God. Their lot indeed is a happy one. From out of their poverty they can see what is of lasting worth. From out of their poverty they can be free to respond to the call of God. From out of their poverty they can build riches. Blessed are the poor, says the optimist.

Blessed are the hungry, says the optimist, for they will be filled. Their lot indeed is a happy one. From out of their hunger they learn the true value of bread. From out of their hunger they glimpse their true dependence on God. From out of their hunger they feed on the Bread of Life. Blessed are the hungry, says the optimist.

Blessed are those who weep, says the optimist, for they will laugh. Their lot indeed is a happy one. Blessed are those who weep, says the optimist.

Optimists and pessimists live in the same world.

Thinking

Reading Luke's sermon on the plain you might be tempted to think that religion is nothing more than opium for the people.

What better opiate is there for the poor than the promise of some heavenly wealth? With such a promise in store there is no immediate call for economic revolution.

What better opiate is there for the hungry than the promise of the eternal, heavenly banquet? With such a promise in store there is no immediate call for snatching food from the tables of the rich.

What better opiate is there for those who weep huge tears than the promise of eternal laughter ringing through the arches of heaven? With such a promise in store there is no immediate call for earthly recompense.

Reading Luke's sermon on the plain you might be tempted to think that religion is nothing more than opium for the people. You might be tempted, but nonetheless you would be wrong. You would be wrong because you misread the power of the Lucan beatitudes.

The beatitudes are not mere promise held out for the future. They are a clear declaration of the way things stand now in the kingdom of God. For when the kingdom of God was made real through the person of Jesus of Nazareth, the new order also dawned.

When the new order dawned the poor should no longer be content with their poverty. In the new order the poor are empowered to claim the kingdom of God.

When the new order dawned the hungry should no longer be content with their hunger. In the new order the hungry are empowered to be filled.

When the new order dawned those who weep huge tears should no longer be content with their sorrow. In the new order those who weep are empowered to claim their share of laughter.

Reading Luke's sermon on the plain you might be tempted to think that religion is nothing more than opium for the people. You might be tempted, but nonetheless you would be wrong. Here is no opiate but a clear call to revolution.

14
Luke 6:20–31

20Then he looked up at his disciples and said:
'Blessed are you who are poor,
for yours is the kingdom of God.
21'Blessed are you who are hungry now,
for you will be filled.
'Blessed are you who weep now,
for you will laugh.
22'Blessed are you when people hate you, and when they exclude you, revile you, and defame you on account of the Son of Man. 23Rejoice on that day and leap for joy, for surely your reward is great in heaven; for that is what their ancestors did to the prophets.
24'But woe to you who are rich,
for you have received your consolation.
25'Woe to you who are full now,
for you will be hungry.
'Woe to you who are laughing now,
for you will mourn and weep.

[26]'Woe to you when all speak well of you, for that is what their ancestors did to the false prophets.

[27]But I say to you that listen, Love your enemies, do good to those who hate you, [28]bless those who curse you, pray for those who abuse you. [29]If anyone strikes you on the cheek, offer the other also; and from anyone who takes away your coat do not withhold even your shirt. [30]Give to everyone who begs from you; and if anyone takes away your goods, do not ask for them again. [31]Do to others as you would have them do to you.'

Context

Luke's sermon on the plain begins like Matthew's sermon on the mount with a set of beatitudes. Then Luke provides a series of practical illustrations about how life is in the kingdom where love reigns.

Sensing

Keep your eyes open for those clear signs of how people treat one another according to the laws of the world.

Keep your eyes open as you drive along the motorway. See the heavy lorry pull out into the path of a fast-moving car. See the car brake sharply. See the driver shake his fist. Hear the angry blast of the horn.

Keep your eyes open as you walk past the school playground. See the careless child bump thoughtlessly into two boys engrossed in conversation. See the anger on their faces. See the clenched fist. Hear the aggressive retaliation.

Keep your eyes open as you walk alone at night through the vandalized city centre. See the hungry and shabby youth threaten a passer-by and steal his wallet. See the quick-witted self-defence. See the tackle that brings the mugger to the ground. Hear the relentless kicking against the mugger's body.

Keep your eyes open as you pass the city square. See the beggars huddled on benches imploring charity from all. See the smartly dressed people hurry past. See the disdain on their faces. Hear their mutterings of contempt.

Keep your eyes open for those incredible signs of how people treat one another according to the guidelines of the kingdom.

Keep your eyes open as you drive along the motorway. See

the fast car flash its lights and sound its horn to intimidate another motorist from the outside lane. See that motorist pull over to let the fast car pass. See the motorist smile kindly to his aggressor. Jesus said, 'Bless those who curse you.'

Keep your eyes open as you walk past the school playground. See the bully kick and punch his helpless victim. See the victim meet aggression with calm and passive acceptance. Jesus said, 'If anyone strikes you on the cheek, offer the other also.'

Keep your eyes open as you walk alone at night through the vandalized city centre. See the mugger strip his victim of his coat. See the victim offer his jacket as well. Jesus said, 'From anyone who takes away your coat do not withhold even your shirt.'

Keep your eyes open as you pass the city square. See the beggar hold out his hand. See the passer-by offer the beggar food and drink. Jesus said, 'Give to everyone who begs from you.'

Keep your eyes open and see the signs of the kingdom.

Intuition

The problem with the word 'love' is that it means so much and it means so little. So what sort of ideas does that four-letter word set running in your mind? What is love, and what does it mean to love your enemies?

In the Greek language in which Luke wrote, he had the choice of at least three different words for love. So I wonder what his choice tells us? The first word Luke could have chosen was *eros*. Eros is erotic love, the love of passion, the love of sensuality, the love of sexuality. What sort of ideas does this kind of love set running in your mind? Can you see your enemy as the object of desire and passion? But Luke did not choose the word *eros*.

The second word Luke could have chosen was *philia*. Philia is that warm affection that binds together close friends, that characterizes the closeness shared by members of the same family. What sort of ideas does this kind of love set running in your mind? Can you see your enemy displacing your closest friend or your nearest family in claims upon your affection? But Luke did not choose the word *philia*.

The third word Luke could have chosen was *agape*. Agape is that gracious, determined, active interest in the welfare of others, that consistent concern for others that is not deterred by their lack of response or by their rejection. What sort of ideas does this kind of love set running in your mind? Can you see your enemy as commanding your constant benevolence and active goodwill, however much your enemy provokes you? Luke could do so. Luke chose the word *agape*.

The problem with the word 'love' is that it means so much and it means so little. So what sort of ideas does that four-letter word set running in your mind?

Feeling

For some people true Christian love is seen at its best in the work of reconciliation, the making of harmony and peace. Do you identify with that view of the gospel?

For such people, the command 'love your enemies' is self-evidently fulfilment of the gospel. In the quest for harmony and peace, no ill should be wished on those who wish ill to you.

For such people, the command 'do good to those who hate you' is self-evidently fulfilment of the gospel. In the quest for harmony and peace, no ill should be done to those who do ill to you.

For such people, the command to 'offer the other cheek' to those who strike you is self-evidently fulfilment of the gospel. In the quest for harmony and peace, pain should be borne without resentment and retaliation should be withheld.

For such people, the command to 'give your shirt' to anyone who takes your coat is self-evidently fulfilment of the gospel. In the quest for harmony and peace, no attempt should be made to protect worldly possessions.

For such people, the command to 'give to everyone' who begs from you is self-evidently fulfilment of the gospel. In the quest for harmony and peace, no question should be asked of those who ask of us. Our generosity should know no limit.

For some people true Christian love is seen at its best in the work of reconciliation, the making of harmony and peace. Do you identify with that view of the gospel?

Thinking

The gospel command to love raises all sorts of practical objections. For some people the radical love described in Luke's sermon on the plain is just plainly unreasonable. It lacks justice. It lacks fairness. It lacks a true view of what people are really like. Do you see that problem with Luke's command to love?

For such people, to love your enemies in times of war, to wish good on those who seek to destroy you is self-evidently madness. What good does it do to hope that those who set out to destroy you will prosper to be effective in their evil intent? Should they not be brought to justice?

For such people, to do good to those who hate you is self-evidently madness. What good does it do to fail to challenge those who make your life hell? Should they not be made to face the truth?

For such people, to offer the other cheek to those who strike you is self-evidently madness. What good does it do to feed their lust for inflicting pain and cruelty? Should they not be challenged to face the errors of their ways?

For such people, to give your shirt to anyone who takes your coat is self-evidently madness. What good does it do to let the thieves imagine they can get away with robbery, thuggery and violence? Should they not face the proper court of justice?

For such people, to give to everyone who begs from you is self-evidently madness. What good does it do to support a subculture of indolence and parasitic existence? Surely such people should be encouraged to take responsibility for themselves?

The gospel command to love raises all sorts of practical objections. For some people the radical love described in Luke's sermon on the plain is just plain unreasonable. It lacks justice. It lacks fairness. It lacks a true view of what people are really like. Do you see that problem with Luke's command to love?

15
Luke 6:27–38

[27]But I say to you that listen, Love your enemies, do good to those who hate you, [28]bless those who curse you, pray for those who abuse you. [29]If anyone strikes you on the cheek, offer the other also; and from anyone who takes away your coat do not withhold even your shirt. [30]Give to everyone who begs from you; and if anyone takes away your goods, do not ask for them again. [31]Do to others as you would have them do to you.'

[32]'If you love those who love you, what credit is that to you? For even sinners love those who love them. [33]If you do good to those who do good to you, what credit is that to you? For even sinners do the same. [34]If you lend to those from whom you hope to receive, what credit is that to you? Even sinners lend to sinners, to receive as much again. [35]But love your enemies, do good, and lend, expecting nothing in return. Your reward will be great, and you will be children of the Most High; for he is kind to the ungrateful and the wicked. [36]Be merciful, just as your Father is merciful.

[37]'Do not judge, and you will not be judged; do not condemn, and you will not be condemned. Forgive, and you will be forgiven; [38]give, and it will be given to you. A good measure, pressed down, shaken together, running over, will be put into your lap; for the measure you give will be the measure you get back.'

Context

Luke's sermon on the plain begins like Matthew's sermon on the mount with a set of beatitudes. Then Luke provides a series of practical illustrations about how life is in the kingdom where love reigns.

Sensing

There are so many ways in which Luke's sermon on the plain makes it clear that the Christian gospel is concerned with the basic practical matters of life. Here is a gospel for the practical person.

In the kingdom of God there is much to be done. Open your eyes and see the people who need your love. See the weary eyes of the child in the playground who knows no deep love at home. See the sorrow in the face of the overseas student separated so far from the love of those back home. See the hurt in the eyes of the middle-aged worker who experiences no love or understanding from those with whom he spends his days. See the loneliness in the face of the elderly widow who returns each evening to an empty house and to an empty bed. See the faces of those who know no love and hear the voice of Jesus say, 'If you love those who love you, what credit is that to you?'

In the kingdom of God there is much to be done. Open your eyes and see the people who need your helping hand. See the refugee imprisoned in bed-and-breakfast accommodation unable to talk the local language. See the young man imprisoned in his flat crippled by the motorcycle accident. See the young woman imprisoned in her smart suburban house paralysed by fear of open spaces. See the elderly widower imprisoned in his terraced house whose zimmer frame can no longer manage the steps down to the street. See the faces of those who need help and hear the voice of Jesus say, 'If you do good to those who do good to you, what credit is that to you?'

In the kingdom of God there is much to be done. Open your eyes and see the people who need your generosity. See the young parents struggling to bring up their hungry children and needing to pay the rent. See the unemployed single mother counting the cost of repairing the broken window pane. See the unkempt homeless traveller begging in the market place. See the sick pensioner struggling to keep warm. See the faces of those who need to borrow and hear the voice of Jesus say, 'If you lend to those from whom you hope to receive, what credit is that to you?'

According to the sermon on the plain there is a lot for the practical person to do in the kingdom.

Intuition

There are so many ways in which Luke's sermon on the plain makes it clear that the Christian gospel is concerned with the fundamental issues of human motivation. Here is a gospel for the imaginative person.

In the kingdom of God there is much to set the mind running and to spark the imagination. What, I wonder, motivates your commitment to the gospel of love? Are you motivated by the philosophy that if you love others, they will love you in return? Are you motivated by the warm feeling deep inside as love pours from you? Are you motivated by the promise that if you love others now, God will love you on the day of judgement? And how do you square your motivation with Jesus saying, 'even sinners love those who love them'?

In the kingdom of God there is much to set the mind running and to spark the imagination. What, I wonder, motivates your commitment to doing good to others? Are you motivated by the philosophy that if you do good to others, they will do good to you in return? Are you motivated by the warm feeling deep inside as good deeds flow from you? Are you motivated by the promise that if you do good to others now, God will do good to you on the day of judgement? And how do you square your motivation with Jesus saying, 'even sinners do good to those who do good to them'?

In the kingdom of God there is much to set the mind running and to spark the imagination. What, I wonder, motivates your commitment to lend to those who stand in need? Are you motivated by the philosophy that if you lend to others, they will repay you in full and with added interest? Are you motivated by the warm feeling deep inside as generosity streams from you? Are you motivated by the promise that, if you lend to others now, God will reckon up your interest ready for the day of judgement? And how do you square your motivation with Jesus saying, 'even sinners lend to sinners, to receive as much again'?

According to the sermon on the plain there is a lot for the imaginative person to reflect on in the kingdom.

Feeling

There are so many ways in which Luke's sermon on the plain makes it clear that the Christian gospel is concerned with the key issues of the human heart. Here is a gospel for the humane person.

In the kingdom of God there is much to touch the human

heart. Take, for example, the quality of mercy. God's people are called upon to be merciful people. God's people are called upon to show mercy to all who stand in need of mercy. 'Show me mercy', cries the child who has disobeyed the parental command. 'Show me mercy', cries the teenager who has failed to do his homework. 'Show me mercy', cries the unfaithful husband. 'Show me mercy', cries the motorist caught speeding. 'Show me mercy', cries a shopworker caught pilfering. God's people are called upon to be merciful people, for they have had mercy shown to them. Jesus said, 'Be merciful, just as your father is merciful.'

In the kingdom of God there is much to touch the human heart. Take, for example, the quality of forgiveness. God's people are called upon to be forgiving people. God's people are called upon to show forgiveness to all who stand in need of forgiving. When jostled and buffeted in the crowd, their instinct is not to jostle back. When cut up at the roundabout, their instinct is not to blast on the horn. When snubbed and insulted at work, their instinct is not to take it out on the perpetrator. When inconvenienced by a forgetful and careless colleague, their instinct is not to snap back. God's people are called upon to be forgiving people, because they are themselves already a forgiven people. Jesus said, 'Forgive and you will be forgiven.'

In the kingdom of God there is much to touch the human heart. Take, for example, the quality of kindness. God's people are called upon to be kind people. God's people are called upon to show kindness to all who stand in need of kindness. The hungry child at the end of your street needs your kindness. The hungry child at the other side of your town needs your kindness. The hungry child in faraway places needs your kindness. God's people are called upon to be kind people, for they have had kindness shown to them. Jesus said of the Most High, 'He is kind to the ungrateful and to the wicked.'

According to the sermon on the plain there is a lot for the humane person to do in the kingdom.

Thinking

There are so many ways in which Luke's sermon on the plain makes it clear that the Christian gospel is concerned with the core issues of the mind. Here is a gospel for the thoughtful person.

In the kingdom of God there is much to engage the human mind. The responsible Christian cannot leave, unasked, questions to do with justice. To respond with open heart to the hungry child at the end of the street without asking why that child is hungry is to be irresponsible. To respond with open hands to the hungry child in faraway places without asking questions about world politics and international policies is to be irresponsible. God's people are called upon to have a passion for justice.

In the kingdom of God there is much to engage the human mind. The responsible Christian cannot leave, unasked, questions to do with fairness. To respond with open heart to the plight of the young parents struggling to feed their children and to pay the rent without asking why there are such inequalities in our society is to be irresponsible. To respond with open hands to the plight of the unemployed and homeless traveller without asking questions about social policy and employment opportunities is to be irresponsible. God's people are called upon to have a passion for fairness.

In the kingdom of God there is much to engage the human mind. The responsible Christian cannot leave, unasked, questions to do with truth. To respond with open heart to forgive the erring child without asking what lesson the child is learning from such forgiveness is to be irresponsible. To respond with open hands to give to the begging stranger without asking what lesson the stranger is learning from such generosity is to be irresponsible. God's people are called upon to have a passion for truth.

According to the sermon on the plain there is a lot for the thoughtful person to consider in the kingdom of God.

16
Luke 7:1–10

¹After Jesus had finished all his sayings in the hearing of the people, he entered Capernaum.

²A centurion there had a slave whom he valued highly, and who was ill and close to death.

³When he heard about Jesus, he sent some Jewish elders to him, asking him to come and heal his slave. ⁴When they came to Jesus, they appealed to him earnestly, saying, 'He is worthy of having you do this for him, ⁵for he loves our people, and it is he who built our synagogue for us.'

⁶And Jesus went with them, but when he was not far from the house, the centurion sent friends to say to him, 'Lord, do not trouble yourself, for I am not worthy to have you come under my roof; ⁷therefore I did not presume to come to you. But only speak the word, and let my servant be healed. ⁸For I also am a man set under authority, with soldiers under me; and I say to one, "Go", and he goes, and to another, "Come", and he comes, and to my slave, "Do this", and the slave does it.' ⁹When Jesus heard this he was amazed at him, and turning to the crowd that followed him, he said, 'I tell you, not even in Israel have I found such faith.' ¹⁰When those who had been sent returned to the house, they found the slave in good health.

Context

This healing story shows that the compassion and care of Jesus is not restricted to those of his own race but is also available to the Gentiles. This Gentile officer, a supporter of the Jewish community at Capernaum, had authority and expected Jesus, as the representative of God, to have similar power to heal his servant. Luke encourages the members of the church to show similar compassion and acceptance to all, especially slaves.

Sensing

In Capernaum today you can sit in the excavated shell of a synagogue and view the bases of the columns of the houses in the main street. Stand next to one and see the elders of the synagogue approach Jesus with eagerness. Hear the dialogue between them: 'A centurion . . . has deep compassion . . . for a valued slave. That officer . . . a good man . . . helped us build our synagogue . . . one good work deserves another . . . please help him . . . come to his house.' Follow the group down the main street.

Watch the procession stop. Some people approach Jesus, speaking for the officer again: 'Authority – I have been given it and I exercise it. My soldiers and my slaves do as I command. Authority – *you* have it and can use it. Those called "Lord" have power from on high, so I trust you to use it to heal my slave.'

Hear the debate among the crowd, 'Slaves are replaceable. Why bother about slaves?' Others say, 'That officer cares for his slaves. His kindness deserves to be rewarded.' The strictly religious are saying, 'If Jesus goes into a Gentile house, he won't be able to come to the synagogue until he cleanses himself.' Feel yourself caught up in the debate.

The chatter stops. See Jesus shake his head in amazement and wonder. 'What faith! I haven't seen such faith – no, not even among God's own people. He told me that I had authority to heal his sick slave – no ifs, no buts; just faith in my compassion and power.' Enter the crowd's debate: 'Faith? Whose faith?'

Listen to the report: 'The slave is better.' This is the outcome of authority. This is the outcome of faith.

Intuition

Some sickness is the result of wrongdoing. Food poisoning can result from lazy hygiene. Smoking causes some cancers and heart congestion. Do you treat the ill as if their sickness was the result of their own sin or the evil of others?

On the other hand sickness can strike the godly. The good can be rewarded with pain. The centurion did not believe this sickness was a punishment for evil and had compassion on his sick servant. What could he do? He had authority in many areas of life but when it came to sickness, he was not in charge. He took the problem to his religious friends for action. They told him about the prophet from Nazareth who had been in their synagogue, teaching with authority and ordering unclean spirits to come out from people. He would be the one to help. His slave recovered. Do we believe the reports that others give us of help that they have received from their faith? Or do we dismiss such reports as impossible?

The difficulty for the officer was that *Jesus* was a Jew and *he* was a Gentile, even if a Gentile who was supportive of the Jewish religion. So the officer made use of his friends: 'You are Jews and Jesus is a Jew, so you ask him on my behalf.' What would you do if your secular neighbour asked you to help in similar circumstances? Would you say, 'You make your own request to God'?

Does the social rank of a person make any difference for us when we are asked to help someone in extreme difficulty? To some extent the value that the officer placed on a slave was exceptional. Slaves were there to produce work and economic benefit. If they became unproductive through advanced age or sickness they were expendable. Is this a common attitude of our society towards employees who become sick? What is the Christian responsibility towards such members of society?

This passage raises many issues for us as individuals and as a society.

Feeling

Look at the relationships in this story through the eyes of the slave. You have worked hard for your master. He is an important officer in the town. He has told you how highly he values you. He has said that if your sickness should lead to your death, that would be a great loss for him. You know that he places more value on you than simply the cost of your replacement; he values you as a person. You can tell that by the attention he has shown to you since you were sick. He has done everything possible, but it does not seem to be enough. He has authority, but not over your sickness. Do you trust him to help you when you might be a burden?

Look at the relationships in this story through the eyes of the slave. Your fellow-slaves tell you that your master has sought help from his religious friends. You are a slave; they are free. You are a Gentile; they are of a different religion. You are considered unholy and worthless because you are a sick slave; they are important holy people in town. You say to yourself, 'What have I done to deserve this?' They probably say the same about you. Do you trust them to help you, the powerful helping the powerless?

Look at the relationships in this story through the eyes of the slave. In your relationship with God in times of sickness you ask yourself, 'Why does God not act to heal me? Why am I always the one to suffer? Is this sickness my fault? Do I lack enough faith in God to be healed?' Do you trust God to help you in your weakness and confusion?

Look at the relationships in this story through the eyes of the slave. What is your relationship with Jesus, the healer? Will he consider you worth healing? 'Jesus, I know that your care is reflected in the care and support of all those around me.' Do you trust Jesus to use his authority to heal *you*, ambivalent about faith?

Look at yourself as the slave in this story. The fever is passing. Something wonderful is happening. You are sure God has a part in all this. You know your healing will make a difference in all your relationships.

When you put yourself in the slave's position, such an experience can transform the way you regard others and the way you look at sickness.

Thinking

What lessons do you think Luke is trying to illustrate by incorporating this passage at the beginning of the 'actions' section of the gospel?

From the record of Acts (Acts 10:34–35) we see the early church recognizing the equality of all people whatever their religious, cultural and racial backgrounds before God. This conclusion was the result of a deep debate. The remembrance of this incident reinforces equality. In these days when we stress the importance of race and culture, how do we demonstrate our equality in Christ?

From the Pauline writings we see the struggle between the concepts of worthiness through works and of righteousness through faith. In this passage faith is highlighted, though works are included. What do we think are the key points in the debate? Is faith shown in works or are we 'saved' even in our unworthiness? In this account the accumulation of works and the depth of faith are shown by the centurion, not by the slave. Do I think that my faith can bring healing to my friend or employee? If so, how should I be involved?

It seems that Jesus was ready and willing to enter the house of a Gentile to care for the sick. Is Luke making the point here that those members of the early church who strictly kept the Jewish traditions should always be ready to follow Jesus' example and visit their Gentile neighbours to bring healing and comfort to the sick? What does this say to ourselves and the church about our policy of visiting the needy in our community? What is your opinion?

The centurion's words do not appear to be an expression of faith. He does not say that he trusts Jesus to heal his slave or that he even believes in God. He talks about himself and his powers. What 'faith' does Jesus refer to?

Thinking about this story, how would you define 'faith' and the ways that people show faith?

17
Luke 7:11–17

11Soon afterwards he went to a town called Nain, and his disciples and a large crowd went with him. 12As he approached the gate of the town, a man who had died was being carried out. He was his mother's only son, and she was a widow; and with her was a large crowd from the town. 13When the Lord saw her, he had compassion for her and said to her, 'Do not weep.' 14Then he came forward and touched the bier, and the bearers stood still. And he said, 'Young man, I say to you, rise!' 15The dead man sat up and began to speak, and Jesus gave him to his mother. 16Fear seized all of them; and they glorified God, saying, 'A great prophet has risen among us!' and 'God has looked favourably on his people!' 17This word about him spread throughout Judea and all the surrounding country.

Context
At Nain, Jesus, this time on his own initiative, shows his compassion and care in the light of tragedy. After the death of her husband this widow had the support and protection of an

only son who has now died. She feels abandoned, although supported by a large crowd who mourn with her. Jesus gives comfort to the widow and then raises the young man from his funeral stretcher. Through the use of the phrase 'He gave him to his mother', the crowd recalls the work of the prophet Elijah (1 Kings 17:23) and hails Jesus as another great prophet.

Sensing

Journey with the disciples and a large crowd of those who followed Jesus from Capernaum as he takes the road around the lake into the low hills that lie to the south. Feel the excitement in the crowd around you. Everyone is asking, 'Who is this man who cares for those in pain, whatever their social standing? Who is this man who has such authority and power?'

Feel pride in your heart as you associate with a man of such compassion and strength. This prophet brings blessings. The crowd is full of hope. It stops at the gate of the town only to hear cries of wailing. Happy thoughts vanish like the mist above the lake. Seeing the bier brings home the facts. Its harsh reality lies before us. Death has destroyed life and hope.

Strain your head over the crowd to see the lonely figure of a woman following the bier. The crowds surround her but there is no one close to hold her with affection. Friends are no substitute for family. Her shoulders are slumped in double hopelessness. Her garments tell us she is a widow, and the cries in the crowd tell us that the body is that of her only son. They complain, 'How could God be so cruel as to strike her twice with such deadly pain?'

Watch Jesus move forward and the widow look up. There is a tear in his eye as he says to her, 'Do not weep.' Jesus seems instinctively to feel fully for her situation. What will he do?

Watch him touch the bier. Hear the gasp of the crowd. Righteous people should not defile themselves with the dead. Listen as he speaks strongly to the corpse as if it would be able to hear him. What is happening? Feel the fear and quaking in your heart and in those around you as the corpse sits up and speaks. Everyone shrinks back. The bearers drop the stretcher to the ground in fright. Who is this that can break the bonds of hopelessness and death?

Hear the people cry, 'A great prophet has brought God's blessing on his people.'

In the face of death and hopelessness there is new life and hope.

Intuition

Can you sense the pain when you read some death notices in the newspaper?

For those who have died in the fullness of years, there is sorrow but also pride. For others the notice records tragedy: a middle-aged man taken suddenly with a heart attack; a wife killed in a car accident; a child lost through cancer. The pain pierces the words of the notice.

Sometimes the pain is doubled in intensity. There is only one notice. This is from the one who loved the most and is left to mourn the most. That person is all alone with the memories of what might have been: 'This was my only son/daughter, my one and only beloved child.' How do you respond when you see such a death notice? Has God deserted those left in such times of death?

What has this passage to say to those in pain? It shows that God does not wait to be asked to show compassion. God understands. Has not God's only Son died? God calls on us not to be overcome with the tears of destitution. Hear God's words: 'Do not weep.' Yet the story does not end with compassion. God also gives the gift of resurrection. Life is to be lived out in the company of those who have been given eternal life. They are not 'lost'. Through the resurrection of Christ they grow to the fullness of life in the life that is beyond death. A great prophet has arisen to tell us this truth from God.

What has this passage to say about the pain of loneliness? It declares that our loneliness is eased not only by resurrection but also by communion. The fellowship of the risen saints and the fellowship of our earthly companions support us. The orphan and the widow find a special place in the heart of the Christian community. They have a new family of brothers and sisters, sons and daughters. The crowd of well-wishers and sympathizers becomes our new family, enfolding us with love. Jesus gave his widowed mother into the care of his best-loved friend.

With Christ's blessing the Christian community embraces the widow and those who mourn. Is this how we touch the bier today?

Feeling

This is a story about the meaning of relationships. Take the place of Jesus and look around you. You must show compassion to those in need. Everyone seems to have such great needs.

Meeting the needs of your disciples, you have taught them the way to live: 'to trust God, mourn, love, give, forgive and have faith'. You must model this way for them to respond to their hopes and live up to their expectations.

The crowds wail with the widow in despair. In their hearts they are complaining at the injustice of God. Your compassion for them will release their compassion. In that way they can live up to the teaching you have given.

The widow has needs. She is broken by this double pain. She has nowhere to go. She has no one to love. She has no one to care for her. You must restore life for her and renew her relationship with others.

You too have needs. You cannot raise expectations beyond the possibility of fulfilment. You must not make people totally dependent on your work and presence. You must empower the compassion of others: to live on even when you are dead. The key lies in restoring relationships, showing 'compassion' in all these different circumstances.

Such is the miracle of resurrection. It opens the door for us to receive love and to give love, and in due time to live fully again. Jesus taught that only love can fill the grave with hope. Too often in grief we shut love out and keep ourselves entombed in our loneliness. Unlock the door and let the blessing of compassion abound.

Thinking

Luke in this passage seems to omit faith from the equation of restoration. Not once does Jesus wait for a sign of faith before the action of God takes place. In most of the biblical cases of healing, faith is required from someone in the process. Having made such a point about faith in the previous passage it seems surprising that there is not even a hint of it here. Do you think that this is to make a contrasting statement, or is there another point to the story? What do you think?

The raising of a corpse seems to be beyond logic. If it did

happen you would have expected a much greater reaction from the crowd. If someone was able to restore a dead person to life today, the news item would be very different from the account in this passage. Society would be overwhelmed. The newswires would be overloaded.

It is true that resuscitation is possible if treatment is applied skilfully and quickly, but that is not the situation described here. The story makes the point that this is a funeral procession and that the corpse is ready for burial. The story in this sense is 'beyond logic', yet it is not to be dismissed. Does it not make the point that there is more to life than death, and death is not to be seen as the end of life?

It is important to note that the word 'rise' is used both about the young man and about the great prophet. The compassion of Jesus gives rise to two outcomes. The first is resurrection for the young man. The second is the 'rising up' of a great prophet. In the compassion of God we are renewed in our hope that God is active among us, renewing life in our midst. When we too act with true compassion people will see the blessing of God active in our midst. The message of resurrection is brought to those who mourn.

When people see God's signs of favour and blessing, then the word of God will spread far and wide.

18

Luke 7:36 to 8:3

36One of the Pharisees asked Jesus to eat with him, and he went into the Pharisee's house and took his place at the table. 37And a woman in the city, who was a sinner, having learned that he was eating in the Pharisee's house, brought an alabaster jar of ointment. 38She stood behind him at his feet, weeping, and began to bathe his feet with her tears and to dry them with her hair. Then she continued kissing his feet and anointing them with ointment. 39Now when the Pharisee who had invited him saw it, he said to himself, 'If this man were a prophet, he would have known who and what kind of woman this is who is touching him – that she is a sinner.' [40]Jesus spoke up and said to him, 'Simon, I have something to say to you.' 'Teacher', he replied, 'speak.' [41]'A certain creditor had two debtors; one owed five hundred denarii, and the other fifty. [42]When they could not pay, he cancelled the debts for both of them. Now which of them will love him more?' [43]Simon answered, 'I suppose the one for whom he cancelled the greater debt.' And Jesus said to him, 'You have judged rightly.' [44]Then turning to the woman, he said to Simon, 'Do you see this woman? I entered your house; you gave me no water for my feet, but she has bathed my feet with her tears and dried them with her hair. [45]You gave me no kiss, but from the time I came in she has not stopped kissing my feet. [46]You did not anoint my head with oil, but she has anointed my feet with ointment. [47]Therefore, I tell you, her sins, which were many, have been forgiven; hence she has shown great love. But the one to whom little is forgiven, loves little.' [48]Then he said to her, 'Your sins are forgiven.' [49]But those who were at the table with him began to say among themselves, 'Who is this who even forgives sins?' [50]And he said to the woman, 'Your faith has saved you; go in peace.'

8 Soon afterwards he went on through cities and villages, proclaiming and bringing the good news of the kingdom of God. The twelve were with him, [2]as well as some women who had been cured of evil spirits and infirmities: Mary, called Magdalene, from whom seven demons had gone out, [3]and Joanna, the wife of Herod's steward Chuza, and Susanna, and many others, who provided for them out of their resources.

Context

Jesus had taught that 'wisdom is vindicated by all her children', meaning that our actions will show whether we have accepted the truth in our hearts. This account shows Jesus fully engaging in the social setting of his day. He responded to the hospitality of the respectable in society as well as to those who felt outsiders. Here the two are brought together, the pure man and the woman who knew (as others knew) that she was a sinner. By their contrasting actions they show their attitude to Jesus and to the truth about themselves.

Sensing

Sense the awkwardness of the situation for Simon. He had invited the visiting rabbi to his house. He was fulfilling one of his religious duties, that of hospitality. Over a meal Simon could engage the rabbi in intelligent conversation. Feel his superiority in having an important visitor in his house.

Feel his shame and annoyance as an uninvited guest turns up. Watch this woman without name slide into the room where the visitors are reclining for the meal with their feet away from the low tables. Simon recognizes her as 'a sinner'. Look at his eyes as he names her as evil. Was she well known in the town for satisfying men? In such a situation was the woman more a sinner than the man? Sense Simon's awkwardness at the presence of the uninvited, but only too-well-known, guest.

Listen as Simon mumbles in his cups, 'A proper prophet would know what sort of woman that is.' Watch his eyes dart around the table. Everyone is looking at one another. Their eyes turn to Jesus. What will he say or do? To be touched by a sinner is to become a sinner. Evil is contagious.

Listen as Jesus looks up and addresses Simon by name: 'Simon, will you listen to me?' 'Rabbi', Simon replies, oh so politely, 'speak on.' Spot the clarity in the story Jesus tells about the two debtors and the forgiving creditor. Simon reluctantly has to admit the truth or appear a real fool. Love is shown in the way people act. Wisdom is vindicated by her children.

Watch Simon squirming in his place. Jesus is applying the story to him and the woman. Simon is shown up for being a poor host. The woman has made up for his sins. Both sets of actions show the heart of a person. One feels superior to Jesus. The other feels accepted by Jesus. Released by love, the woman can show a proper kind of love. Watch the woman's face smile to reflect a heart at peace. Watch the man scowl to reflect his heart in turmoil.

The gospel message about judgement and forgiveness strikes home. Faces and deeds show up the truth.

Intuition

Here are good examples of judgement and forgiveness in action.

Forgiveness is a difficult matter. It seems to run counter to the concept of justice. We all want to be free from sin and live holy lives. That makes us feel worthy and acceptable. People will admire our goodness. We will be confident in our own acceptability. Most folk put on a mask of respectability. However, in the end what is underneath does show!

The woman did not need a word of judgement. She was well aware of her shame. Driven to it, or inviting it, we will never know, but she was clearly one of the village sinners. It was a hopeless situation. Even if she turned over a new leaf, no one would ever let her forget her sins. If she tried to be accepted by others, 'they' would shun her. Everyone was ready to judge. Do you know of situations like this? Do you know of employers wanting to see references? Do you know of young people expelled from one school having difficulty finding another? Can you find other examples in your community?

Simon could not see that he was a sinner, for his were sins of omission. He had failed to supply the comforts of cooling water and fragrant oil for his visitor. He had kept his distance and never given him the kiss of acceptance or even affection. He honoured himself rather than his guest. It seems strange that sins of omission are never considered as important because they seem less damaging. Do sins of omission stand out in the ministry of hospitality in your church or your home?

In the story Jesus told about judgement and forgiveness, do you identify with the one in debt for the large or the small amount? There is a vast difference in the amounts: one is one hundred times the other.

The outcomes for the two people are as striking in contrast as the sums of money stated. Simon is left in confusion and loss of face. The woman is left with peace and a new opportunity to live and love. All this happened because they met with Jesus. Judgement and forgiveness are shown up clearly.

Feeling

How do you feel towards those in your church community? Who would you invite to dinner? Many of us would have sympathy with Simon. Everyone likes the honour of inviting the church leaders to their homes. It gives us satisfaction and pride and an occasion for learning. But would we be likely to invite the church members who dress badly or who have been battered and bruised by life's circumstances? Their presence would make us feel uncomfortable, would it not?

Do we measure our relationships by respectability or faith? Jesus points out that the faith of the woman in the story has saved her. Do we feel that faith is a more attractive virtue than outward righteousness?

How do we feel towards the mixture of people we meet in the company of Jesus? There are women and men of different backgrounds, temperaments and cultures. Remember that the disciples and followers of Jesus were a mixed bunch: zealots and peacemakers, scholars and simple folk, city dwellers and country fishermen, older and younger persons all together. It couldn't have been an easy group to be in. Yet, God must delight in variety. The women as well as the men came from different backgrounds. In this passage are mentioned a strange woman with psychological problems from a tiny village and a high-born woman from the court of a king. What a mixed group. Is it any different in your congregation? How do you relate to them? Do you classify them by their backgrounds or their faith?

How do you feel about your own position in the church community? Are you secure in your forgiveness for whatever sins you have committed or for those sins of omission which you have confessed? Do you expect others to forgive you, or do you keep your distance? How do you show that you know you are forgiven through the saving grace of Jesus Christ?

Thinking

When we think about it, this passage almost makes it righteous to sin. Saint Paul had to tackle this intellectual question with careful reasoning to prevent people being swept away by their emotions. Paul refutes the idea that it would be good to sin more so that the grace of forgiveness would abound. It is illogical to reverse the statement that the greater the sin, the greater the sense of forgiveness and therefore the greater the love shown by the forgiven sinner. We can see that it is stupid to promote sin in order to show that forgiveness leads to love.

In the light of Christ's judgement we are all sinners, whether by commission or omission. We know that we do not have to try very hard to be good sinners! Yet we do have to try very hard to admit that we can act as sinners. We would rather avoid the issue, making excuses and blaming others. Did Simon blame his servants for the lack of good hospitality or a shortage of oil?

Paul encouraged his readers to come to terms with the fact that we are all sinners.

Isn't this story about us? At times we will act like Simon and at other times like the woman. We can keep Jesus at a distance or we can accept him as Saviour, freeing us from the immobilizing effects of our sins.

The story also tells us that our rational faculty is capable of seeing the truth. Simon could see the truth in his mind but was reluctant to apply it to his own heart. He preferred to hide behind his own respectability. He could not bring himself as an intelligent hardworking person to admit he needed forgiveness. It is a hard lesson to learn. To receive forgiveness we must trust God rather than our own power to give us new life. Can you see the truth in that? How will it show in your life?

19

Luke 8:22–25

²²One day he got into a boat with his disciples, and he said to them, 'Let us go across to the other side of the lake.' So they put out, ²³and while they were sailing he fell asleep. A gale swept down on the lake, and the boat was filling with water, and they were in danger. ²⁴They went to him and woke him up, shouting, 'Master, Master, we are perishing!' And he woke up and rebuked the wind and the raging waves; they ceased, and there was a calm. ²⁵He said to them, 'Where is your faith?' They were afraid and amazed, and said to one another, 'Who then is this, that he commands even the winds and the water, and they obey him?'

Context

Luke records a series of incidents that illustrate the need for faith. This first incident is located on the large inland lake of Galilee. Found in each of the first three gospels, the story must have been widely circulated in the early church. As we know from Saint Paul's journeys, the expansion of the gospel community called for much travel, often in stormy conditions. This passage would encourage faith and trust in God in the midst of storms, both on the sea and in the events of life.

Sensing

Step into the boat as one of the disciples. You have been brought up with boats. You know the moods of the lake and the fickle nature of the wind which whistles down the gullies between the hills that surround the lake.

Take the oars to put off from the beach. Jesus is on the move, eager to teach and heal in places around the lake. Today he is in Gentile territory, across from Tiberias. He is exhausted from his ministry, having given out all day. You have trusted him to carry out his task.

Hear him saying to you, 'Sailing is your area of expertise. I trust you to do your work well.' See him nodding off on a cushion at the rear of the ship, well away from the sails and the work.

Feel your stomach pitch and toss as the wind suddenly rises and a black storm sweeps down from the hills. 'Here's trouble, get the sail down', you hear Peter say. The waves are rising and the water is wet on your feet. Feel the anxiety rising, then the panic. Will the boat hold? Will you have to swim for it? You are fighting for your life.

John is angry. He shouts at Jesus over the wind, trying to wake him up from the depth of sleep: 'Master we are perishing! Master you are in charge of everything, why will you let us drown?'

Watch Jesus shake the sleep from his eyes and raise his hand. 'Stop, let there be calm.' Is he shouting at the wind or your fears or both? Feel the wind drop as suddenly as it arose. Feel your fears subside and your heart return to its normal beat. You and your fellow-seamen look sheepish as Jesus says: 'Where is your faith? I trust in you and in God. Where is *your* faith?'

Turn to one another and say, 'Who is this? What do you believe about Jesus? What do you believe about life?'

Step out of the boat and thank God for a safe crossing.

Intuition

Faith: what happens to it when we meet the storms of nature
and storms of life? Why does our faith seem to sink to the
bottom of the sea at such times? Is ours a fair-weather faith,
strong when life is going well and lacking when life is in
turmoil?

Storms: why do we panic so quickly when faced with the
storms of life? We have been brought up to be realistic about
life's ups and downs. We know that the circumstances of life
come and go. Most of us will experience some measure of
sickness, grief and hardship. Why do we pretend that it is not
so?

All is calm, all is bright. Is that true? Has modern science
created an illusion, promising us fix–its for every trouble? We
have so many medicines and counsellors that we may be
tempted to think that life can be a dream come true, all calm
and no storms. The cross, the experience of others and our own
experiences tell us otherwise.

Protection: does God protect us from storms or bring us
through them with courage and faith? Is the lesson of this
passage that turmoil and storms are part of human existence
but we have no need to panic in the face of them? Christ is in
the storm with us, expecting us to use our skills to sail a way
through, and if necessary giving us new courage and strength
to endure until normality returns. What do we understand
about the system of creation? Do we accept the earthquake and
the storm as necessary to the whole but not as the usual state of
creation? Do we believe that there is a good purpose in all that
happens in creation, and that calm and balance is its achievable
goal?

What do we mean by storms? What do we mean by faith?
What do we mean by protection?

Feeling

Put yourself on the pillow beside Jesus. It will help you see how
to relate to the others in the boat. It will test how you learn to
trust others and their skills when there is danger. It will reveal
your relationship with God in times of trouble.

There on the pillow, out of the way of those entrusted with
the task of getting everyone safely across the lake, you can

remain calm. You know these sailors are resourceful. They have the experience of working in stormy weather. They know the procedures to follow. They are the experts. You can put your life in their hands. Keeping calm and keeping faith with them will help them concentrate on the difficult task.

There on the pillow watch Jesus at rest. He does not interfere with those who know what they are doing. He does not try to take over. He is a partner with them, not a usurper of their power. He lies there beside you trusting in their human skills to match nature's fury. Can you too remain calm beside him?

The sailors call out to you on the pillow. Can you give them a hand? Have you learnt the skills of survival, able to follow the commands of the experts with calmness and cooperation? Are you frozen with fright or equipped for action through faith and experience? There on the pillow do you feel close to Jesus with his total faith in God and his friends? When called into action can you respond?

From your pillow hear Jesus rebuke the turmoil, bringing calm to sailors and storm. Indeed it is right to call him 'Master' of both. He felt for the needs of all in the boat. He acted when they called on him. He showed that God responded to their cries. He did not leave them comfortless. Peace returns to both nature and human hearts.

Is this how you relate to Jesus? Is this how you relate to storms? Storms are part of life and part of nature. Your reaction to them, and in them, will show how you relate to God, to others and to yourself in a crisis.

Thinking

Those who live beside Lake Galilee will tell you that sudden storms stir up its waters which later quickly return to a still calm. It is a fickle lake. Boats still cross it. Fishermen still fish there. Across the water from Capernaum the land rises steeply and is broken by steep gullies that lead down to the water's edge. Down these gullies the wind, coming in from the hot hinterland, sweeps to churn up the waters in the deep basin of the lake. Once the windstorm has passed over, the lake resettles into its calm.

Storms are common. Some are clearly worse than others. Then fishing vessels run for the shore. Usually the boats weather the storm with sails furled and prow kept firmly facing into the waves. The seamen with Jesus should have known their boat and the lake well; they should have handled the situation effectively.

With storms so common, why do you think that the incident was remembered and recorded in the first three gospels? Was it because the disciples and the early church saw it as a key step in their understanding of who Jesus might be? The way that Jesus handled the storm showed the trust he had in the Creator God. Storms have a purpose. The wind and the waves might sting his face but they could not dent his spirits. The disciples remembered that vividly.

The disciples also remembered the story as teaching them an important lesson about faith. With faith, the early Christians learnt to deal with the storms of travel as they spread the gospel. With faith they learnt to deal with storms of persecution. They became steadfast in both.

The story was applicable to so many situations in the early church. It has helped disciples in every age to discover who Jesus is, how Jesus can come to our aid and how to maintain faith during the storms. For many it is possible to call Jesus 'Master' because he keeps us 'in control'. It is our faith which helps us to see Jesus act in this way. What do you think Luke was trying to teach through the inclusion of this incident?

20
Luke 8:26–39

²⁶Then they arrived at the country of the Gerasenes, which is opposite Galilee. ²⁷As he stepped out on land, a man of the city who had demons met him. For a long time he had worn no clothes, and he did not live in a house but in the tombs. ²⁸When he saw Jesus, he fell down before him and shouted at the top of his voice, 'What have you to do with me, Jesus, Son of the Most High God? I beg you, do not torment me' – ²⁹for Jesus had commanded the unclean spirit to come out of the man. (For many times it had seized him; he was kept under guard and

bound with chains and shackles, but he would break the bonds and be driven by the demon into the wilds.) [30]Jesus then asked him, 'What is your name?' He said, 'Legion'; for many demons had entered him. [31]They begged him not to order them to go back into the abyss.

[32]Now there on the hillside a large herd of swine was feeding; and the demons begged Jesus to let them enter these. So he gave them permission. [33]Then the demons came out of the man and entered the swine, and the herd rushed down the steep bank into the lake and was drowned. [34]When the swineherds saw what had happened, they ran off and told it in the city and in the country. [35]Then people came out to see what had happened, and when they came to Jesus, they found the man from whom the demons had gone sitting at the feet of Jesus, clothed and in his right mind. And they were afraid. [36]Those who had seen it told them how the one who had been possessed by demons had been healed. [37]Then all the people of the surrounding country of the Gerasenes asked Jesus to leave them; for they were seized with great fear. So he got into the boat and returned. [38]The man from whom the demons had gone begged that he might be with him; but Jesus sent him away, saying, [39]'Return to your home, and declare how much God has done for you.' So he went away, proclaiming throughout the city how much Jesus had done for him.

Context

Luke's gospel shows that Jesus had authority over the storms of creation and over the disturbing storms that can stir up serious turmoil in the mind. This account of the restoration of a man driven to distraction by an army of 'demons' ends with the man giving witness to the saving power of Jesus. It has some difficulties of interpretation for modern readers.

Sensing

Imagine the scene. Jesus stepped ashore after the stormy crossing and immediately he was faced with the storm in the mind of a man. Once he had been a cultured person (a man of the city), here he was naked and leaping from tomb to tomb. See everyone shrink back in fear. This man is dangerous and should not be approached. He charges up to Jesus and falls at his feet writhing around and shouting at the top of his voice as Jesus challenges the unclean spirit to leave him.

Watch him quieten as Jesus speaks calmly to him, 'What is your name?' Does this man remember having a name, an identity and a value in the eyes of others? Listen to the reply, 'Legion', a regiment in the Roman imperial forces. This response could imply that he considered himself captured by a regiment of demons who had marched into his life and taken it over, or it may subconsciously recall a Roman legion that swept into his town, pillaging and murdering, shattering the settled life of his family. Whatever the reason he is a broken human being, bent on the destruction of himself and others.

Watch Jesus take him seriously without argument or rebuke. Jesus takes his word for it that demons are like a legion within him. How can they leave him for good? Watch Jesus bend down to listen to him again. The man feels the demons are speaking from inside him: 'We must not be put in prison, we must be totally destroyed.'

Hear the squeal of pigs on the opposite hillside. Remember we are in Gentile territory. To a Jew, pigs are unclean. The man's agitation terrifies them. The demons in his voice cry out to be released into them. Watch the herd rush headlong down the steep gully into the deep water of the lake. Everything is happening at once. The man runs at the swine. The swine run down the bank to destruction. The swineherds run off in terror.

Within minutes see the man calmly sitting at the feet of Jesus. Someone has thrown a cloak over his shoulders. He is carrying on a rational conversation. He looks like one of the disciples sitting at the feet of the Master. Humanity is restored. Feel the calmness and dignity in the scene. Observe the joy in the faces of Jesus and the other disciples. Another one of God's people has found life.

Intuition

Mental illness is one of the most disturbing features of modern life. Previous generations tried asylums to protect and care for the mentally ill. They tried chains to stop people hurting themselves and hurting others. Today we see locking people away as a last resort.

We have tried to treat the mentally ill by counselling and drugs. There has been some success and we can rejoice in that.

But mental illness still returns for many. Drugs have positive and negative effects. No one is quite sure about them. Counselling has been very effective in some cases but it is a long and expensive process.

How much money is society prepared to allocate to the treatment of the mentally ill? Are we sometimes angry and frightened like the swineherds were at the cost of care and cure? What obligations have we towards the mentally ill?

What is the place of healing by the Spirit in the ministry to the mentally ill? Why do we talk of possession when the New Testament merely uses the word 'had demons', stating a fact without using emotive language? This passage shows that Jesus is not overawed by the demons, and it is they who take the initiative in leaving the man and finding a way to be gone for good. Why do spiritual healers try to drive out demons in what appears a shouting match between the two? Here is dignified calm and the fear is in the swineherds, not in the ill man. What is our approach to the mentally ill?

In today's society many are traumatized by the violence they experience or witness. How do we handle our 'legions'? How do we restore humanity to its right mind?

Feeling

Imagine yourself as the man in the story. Feel the strain on your relationships with others. How would you feel about yourself? It is very hard to lose control of your dignity and mental faculties, whatever the reason. You cry out to be free but feel chained inside. Approaching others for help fills them with panic and fear. They seem to sink with you into depression. You hurt those you love most and hate yourself all the more for it.

If you were the man in the story, how would you feel towards others? No doubt you would seek from them stability. You would hope they might treat you as a human being and not as some animal out of control. You would want them to be a stable point of reference in a confused world. You would want them to bear without grudging the cost of your restoration to full humanity. It is not your fault that you are ill; it could happen to anyone. You do not want to be left to drift from one specialist to another, from one sheltered accommodation to another. You want to restore relationships as far as possible.

If you were the man in the story, how would you feel about God? Would you attack God for causing your illness? It is hard to achieve a balance between expecting God to restore us and cursing God for making our minds so frail. Can we let go of the desire for instant results and see God at work in many different ways? Is the faith we need any different from that of others facing their storms and traumatic moments?

If you were the man in the story, how would you relate to those who bear the 'cost' of your illness? It is hard to be a doctor or counsellor for the mentally ill. They are overburdened and must listen and empathize with the legion of stories about violence and abuse. How can they be repaid for their skill and dedication? What support does the church give them for their work?

If you were the man in the story, how would you relate to yourself and others?

Thinking

This story has many illustrations of clashes of cultures and motives.

The man seems to be a Jew living in an area with a mixture of Gentiles and Jews. The mention of pigs in the story illustrates this. Pigs were only kept by non-Jews. The man's description of Jesus and his language about demons puts him within the Jewish culture. The clash of cultures leaves a gulf between opposing values. For some, one man is not worth the sacrifice of so many precious pigs. The swineherds and townspeople want this Jesus to leave. The gospel writer has a different set of values. The restoration of one human being is the purpose of creation and the purpose of the cross. Is this the prevalent value in your society? What is it worth to rescue climbers lost on a mountain? What is it worth to provide adequate treatment and care for the mentally ill?

There is a clash of values between the restored man and Jesus. The man wants to join the worldwide mission of the disciples. Jesus wants him to undertake mission at home. Is this clash still present in your local church? Do you give priority in finance and honour to overseas mission, even when there are also major challenges at home? How do you think you can retain a balance between the two?

Luke stresses the lack of response by the local people to the dramatic salvation of this man. Is this a reminder that the gospel creates opposition as well as acceptance? This is a common experience for the church in every age. How do you think Christians should respond to such opposition in these circumstances?

The gospel from the beginning has caused a clash of values and cultures. In what ways do you think your own culture stops people readily accepting the gospel today?

———————⟫⊱-◉-⊰⟪———————

21

Luke 9:28–36

28Now about eight days after these sayings Jesus took with him Peter and John and James, and went up on the mountain to pray. 29And while he was praying, the appearance of his face changed, and his clothes became dazzling white. 30Suddenly they saw two men, Moses and Elijah, talking to him. 31They appeared in glory and were speaking of his departure, which he was about to accomplish at Jerusalem. 32Now Peter and his companions were weighed down with sleep; but since they had stayed awake, they saw his glory and the two men who stood with him. 33Just as they were leaving him, Peter said to Jesus, 'Master, it is good for us to be here; let us make three dwellings, one for you, one for Moses, and one for Elijah' – not knowing what he said. 34While he was saying this, a cloud came and overshadowed them; and they were terrified as they entered the cloud. 35Then from the cloud came a voice that said, 'This is my Son, my Chosen; listen to him!' 36When the voice had spoken, Jesus was found alone. And they kept silent and in those days told no one any of the things they had seen.

Context

In Luke chapter nine three important events happen in sequence. Peter speaks out his recognition of Jesus as the Messiah. Jesus foretells his death and resurrection. Peter, John and James see Jesus' glory revealed on the mount of transfiguration.

Sensing

Picture three events in Luke's gospel and see how they fit so closely together.

Begin by walking down to the river Jordan. There in the distance you hear the stern and impelling voice of John the Baptist proclaiming the good news of the coming Messiah. 'I baptize you with water', says John, 'but one who is more powerful than I is coming . . . He will baptize you with the Holy Spirit and with fire.' See Jesus step out of the crowd, descend into the water, submit to the baptism of John and withdraw from the Baptist.

Now see Jesus fall to his knees in prayer. Keep your eyes firmly on Jesus as he becomes absorbed in that prayerful relationship with the Father. See the heavens open. See the Holy Spirit descend upon him in bodily form like a dove. Now hear the voice from heaven saying, 'You are my Son, the Beloved, with you I am well pleased.' Note how the voice is addressed to Jesus.

Continue by walking up the mountain slope, the mount of transfiguration. There in the distance you hear the hushed conversation of Peter, John, James and Jesus. See Jesus step away from the others. Now see Jesus fall to his knees in prayer. Keep your eyes firmly on Jesus as he becomes absorbed in that prayerful relationship with the Father. See his disciples struggle to keep awake, but awake they remain. See the appearance of Jesus' face change and his clothes become dazzling white. Hear Moses and Elijah speak to Jesus about his departure, his exodus, at Jerusalem. Now hear the voice from heaven saying, 'This is my Son, my Chosen; listen to him!' Note how the voice is addressed to you.

Continue by walking up another mountain slope, the Mount of Olives. Now is the time of exodus, for the Passover meal has already been eaten in the upper room. There in the distance you hear the hushed conversation of the disciples. See Jesus step away from the others. Now see Jesus fall to his knees in prayer. Keep your eyes firmly on Jesus. In his anguish he prays more and more earnestly and his sweat becomes like great drops of blood falling down to the ground. See his disciples struggle to keep awake, and fall into deep slumber. Now see Judas approach Jesus with the betrayer's kiss. This time there is no voice from heaven.

Picture three events from Luke's gospel and see how they fit so closely together.

Intuition

Here is a narrative about divine revelation, a narrative about God breaking in on human lives. How easy is it for God to break in on your life?

Here is a narrative about three disciples taking time off together to walk with Jesus. How important do you think it is for Christian people to explore their faith together? Do you make time for that?

Here is a narrative about making pilgrimage to the mountain-top where heaven and earth draw closer together. How important do you think it is for Christian people to recognize holy places and holy sites? Do you make time for that?

Here is a narrative about Jesus going away to pray and losing himself in prayer. How important do you think it is for Christian people to take prayer seriously? Do you make time for that?

Here is a narrative about linking present experience with the great traditions and characters of the bible. How important do you think it is for Christian people to be steeped in the biblical tradition? Do you make time for that?

Here is a narrative about fighting off the overwhelming desire for sleep in order to stay awake to the voice of God. How important do you think it is for Christian people to keep holy vigil? Do you make time for that?

Here is a narrative about disciples facing profound fear as they approach and allow themselves to enter the cloud of revelation. How important do you think it is for Christian people to allow themselves to cross the threshold of God's holy presence? Do you make time for that?

Here is a narrative about divine revelation, a narrative about God breaking in on human lives. How easy is it for God to break in on your life?

Feeling

Step into the shoes of those three chosen disciples, Peter, John and James, and experience the transfiguration from the inside.

Here are three people who have been chosen, set apart for a special closeness to Jesus himself. Share their sense of intimacy.

Here are three people who have been climbing the mountain path. Already their limbs have grown weary, their breathing has grown heavy. Share their sense of exhaustion.

Here are three people who are weighed down by sleep, yet struggle to keep awake, to keep their senses alert. Share their sense of drifting between sleep and wakefulness.

Here are three people whose eyes are open to the vision of holiness. They see the face of Jesus changed and his clothes become dazzling white. They see the faces of Moses and Elijah made present from the past. They see the glory of God stretched out on the mountainside. Share their sense of the vision of divine revelation.

Here are three people whose ears are open to the sounds of holiness. They hear the voice of Jesus and the voices of Moses and Elijah discussing events yet to come. They hear the voice of God command their attention, 'This is my Son, my Chosen, listen to him!' Share their sense of receiving the word of divine revelation.

Here are three people who are stunned by coming face to face with the divine presence on the mountain-top. They embarrass themselves by what they say. They embarrass themselves by what they do. Share their sense of inadequacy.

Step into the shoes of those three chosen disciples, Peter, John and James, and experience the transfiguration from the inside.

Thinking

The account of the transfiguration is one of those occasions when Luke consciously redrafts his Marcan source. I wonder what that tells us about Luke's theology?

Both Mark and Luke clearly date the transfiguration. In Mark the transfiguration occurs six days after Peter's confession of faith in Jesus as the Messiah. In Luke the transfiguration occurs eight days later. Do eight days bring Luke to the first day of the week, the day of resurrection?

Both Mark and Luke name the same three disciples. Mark speaks of Peter, James and John. Luke speaks of Peter, John and James. Is Luke deliberately bringing the disciples into the order of importance they assume in his second volume, the Acts of the Apostles?

Both Mark and Luke bring Jesus and the disciples to the mountain. Mark leads them there to be apart from the others. Luke leads them there to pray. Is Luke deliberately emphasizing the theme of the prayerful Jesus seen so clearly elsewhere in his gospel?

Both Mark and Luke note the effect of the events on Jesus. Mark says that Jesus was transfigured. Luke says that the appearance of his face changed. Is Luke deliberately distancing his account from the metamorphoses of the Greek gods?

Both Mark and Luke describe Moses and Elijah talking with Jesus. But only Luke relates the substance of their discourse as Jesus' departure (exodus) which he was about to accomplish at Jerusalem. Is Luke deliberately linking Jesus' last Passover meal with a new exodus of God's people?

Both Mark and Luke give prominence to Peter. But only Luke describes Peter and the disciples as weighed down with sleep yet managing to stay awake. Is Luke deliberately linking this occasion on the mount of transfiguration with the occasion, on the Mount of Olives after the Passover meal, when the disciples fell asleep and Jesus was arrested?

Both Mark and Luke describe the cloud and the voice. But only Luke says clearly that they saw Jesus' glory. Is Luke making more explicit his theme that the presence of God known in the Old Testament now clearly shines through the person of Jesus?

The account of the transfiguration is one of those occasions when Luke consciously redrafts his Marcan source. I wonder what that tells us about Luke's theology?

22

Luke 9:51–62

⁵¹When the days drew near for him to be taken up, he set his face to go to Jerusalem. ⁵²And he sent messengers ahead of him. On their way they entered a village of the Samaritans to make ready for him; ⁵³but they did not receive him, because his face

was set towards Jerusalem. [54]When his disciples James and John saw it, they said, 'Lord, do you want us to command fire to come down from heaven and consume them?' [55]But he turned and rebuked them. [56]Then they went on to another village.

[57]As they were going along the road, someone said to him, 'I will follow you wherever you go.' [58]And Jesus said to him, 'Foxes have holes, and birds of the air have nests; but the Son of Man has nowhere to lay his head.' [59]To another he said, 'Follow me.' But he said, 'Lord, first let me go and bury my father.' [60]But Jesus said to him, 'Let the dead bury their own dead; but as for you, go and proclaim the kingdom of God.' [61]Another said, 'I will follow you, Lord; but let me first say farewell to those at my home.' [62]Jesus said to him, 'No one who puts a hand to the plough and looks back is fit for the kingdom of God.'

Context

According to Luke, at the transfiguration Moses and Elijah talked with Jesus about his departure (exodus) in Jerusalem. Now the whole section 9:51 to 19:28 is set on the road to Jerusalem.

Sensing

Here are three messages about the nature of discipleship. Have you heard them?

See Jesus walking along the road with his face toward Jerusalem. See an enthusiastic bystander run up to Jesus and engage him in conversation. Hear his declaration of discipleship. 'Master', he says, 'I will follow you wherever you go.' Hear Jesus reply, 'Foxes have holes, and birds of the air have nests; but the Son of Man has nowhere to lay his head.' Here is the first message about the nature of discipleship. Jesus offers no false hopes of an easy journey.

See Jesus walking along the road with his face toward Jerusalem. See Jesus turn to an interested enquirer. Hear Jesus challenge his allegiance. 'Follow me', says Jesus. Hear the man's reply, 'Lord, first let me go and bury my father.' Then hear Jesus' sharp retort, 'Let the dead bury their own dead; but as for you, go and proclaim the kingdom of God.' Here is the second message about the nature of discipleship. Jesus' call demands a prompt and immediate response that cannot be delayed because of other priorities.

See Jesus walking along the road with his face toward Jerusalem. See yet another bystander run up to Jesus and engage him in conversation. Hear his shout of commitment. 'I will follow you, Lord; but let me first say farewell to those at my home.' Then hear Jesus' sharp retort, 'No one who puts a hand to the plough and looks back is fit for the kingdom of God.' Here is the third message about the nature of discipleship. Jesus' call demands a consistent and single-minded approach.

Here are three messages about the nature of discipleship. Have you heard them?

Intuition

How tolerant are you willing to be?

There was a time when Samaritans and Jews engaged in bitter conflict. They would willingly call down fire from heaven to support their claims. So how tolerant are you?

There was a time when Catholics and Protestants engaged in bitter conflict (and perhaps still do). They would willingly call down fire from heaven to support their claims. So how tolerant are you of other denominations?

There was a time when Christians and Moslems engaged in bitter conflict (and perhaps still do). They would willingly call down fire from heaven to support their claims. So how tolerant are you of other faiths?

There was a time when children who attended different schools engaged in bitter conflict (and perhaps still do). They would willingly call down fire from heaven to support their claims. How tolerant are you of those who belong to other groups?

There was a time when people from different races engaged in bitter conflict (and perhaps still do). They would willingly call down fire from heaven to support their claims. So how tolerant are you of other races?

There was a time when people from different social backgrounds engaged in bitter conflict (and perhaps still do). They would willingly call down fire from heaven to support their claims. So how tolerant are you of other classes?

There was a time when people of different sexual orientations engaged in bitter conflict (and perhaps still do). They would willingly call down fire from heaven to support their claims. So how tolerant are you of others' sexuality?

How tolerant are you willing to be?

Feeling

It was not for nothing that James and John earned the nickname Boanerges, 'Sons of Thunder'. Look at the world through their eyes and appreciate their fiery response.

Take, for example, how they felt when the villagers rejected them and taunted them as they passed through Samaria en route to Jerusalem. Here are two people whose personal pride is attacked. If only they could have called down fire from heaven to vindicate their personal honour, they would have done so there and then. It was not for nothing that James and John earned the nickname Boanerges, 'Sons of Thunder'.

Take, for example, how they felt when the Samaritans rejected their fellow Jewish travellers as they passed through en route to Jerusalem. Here are two people whose notion of identity is attacked. If only they could have called down fire from heaven to vindicate their national honour, they would have done so there and then. It was not for nothing that James and John earned the nickname Boanerges, 'Sons of Thunder'.

Take, for example, how they felt when the Samaritans rejected their Lord and master as they passed through en route to Jerusalem. Here are two people whose religious faith is attacked. If only they could have called down fire from heaven to vindicate their spiritual honour, they would have done so there and then. It was not for nothing that James and John earned the nickname Boanerges, 'Sons of Thunder'.

But now look at the Sons of Thunder through Jesus' eyes. Here are two men whom Jesus had called to become his closest companions and leaders of the new people of God. Here are two men whose zeal Jesus well knows and well accepts. Here are two men whose thunder Jesus transforms for the growth of his kingdom. Today Jesus rebukes them. And tomorrow he schools them further in his ways of acceptance and peace.

It was not for nothing that Jesus called Boanerges, 'Sons of Thunder', among his closest companions.

Thinking

Earlier on in chapter nine Jesus was listening to what the crowds were saying about him. Some said that he was Elijah. Can you understand their mistake?

Now, later in chapter nine, Jesus set his face to go to Jerusalem, for there he was 'to be taken up'. The Greek work used by Luke, *analempseos*, means an assumption, a reception up into heaven. Do you recall the account in 2 Kings 2 when a chariot of fire and horses of fire came for Elijah and he was carried up in a whirlwind into heaven? Some of the crowd said that Jesus was Elijah. Can you understand their mistake? But Jesus' ascension was not like Elijah's assumption.

Now, later in chapter nine, Jesus and his disciples met with rejection as they travelled the road to Jerusalem. When James and John, the Sons of Thunder, saw this rejection of their master, they said, 'Lord, do you want us to command fire to come down from heaven and consume them?' Do you recall the account in 2 Kings 1 when Elijah called fire down from heaven to consume the captain of fifty with his fifty men? Some of the crowd said that Jesus was Elijah. Can you understand their mistake? But Jesus rebuked James and John for their suggestion.

Now, later in chapter nine, as Jesus and his disciples journeyed toward Jerusalem, a man said to him, 'I will follow you, Lord; but first let me say farewell to those at my home.' Do you recall the account in 1 Kings 19 when Elijah called Elisha away from his plough? Elisha said, 'Let me kiss my father and mother, and then I will follow you.' And Elijah gave him permission so to do. Some of the crowd said that Jesus was Elijah. Can you understand their mistake? But Jesus refused the request and said, 'No one who puts a hand to the plough and looks back is fit for the kingdom of God.'

Earlier on in chapter nine Jesus was listening to what the crowds were saying about him. Some said that he was Elijah. Can you understand their mistake?

23
Luke 10:1–11, 16–20

¹After this the Lord appointed seventy others and sent them on ahead of him in pairs to every town and place where he himself intended to go. ²He said to them, 'The harvest is plentiful, but the labourers are few; therefore ask the Lord of the harvest to send out labourers into his harvest. ³Go on your way. See, I am sending you out like lambs into the midst of wolves. ⁴Carry no purse, no bag, no sandals; and greet no one on the road. ⁵Whatever house you enter, first say, "Peace to this house!" ⁶And if anyone is there who shares in peace, your peace will rest on that person; but if not, it will return to you. ⁷Remain in the same house, eating and drinking whatever they provide, for the labourer deserves to be paid. Do not move about from house to house. ⁸Whenever you enter a town and its people welcome you, eat what is set before you; ⁹cure the sick who are there, and say to them, "The kingdom of God has come near to you." ¹⁰But whenever you enter a town and they do not welcome you, go out into its streets and say, ¹¹"Even the dust of your town that clings to our feet, we wipe off in protest against you. Yet know this: the kingdom of God has come near."

¹⁶'Whoever listens to you listens to me, and whoever rejects you rejects me, and whoever rejects me rejects the one who sent me.'

¹⁷The seventy returned with joy, saying, 'Lord, in your name even the demons submit to us!' ¹⁸He said to them, 'I watched Satan fall from heaven like a flash of lightning. ¹⁹See, I have given you authority to tread on snakes and scorpions, and over all the power of the enemy; and nothing will hurt you. ²⁰Nevertheless, do not rejoice at this, that the spirits submit to you, but rejoice that your names are written in heaven.'

Context

While Mark and Matthew describe Jesus sending the twelve on a missionary journey, Luke provides a second account about Jesus sending out seventy others.

Sensing

Here is a story about seventy people with a real sense of mission. They are full of energy for the task ahead. Sense the urgency in their footsteps.

See how they travel light. They are weighed down by no excess baggage. There is no bag in their hands. There is no purse in their belt. There is no spare pair of sandals for their feet. See how they travel light. Sense the urgency in their footsteps.

See how they press on with their journey. They pause to greet no one on the road. They stop for no leisurely conversation with fellow travellers. They ignore the oriental etiquette of their day when greeted by others. See how they press on with their journey. Sense the urgency in their footsteps.

See how they waste no time with those who reject them. They proclaim 'peace' to the strangers' house and the peace returns to them if no son of peace resides there. They proclaim 'peace' to the strangers' town and when they receive no welcome they shake the dust of that town from their feet. See how they waste no time with those who reject them. Sense the urgency in their footsteps.

See how they disregard the time-consuming ritual scruples of their race. When they are welcomed into a strange house, they accept what they find. When food is placed in front of them, they eat what they are given. When drink is poured for them, they consume what is provided. See how they disregard the time-consuming ritual scruples of their race. Sense the urgency in their footsteps.

Here is a story about seventy people with a real sense of mission. They are full of energy for the task ahead. Sense the urgency in their footsteps.

Intuition

Here is a story about personal security. How secure are you? And from what do you derive your sense of security?

Some people build their security around possessions. How important are possessions to you for your sense of identity and sense of security? How important are the right clothes and the right shoes? How important are the right bag and the right accessories? How important are the right car and the right house? Some people build their security around possessions. But Jesus said, 'Carry nothing for the journey.'

Some people build their security around meeting with other people. How much do you need the company of others? How much do you need the conversation of others? How much do you need others to affirm and value you? How much can you face up to your own company? How much can you feed off your own resources? Some people build their security around meeting with other people. But Jesus said, 'Greet no one on the road.'

Some people build their security around personal success. How much do you need to succeed in all you do? How able are you to accept defeat in an argument? How able are you to be the loser in a game? How much do you strive to convince others that you are in the right? How competitive are you in your professional and personal life? Some people build their security around personal success. But Jesus said, 'If one town fails to listen to you, move on to another.'

Some people build their security around personal control. How much do you need to be in charge of your own environment? How much do you need to know that your home is your castle? How much do you need to be in control of what and where and when you eat? Some people build their security around personal control. But Jesus said, 'Eat and drink whatever they provide.'

Here is a story about personal security. How secure are you? And from what do you derive your sense of security?

Feeling

According to Luke, the ministry and mission of the church is not something individuals are asked to undertake alone. Seventy people were commissioned, but they were sent out as thirty-five pairs. Even in a time of great urgency and haste, shared ministry was no luxury but a fundamental key to survival and to success.

Put yourself in the shoes of those chosen seventy. When they were sent out they knew that the harvest was plentiful but the labourers were few. Surely shared ministry was essential to keep hope alive when the task was so immense.

Put yourself in the shoes of those chosen seventy. When they were sent out they knew that they were sent as lambs into the midst of wolves. Surely shared ministry was essential to keep spirits up when the dangers were so great.

Put yourself in the shoes of those chosen seventy. When they were sent out they were commanded to take no purse, no bag, no spare sandals for the journey. Surely shared ministry was essential to survival when the resources were so scarce.

Put yourself in the shoes of those chosen seventy. When they were sent out they were commanded to greet no one on the way. Surely shared ministry was essential to maintain fellowship and social support.

Put yourself in the shoes of those chosen seventy. When they were sent out they were commanded to stay with the strangers who welcomed them. Surely shared ministry was essential to keep faith alive in unfamiliar homes.

Put yourself in the shoes of those chosen seventy. When they were sent out they were commanded to work among the sick, the possessed and the deranged. Surely shared ministry was essential to protect their own sanity in such situations.

According to Luke, the ministry and mission of the church is not something that individuals are asked to undertake alone. So are you ready for shared ministry?

Thinking

Luke, and Luke alone among the gospel writers, tells how Jesus appointed seventy others and sent them on ahead of him in pairs to every town and place where he himself intended to go. I wonder what significance Luke saw in this group of seventy? What do you think?

Perhaps minds steeped in the Old Testament would think immediately of Genesis chapter ten, where the authority of scripture lists the Gentile nations of the world. When rabbinic convention counted the names of these nations they totalled seventy. Now, Luke is particularly concerned to show that the Christian faith is destined for the Gentile world, destined even for Rome itself. So what do you think Luke had in mind?

Perhaps minds steeped in the Old Testament would think immediately of Exodus chapter one, where the total number of people born to Jacob totalled seventy. Here were the seventy Israelites going into Egypt as the seed of the future people of God. Now, Luke is particularly concerned to show that the Christian faith constitutes the new people of God, a new beginning for God's continuing activity. So what do you think Luke had in mind?

Perhaps minds steeped in the Old Testament would think immediately of Numbers chapter eleven, where the Lord said to Moses, 'Gather for me seventy of the elders of Israel, whom you know to be the elders of the people and officers over them.' These were the seventy elders who accompanied Moses upon the holy mount and who received a portion of his prophetic spirit. Now, Luke is particularly concerned to show that Jesus is the new Moses who leads the people of God through a new exodus to a new beginning. So what do you think Luke had in mind?

Luke, and Luke alone among the gospel writers, tells how Jesus appointed seventy others. I wonder what significance Luke saw in the group of seventy? What do you think?

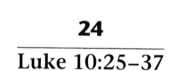

24

Luke 10:25–37

²⁵Just then a lawyer stood up to test Jesus. 'Teacher', he said, 'what must I do to inherit eternal life?' ²⁶He said to him, 'What is written in the law? What do you read there?' ²⁷He answered, 'You shall love the Lord your God with all your heart, and with all your soul, and with all your strength, and with all your mind; and your neighbour as yourself.' ²⁸And he said to him, 'You have given the right answer; do this, and you will live.'

²⁹But wanting to justify himself, he asked Jesus, 'And who is my neighbour?' ³⁰Jesus replied, 'A man was going down from Jerusalem to Jericho, and fell into the hands of robbers, who stripped him, beat him, and went away, leaving him half dead. ³¹Now by chance a priest was going down that road; and when he saw him, he passed by on the other side. ³²So likewise a Levite, when he came to the place and saw him, passed by on the other side. ³³But a Samaritan while travelling came near him; and when he saw him, he was moved with pity. ³⁴He went to him and bandaged his wounds, having poured oil and wine on

them. Then he put him on his own animal, brought him to an inn, and took care of him. ³⁵The next day he took out two denarii, gave them to the innkeeper, and said, "Take care of him; and when I come back, I will repay you whatever more you spend." ³⁶Which of these three, do you think, was a neighbour to the man who fell into the hands of the robbers?' ³⁷He said, 'The one who showed him mercy.' Jesus said to him, 'Go and do likewise.'

Context

The well-known parable of the good Samaritan is unique to Luke's gospel, where Jesus tells the story in response to a debate about interpreting the scope of the commandment to love God and to love your neighbour.

Sensing

The answer, of course, does not always fit the question. First, listen to the question. 'Who is my neighbour?' asked the lawyer. 'Who is my neighbour?' Then, listen to the answer.

'Who is my neighbour?' asked the lawyer. 'Well', said Jesus, 'there was a traveller going down the steep, winding and dangerous road from Jerusalem to Jericho and the traveller was travelling alone. Look into the eyes of that traveller and see there an answer to the question. *There* is your neighbour.'

'Who is my neighbour?' asked the lawyer. 'Well', said Jesus, 'there were robbers going down the steep, winding and dangerous road from Jerusalem to Jericho and the robbers set upon the traveller. Look into the eyes of those robbers and see there an answer to the question. *There* is your neighbour.'

'Who is my neighbour?' asked the lawyer. 'Well', said Jesus, 'there was a priest going down the steep, winding and dangerous road from Jerusalem to Jericho and the priest passed by on the other side. Look into the eyes of that priest and see there an answer to the question. *There* is your neighbour.'

'Who is my neighbour?' asked the lawyer. 'Well', said Jesus, 'there was a Levite going down the steep, winding and dangerous road from Jerusalem to Jericho and the Levite passed by on the other side. Look into the eyes of that Levite and see there an answer to the question. *There* is your neighbour.'

'Who is my neighbour?' asked the lawyer. 'Well', said Jesus, 'there was a Samaritan going down the steep, winding and dangerous road from Jerusalem to Jericho and the Samaritan stopped and did all he could to help the wounded traveller. Look into the eyes of this Samaritan, a despised foreigner, and see there an answer to the question. *There* is your neighbour.'

The answer, of course, does not always fit the question. 'Who is my neighbour?' asked the lawyer. 'Go and be the good neighbour to those who stand in need', came Jesus' short reply.

Intuition

Here is a story about flawed human beings. Examine the flaws. Do you see yourself there in the cracks?

Here is a story about a flawed and foolhardy traveller. No one who took proper responsibility for his own life would have set out alone on that dangerous and hazardous road. This flawed human being put himself at risk and put at risk the security of his family and his dependants. Examine the flaws. Do you see yourself in the cracks?

Here is a story about a flawed and villainous set of robbers. Here are people who made their living off the misfortune of others, off the bad luck of their fellow travellers. These flawed human beings put self first, completely disregarding the good and the wellbeing of those around them. Examine the flaws. Do you see yourself in the cracks?

Here is a story about a flawed and pious priest. Here is a man whose head is so far into heaven that his heart has lost touch with the ground. This flawed human being is so committed to fulfilling and displaying love for God that he fails to fulfil and display love for his neighbour. Examine the flaws. Do you see yourself in the cracks?

Here is a story about a flawed and anxious Levite. Here is a man whose concern for his own safety erodes his concern for the safety of others. This flawed human being is so concerned not to fall into a trap set by robbers that he gives no time to assess the real needs of the victim. Examine the flaws. Do you see yourself in the cracks?

Here is a story about a flawed and fame-seeking Samaritan. Here is a man whose concern for glamour and commendation allows him to become the hero of the story. This flawed human being is so concerned to have the story named after himself that he overlooks how his own good deeds were entirely dependent upon the strong back of his donkey and upon the good faith of the innkeeper. Examine the flaws. Do you see yourself in the cracks?

Here is a story about flawed human beings. Examine your flaws and seek God's forgiveness.

Feeling

The parable of the good Samaritan epitomizes the practical heart of the Christian gospel.

Come and stand alongside the victim and open your heart to the trauma of his experience. Here is a man who has been robbed of all the possessions he was carrying with him. Here is a man who has lost all that he had. Feel his grief.

Come and stand alongside the victim and open your heart to the trauma of his experience. Here is a man who has been robbed of his self-respect. Here is a man who has been stripped naked and left vulnerable to the public gaze. Feel his humiliation.

Come and stand alongside the victim and open your heart to the trauma of his experience. Here is a man who has been kicked and beaten within inches of his life. Here is a man who has been left for dead. Feel his pain.

Come and stand alongside the victim and open your heart to the trauma of his experience. Here is a man who has been ignored by the priest. Here is a man who has been treated as of no value by the Levite. Feel his hurt.

The parable of the good Samaritan epitomizes the practical heart of the Christian gospel.

Come and stand in the shoes of the hero and open your heart to the humanity of his experience. Here is a man whose heart was moved with pity. Here is a man who empathized with the suffering of his fellow traveller. Feel his empathy.

Come and stand in the shoes of the hero and open your heart to the humanity of his experience. Here is a man who bandaged the wounds of the injured. Here is a man who stained his own hands with the blood of the bleeding. Feel his compassion.

Come and stand in the shoes of the hero and open your heart to the humanity of his experience. Here is a man who used his own beast to carry the victim. Here is a man who paid for the victim's lodging from his own pocket. Feel his generosity.

The parable of the good Samaritan epitomizes the practical heart of the Christian gospel. Come and stand alongside the victim. Come and stand in the shoes of the hero.

Thinking

How fair are you being to the characters in the parable of the good Samaritan? Take a sideways look and think again.

How fair are you being towards the robbers? Are they really the unambiguous villains of the tale? Do you know enough about the economic constraints placed on life on that barren and tortuous road to condemn these men out of hand? Were they driven to a life of crime by sheer necessity?

How fair are you being towards the priest? Is he really without redeemable qualities? Do you know enough about the religious obligations he carried for the people of God to judge his actions so severely? Suppose the priest had been defiled by contact with a corpse; who then would have fulfilled the religious obligations?

How fair are you being towards the Levite? Is he really so unforgivably callous? Do you know enough about his previous experiences on this perilous road to question his judgement about unnecessary delay? Suppose the wounded traveller had been a decoy to trap the unwary?

How fair are you being towards the innkeeper? Would the good Samaritan really have been the hero of the tale had not the innkeeper welcomed a foreigner and stranger? Would the good Samaritan really have been the hero of the tale had not the innkeeper given credit and taken him so clearly on trust? Should not the story really be renamed 'The parable of the good innkeeper?'

So how fair are you being to the characters in this parable? Take a sideways look and think again.

25
Luke 10:38–42

³⁸Now as they went on their way, he entered a certain village, where a woman named Martha welcomed him into her home. ³⁹She had a sister named Mary, who sat at the Lord's feet and listened to what he was saying. ⁴⁰But Martha was distracted by her many tasks; so she came to him and asked, 'Lord, do you not care that my sister has left me to do all the work by myself? Tell her then to help me.' ⁴¹But the Lord answered her, 'Martha, Martha, you are worried and distracted by many things; ⁴²there is need of only one thing. Mary has chosen the better part, which will not be taken away from her.'

Context

The long journey to Jerusalem remains key to the structure of Luke's gospel. Within this journey, Luke locates Jesus' encounter with the two sisters, Mary and Martha. These two sisters are very different types of people.

Sensing

Jesus has a strong eye for psychological type. Look with care at the two powerful portraits of Martha and Mary. See how these two types contrast so clearly.

Martha is the archetypal *extravert*. See how she is excited by the arrival of the visitor. See how she is occupied with all the social interaction. Hear how she chatters and expresses her thoughts. Sense how she draws her energy from the outside world. Mary is the archetypal *introvert*. See how she quietly withdraws into herself when the visitor arrives. See how quickly she is exhausted by the social interactions. Hear how she becomes the centre of stillness and quiet, sitting at the visitor's feet. Sense how she draws her energy from the inside world. Jesus knew how extraverts and introverts have problems understanding one another.

Martha is the archetypal *sensing* person. See how she is concerned with all the practical details of hospitality. See how she prepares the food. Hear the clatter of her utensils. Sense how she is alert to her environment. Mary is the archetypal *intuitive* person. See how she is concerned with all that Jesus has to say and to express. Hear her wide-sweeping and far-reaching questions. Sense how Jesus' conversation sparks her own thoughts and imagination. Jesus knew how sensing people and intuitive people have problems understanding one another.

Martha is the archetypal *feeling* person. See how she is much given to be concerned about the wellbeing of her guest. See how she wants to know about her guest's feelings and concerns. Hear how she, too, needs affirmation and approval. Sense her concern for the world of people. Mary is the archetypal *thinking* person. See how easily she is able to distance herself from her sister's concerns with the guest and with herself. See how she sets her own priorities and prizes the challenge of Jesus' teaching. Sense her concern for the world of ideas. Jesus knew how feeling people and thinking people have problems understanding one another.

Martha is the archetypal *judging* person. See how she wants her outside world well organized and disciplined. See how she puts the supper in its place. Hear how she puts her sister in her place. Sense her need for order and routine. Mary is the archetypal *perceiving* person. See how she wants her outside world to remain flexible and spontaneous. See how she gives supper second place to the new agenda of Jesus' conversation. Hear how she allows new circumstances to change her plans. Sense her need for flexibility and spontaneity. Jesus knew how judging people and perceiving people have problems understanding one another.

Jesus has a strong eye for psychological type. Look with care at the two powerful portraits of Martha and Mary.

Intuition

Martha thought that she had her relationship with Jesus well thought through, well established. All was settled in her soul until at long last she gave Jesus time to speak to her. Would you dare run such a risk? Would you give Jesus time to speak to you?

Martha thought that she had her relationship with Jesus well thought through, well established. She thought that Jesus would approve of her personal priorities and her way of life. She paused just long enough to seek Jesus' personal affirmation. She received Jesus' personal criticism. Would you dare run such a risk? Would you give Jesus time to criticize you?

Martha thought that she had her relationship with Jesus well thought through, well established. She thought Jesus would be impressed by her dedication, by her frenzied activity, by her ministry of service. She paused just long enough to check. She learnt that she had not got it entirely right. Would you dare run such a risk? Would you give Jesus time to evaluate your service and your ministry?

Martha thought that she had her relationship with Jesus well thought through, well established. She thought Jesus would share her judgement of her sister as idle and unhelpful. She paused just long enough to let Jesus agree with her. She learnt that Jesus thought otherwise. Would you dare run such a risk? Would you give Jesus time to challenge your judgements made in his name?

Martha thought that she had her relationship with Jesus well thought through, well established. She thought Jesus would look into her soul and be well pleased with all that he found there in her spiritual formation. She paused just long enough to hear Jesus say, 'Martha, Martha, you are worried and distracted by many things.' Is there any chance that Jesus has a similar message for you?

Feeling

Here is a story about how to welcome guests, and about how not to welcome guests.

Martha knew how to make a guest really feel at home. As an extravert, Martha knew that every guest would be refreshed by a warm welcome and a great deal of conversation. As a sensing person Martha knew that every guest would be concerned with a fine meal, well prepared and set out in an appropriately prepared environment. As a feeling person Martha knew that every guest would be occupied with matters of human values, harmony and cooperation. As a judging person Martha knew that every guest would want to be welcomed into an organized and structured home where the meal was ready on time.

Here is a story about how to welcome guests, and about how not to welcome guests.

Mary knew how to make a guest really feel at home. As an introvert, Mary knew that every guest would be refreshed by a quick welcome and space to be by themselves. As an intuitive person Mary knew that every guest would be concerned with stimulating ideas and hardly notice their environment. As a thinking person Mary knew that every guest would be occupied with matters of truth, fairness and justice. As a perceiving person Mary knew that every guest would want to be welcomed into a flexible and spontaneous home free from all tyranny of routine and fixed times.

Here is a story about how to welcome guests, and about how not to welcome guests. The problem is that each guest differs and has his or her own specific requirements, needs and expectations.

Thinking

Here is a story about the management of conflict in the early church. Martha seems to have been concerned with a socially engaged church. Mary seems to have been concerned with a contemplative church. Conflict between these two traditions seems well established.

Martha's socially engaged church is much given to hospitality. Strangers are welcomed. Hungry bodies are fed. The poor are clothed. The kingdom of God is made present through proper material concerns. Surely Jesus himself set just such an example when the five thousand were fed.

Mary's contemplative church is much given to quiet reflection. Strangers are seated at the feet of the teacher. Hungry souls are fed. The poor are enriched in mind. The kingdom of God is made present through proper spiritual concerns. Surely Jesus himself set just such an example when the crowds were taught in the sermon on the plain.

Here is a story about the management of conflict in the early church. On this occasion it was Martha's socially engaged church which convened the sacred synod and invited Jesus to rule against Mary's contemplative church. Jesus heard the case and refused to support the judgement. For Jesus there remained room for Martha's church and for Mary's church to continue to grow side by side.

Here is a story about the management of conflict in the early church. Martha seems to have been concerned with one style of church. Mary seems to have been concerned with a different style of church. Perhaps similar conflicts still exist in the church of Christ today? So I wonder how well Jesus' method of managing such conflict can still be applied?

26
Luke 11:1–13

¹He was praying in a certain place, and after he had finished, one of his disciples said to him, 'Lord, teach us to pray, as John taught his disciples.' ²He said to them, 'When you pray, say:
Father, hallowed be your name.
Your kingdom come.
³Give us each day our daily bread.
⁴And forgive us our sins,
for we ourselves forgive everyone indebted to us.
And do not bring us to the time of trial.'
⁵And he said to them, 'Suppose one of you has a friend, and you go to him at midnight and say to him, "Friend, lend me three loaves of bread; ⁶for a friend of mine has arrived, and I have nothing to set before him." ⁷And he answers from within, "Do not bother me; the door has already been locked, and my children are with me in bed; I cannot get up and give you anything." ⁸I tell you, even though he will not get up and give him anything because he is his friend, at least because of his persistence he will get up and give him whatever he needs.
⁹'So I say to you; Ask, and it will be given to you; search, and you will find; knock, and the door will be opened for you. ¹⁰For everyone who asks receives, and everyone who searches finds, and for everyone who knocks, the door will be opened. ¹¹Is there anyone among you who, if your child asks for a fish, will give him a snake instead of a fish? ¹²Or if the child asks for an egg, will give a scorpion? ¹³If you then, who are evil, know how to give good gifts to your children, how much more will the heavenly Father give the Holy Spirit to those who ask him!'

Context

Luke sees prayer as a central part of the gospel message. This passage illustrates the duty of focusing through prayer on our relationship with Jesus, which he earlier praised in the actions of Mary. It contains three examples of Jesus' teaching on prayer: a model prayer, a parable about persistence in prayer, and an encouragement to see God as wanting to respond to our prayers.

Sensing

It is midnight. You are lying on your bed. Hear the sound of banging on your door. Turn over in the hope that it is only a dream! Listen to the doorbell clamouring for attention. Hear yourself curse it for waking up the kids. You are more awake now. Listen, there is a shout. Isn't that the neighbour's voice? What does he want? He is calling your name and banging again. Listen to the cry, 'I want you to help now! I have run out of bread, and my friend has arrived late and is starving. Just lend me three portions.'

Feel your anger rising as the banging continues. You cannot sleep. He keeps shouting, 'What sort of friend are you? I have responded to my friend's need, why can't you help a little?' Then the doorbell again, then the shouting, then the banging. There is no end to it. Hear yourself saying, 'This guy is not going to go away. I might as well get up and give him the bread before all the kids are awake and crying too.'

Feel yourself yawn and stretch, go downstairs in your dressing gown. 'Why am I doing this?' you ask yourself. 'He has no right to disturb me at this hour.' Open the door and let him in. He looks as tired as you do. His face is lined with worry and apology. Listen to his explanation. 'I just had to help my friend. He has travelled all day to seek my help, and he needs food now. Three small flat loaves, the daily ration, will do.' See the look in his eyes. He is determined and trusts you to help. His persistence proves his faith in your generosity. He is only taking his duty of hospitality seriously. Feel a smile covering your face as you say, 'Friendship would not raise me from sleep but your persistence is irresistible.'

Take the loaves from your basket and give him the daily bread for his friend. Pat him on the shoulder in admiration and affection. Bolt the door and climb the stairs to bed again. Lie down and snuggle in. Your mind ticks over: friendship . . . persistence . . . generosity . . . sleep.

Intuition

Asking: what are the rules about asking in prayer? Is it right to pester God for what we need? Does it depend on what you are asking for?

Obviously we ought to ask for our basic needs: for food and shelter, love and support, the water of life and some wine for celebration. We ask not only for ourselves as individuals but also for ourselves as community. By our requests for such things we show our intimate relationship with creation and the Creator God. Our lives are linked to nature and to one another through the basic needs of human life. The Creator God, like any good parent, desires to provide for the needs but not the wants of all. Being open to receive these gifts will open our hearts to be generous in sharing them.

'Ask and you shall receive.' Is this an open cheque from God? Will all the whims of our childish behaviour be satisfied by an indulgent God? Heaven forbid! No wonder some of our requests are met with silence, not because of a lack of generosity from God but from the lack of appropriateness in our request. Silence will help us think through the consequences of our request: 'If we had that, who would have to do without? If we were given power to do that, what damage would it do to others and to nature?'

Asking: do we have to hammer on the door of God's heart? Is this the only way we can work out our priorities, sifting the wants from the needs?

Asking: what do we want most of all from God? Is it not the gift of the Spirit, which God offers us for our own good and the good of all? That gift of the Spirit includes the gift of relationship with God: faith, trust, peace; the gift of restraint: from violence, greed, intimidation, self-seeking and self-destruction; and the gift of spiritual awareness: joy, prayer, hope, truth and insight into the Being of God. Faithfully we can ask. Faithfully God will give us this greatest gift of all: God's Spirit and God's Self.

Feeling

What part does the Lord's Prayer play in your relationship with God? It begins with one of the most personal affirmations in scripture: 'Abba'. We are linked to God as lovingly and firmly as we are to our parents. Is that how you feel when you begin the Lord's Prayer?

How do you feel about your relationship with God when you ask for the coming of the kingdom? Are you looking for miracles or for opportunities? Do you see the request as involving *you* in change or only changing others? How can you discover and do the will of God unless the Spirit of God dwells in you?

How do you feel when you ask for daily rations? Does that make you feel you are dependent on handouts or are you simply being realistic about the providence of God through nature? Does this prayer help you to distinguish needs from wants? Are you tempted to sit back and let others provide or do your share in the work of sowing and harvesting? The garden of paradise needs our attention but we can never create it.

How do you feel when you ask for forgiveness? Does it strengthen your relationship with God and with others? Do you feel a new freedom through forgiveness to take up both relationships again? Or are you overwhelmed by the shame of sin?

How do you feel about your relationship with God when you are faced with trials and persecution? What do we mean by our request for God's protection? Are we asking for safety or comfort or strength to survive? If we were to avoid life's challenges how could we grow? In our times of trial we can rightly ask the Jesus of the cross to stay by our side to bring comfort and strength. Is not his promise to the faithful, 'Lo, I am with you always, even to the end of all things'?

How does the Lord's Prayer help your relationship with God?

Thinking

Do you think that there is any point in prayer? Are we just talking to ourselves, a sort of whistling in the dark?

What is Luke trying to share with his readers in these sayings about prayer? Clearly the Lord's Prayer was a favourite with many in the early church. When you examine the words you can see why. It summarizes the various forms of prayer activity: relationship, praise, respect, union with God, vision, will, supplication, confession, mutual forgiveness, protection from external and internal evil.

Jesus' parable about the householder and his neighbour at first seems confusing. Is God a reluctant neighbour who has no sense of the obligations of friendship and only responds out of self-interest to troublesome persistence? Our mind tells us that this is contrary to the wider picture of God in the teaching of Jesus. What then are we overlooking in this story? The praise given is for persistence. The neighbour refuses to give up on the task of getting help for his friend. He has worked out his priorities: not his own comfort but the needs of his community. When you think about it that way, you see that prayer is a vital part of attaining a sense of priority in life: focusing on the real and the possible. In the daily struggle, we work out what is really necessary and we are invited to work for it.

The balance between these two aspects of prayer is vital. We must work for what we pray for, and we will receive what we work for. God is ready to give, but not with indulgence. We must be open to receive, but not make it an excuse for laziness. Taken together the words make sense. Taken separately the ideas can be distorted. We must read scripture as a whole and use our minds to achieve a balanced interpretation.

27
Luke 12:13–21

13Someone in the crowd said to him, 'Teacher, tell my brother to divide the family inheritance with me.' 14But he said to him, 'Friend, who set me to be a judge or arbitrator over you?' 15And he said to them, 'Take care! Be on your guard against all kinds of greed; for one's life does not consist in the abundance of possessions.'

16Then he told them a parable: 'The land of a rich man

produced abundantly. [17]And he thought to himself, "What should I do, for I have no place to store my crops?" [18]Then he said, "I will do this: I will pull down my barns and build larger ones, and there I will store all my grain and my goods. [19]And I will say to my soul, 'Soul, you have ample goods laid up for many years; relax, eat, drink, be merry.'" [20]But God said to him, "You fool! This very night your life is being demanded of you. And the things you have prepared, whose will they be?" [21]So it is with those who store up treasures for themselves but are not rich towards God.'

Context

In some religions riches have been seen as a sign of blessing from God, given as a reward for goodness. Those who were rich received honour and respect, and possessed the resources to make others dependent on them.

Judges also were held in honour as being capable of expressing God's justice for all. Luke in his gospel helps his readers to see that riches can trap the wealthy in folly. Riches can be acquired by inheritance or good fortune. Neither brings the reward of a full life. Only a relationship with God can do that.

Sensing

Look out over your land. The land is rich and fertile and it has made you a rich farmer. The heavy crops are the result of the soil and the climate rather than your struggle and hard work. This year you have been especially fortunate. There will be a large surplus for you to enjoy.

Look over your buildings. They have been big enough for the crops in the past but they are too small for this bumper harvest. You will have more than you need this year and you want to store up the surplus for the years to come. That will mean bigger barns and silos to store it all. The surplus could make you rich and idle in the future: no more work; lots of time for fun and frivolity; no need to think of others or God, only yourself. There is a large surplus for you to enjoy.

Look into your soul. You have all you need materially. You must feel wonderful in those expensive clothes with the latest labels. How can all this surplus make you a better person? How can you build a bigger soul? There is a large surplus for your soul to enjoy.

Look into the future. Someone will inherit all of the surplus you have stored up. Imagine what will it do to them. Listen to the squabbles among your descendants. Hear their voices: 'What is my share?' The surplus will add to the family difficulties.

Look into your heart. See the uncertainty. I cannot tell what will happen to me. I cannot foretell what will happen to all I have stored up. Decisions about the surplus will challenge my descendants. The surplus is a problem. Should I give it to those in need? I would rather be compassionate than complacent.

Will you be wise or will you be foolish in handling the surplus?

Intuition

You must be desperate if you ask a visiting teacher to judge a family dispute. What does he know about the delicacy of the family history? No doubt you hope his ignorance will tip the balance in your favour. You would not have asked him if you were satisfied with your rightful share. How do you deal with problems in your family? Do you sort them out yourselves or ask some stranger to provide an answer in your favour?

What do we mean by looking to Jesus to be our judge? Who do we want him to sort out, other people or ourselves? Can't you hear Jesus challenge you with his question, 'Who set me to be a judge over you?' You must have made that decision; is that what you really want? If so, listen to me as I explain the truth about life, your life in particular.

What do you judge you can do with money? Possession of it can lead to all sorts of problems. When you have too little you think that money will solve all your problems. When you have more than enough you know it will not. Can you handle money so that it brings you a sense of being rich with God?

How do you guard against greed? It creeps upon us so easily. How do you keep it in check? Wisely, Jesus warns us to be on our guard. We must be as vigorous and vigilant as a boxer or a fencer to ensure that the decisive blow does not slip under our guard. How do you protect yourself from the most severe of modern pressures, to acquire more and more money? Remember it is how you handle money, not money itself, which is the test.

If you say to your *soul* that you have ample goods laid up for many years, and then think of material wealth, you show that you do not understand the things of the soul. Ample goods for the soul would be spiritual gifts, not material ones. How easy it is to be blinded by false values. Judge carefully!

Feeling

Imagine what it feels like to be rich. When you have more than enough it should be easy to relate to others. When you are comfortably off it should be easy to relate well to God. When you can take pride in your crop you can value yourself highly.

Imagine what it feels like to be rich. The stories lucky gambling winners tell should warn you of the difficulties. They speak of false friends, grasping neighbours, loneliness and a constant sense that they are only valued for their money. They tell how hard it is to appear in public without being pestered. What is your attitude to others now you are rich?

Imagine what it feels like to be rich and to say your prayers to God. Would you thank God for the resources entrusted to you for the good of all, or for giving you plenty for your own pleasure? In the story, the farmer's abundance was given to him without any sign that he had to work harder than usual. In the story the farmer enjoyed a major surplus, not an adequate sufficiency. In times of surplus who should benefit, those with enough or those in need? Your answer reveals your feelings for others.

Look at yourself now that you are rich. What do you feel about yourself? Do you value yourself all the more because you have money in your pocket? Do you feel especially blessed by God? If you inherit the largest portion of the family wealth, do you feel the most highly favoured one? What would make you feel really good about yourself? Your answer reveals your attitude to yourself and your worldly possessions.

You have lots of money in your pocket to protect you from the tragedies of life, yet the story makes it clear that the rich are not able to cope more easily with accidents than the rest of us. Are you anxious that riches may cause such strain that there is more likelihood that your life will be required of you? The text here points to a belief that we will all be required to explain to God what difference our money made to our way of life.

In the end the way you use your money will show the values you hold.

Thinking

How do you see the connection between the statements 'poor in spirit' and 'rich towards God'? Sometimes it is hard to explain these words. It seems that 'poor in spirit' is best interpreted as knowing one's needs before God. If we are poor in spirit we will understand how God cares for us, supports us, inspires us and gives us value. This gives us true humility, seeing our place in the whole as it really is.

'Rich towards God' may be explained as giving value to God and to the will of God above all else. We will measure material things by the values of God's kingdom, not by the values of the world. We will be able to mirror God's generosity to others and with them rejoice in what we can enjoy together. We will value our relationship with God above all other priorities.

This story makes you think about such values and the balance we can achieve between treating money as dirty and seeing it as useful to fulfil the purposes of God. Luke does not say that money is sinful, but that greed is the problem. Selfishness in God's communal world is destructive of all. Greed leads to war and to violence in families and in nature. Generosity leads to new resources with which to meet the needs of the community and build up interdependent relationships. We may see the logic in this but be blind to the advantages and dangers before us.

When you consider the passage thoughtfully you can see that Jesus did act as judge for the family member. He pointed out to him the danger in his request to settle the family dispute. If the motive was selfishness and greed then a decision could destroy all the members of the family. The parable indeed was the appropriate reply. How else do you think Jesus might have responded? How would you point out the folly of riches?

28
Luke 12:32–40

[32]'Do not be afraid, little flock, for it is your Father's good pleasure to give you the kingdom. [33]Sell your possessions, and give alms. Make purses for yourselves that do not wear out, an unfailing treasure in heaven, where no thief comes near and no moth destroys. [34]For where your treasure is, there your heart will be also.

[35]'Be dressed for action and have your lamps lit; [36]be like those who are waiting for their master to return from the wedding banquet, so that they may open the door for him as soon as he comes and knocks. [37] Blessed are those slaves whom the master finds alert when he comes; truly I tell you, he will fasten his belt and have them sit down to eat, and he will come and serve them. [38]If he comes during the middle of the night, or near dawn, and finds them so, blessed are those slaves.

[39]'But know this: if the owner of the house had known at what hour the thief was coming, he would not have let his house be broken into. [40] You also must be ready, for the Son of Man is coming at an unexpected hour.'

Context

Luke has made a collection of the sayings of Jesus which advise disciples how to act 'in the end times'. Major upheaval is expected and the disciples of every age need to be ready for it. Possessions will not be required in such times, and they should be replaced by treasures that will last for heaven. It is difficult for some people in our times to imagine what such instability would be like. Others are all too familiar with political, social and economic upheaval. Readiness is the key to any uncertainty.

Sensing

You are an employee of a major firm expecting restructuring. You work in the office as Personal Assistant to the Manager.

You do not know whether you will have a job or what you might be asked to do by the end of this day. Shake the sleep from your eyes and choose your wardrobe for this crisis day. Flick the garments over on the rack and choose those most suitable for a day of action. Go downstairs and take a quick breakfast. What equipment will you need? Put it into your bag. Will you be ready for anything?

Arrive at work and put the place in order. The Managing Director has a board meeting at ten. Expect him any time after that to bring news of what will happen to you all. Feel the tension rising at noon when he still has not returned. The others in the workplace are bored with waiting. They keep slipping in and out to do a bit of personal shopping. The tension builds as the afternoon passes. You keep on with the tasks in hand. More and more staff are slipping away, saying that there is no point in working if we are all going to be redundant tomorrow. You keep on with the job.

Hear the phone ring. You answer it. The Managing Director is speaking: 'Come across and join me in the cafeteria.' 'Coming', you reply as your heart beats furiously. Whatever will happen now?

See the Managing Director draw up a chair for you to sit on. He is all politeness: 'What would you like to eat and drink?' What does this reversal of roles mean, you think to yourself. He brings the tea and cakes and sits down beside you. 'There is to be a restructuring', he confirms. 'We are all to share in every task: you in mine and I in yours. It is a bit of a surprise. We are all equal in this new structure. Our new company motto is "To serve each other". Have some more tea.'

Feel the shock at the actions and the words. What are you going to say in reply?

Intuition

Be prepared is the scouting motto. 'Prepared for what?' we may ask. 'Everything', is the bold reply. The stark truth about life's journey is that we cannot see round the corner to know exactly what is coming. For Christians this should be a fact, not a fear. We know that if we develop our trust in God and our spiritual gifts we will be ready to face every eventuality.

Be ready! The motto for the Christian is: *Be dressed for action and have your lamps lit.* What does 'to be dressed for action' mean for you? Are you ready to go anywhere at any time in obedience to God's call? Will you be fit in body, mind and soul and thus be equipped for every situation? What does 'to have your lamps lit' mean for you? Will it give you light to respond to any situation? In what way is the scripture a 'light unto my path'? How can your lamp be a light to others who are overcome by the darkness?

Is your soul ready to counter invasion, distraction and evil? If not, all our plans for good will be stolen away from us. Like the watchful house-owner we must take the precautions necessary to defend our property. We must put a guard on every possible entrance. We must build up all our different spiritual resources: prayer, bible reading, intercession, meditation, sacramental relationship with God, guidance on ethical issues, service of others in need and fellowship with our fellow Christians. We cannot leave any weaknesses unrepaired. We know that the times to come will see all the regular supports stripped away, and in the chaos we will have to stand firm.

Are you fully prepared? The whole point in these sayings is to help us understand that we can never rest on our laurels and expect a smooth path before us. Every Christian is to expect the unexpected and to be equipped to deal with every eventuality. Our minds must be prepared by thought and study, our wills prepared by closer union with the divine will, and our souls prepared by sacramental grace and prayer.

In all things *Be prepared*!

Feeling

What do you value? Write a list of what you value most in life. As a person with a *feeling* preference you will probably put relationships in front of possessions. That is certainly important in the establishment of Christian priorities, but which relationship tops the list? Is it your relationship with yourself or with significant others or with God? Be honest now with yourself!

What makes you feel valued? Do you feel most valued when people serve you, do things for you and give you priority in attention? Or do you feel most valued when you have a chance to help others, do things for them and make them feel highly important?

Sell what you value. Your possessions might be of lesser value to you, but how do you feel when the scripture says, 'Sell your possessions and give alms', that is, provide for the needs of the poor, the frail, the powerless and the despised? Are you excited by the prospect or dejected at the loss? You value these possessions when they bring back memories of people and places which you treasure. Do we have to break such bonds to make a new bond with the needy?

Do you feel that this saying only applies to the 'end times', when possessions will be useless due to the instability? We may be driven from our homes or our goods might be shattered in the earthquake and the storm. Surely what counts then is the strength of the community that faces the disaster together. That is when there is need for a kingdom community of those who will follow the way of God, who are prepared by common work and prayer for such a time. How can you ensure that you give this community the most valuable of all your possessions?

Thinking

These sayings could be assigned to Apocalyptic literature, material that relates to end times when the current order of society will be shattered and a new era of existence will begin. In such literature there is often portrayed a sharp contrast between the settled nature of the society we enjoy and the turmoil of the future. The old and familiar is abandoned and the new embraced.

For those who can foresee that the end times are at hand, there is a strong message to be ready to live in a world that will be turned upside down. The master acts like the servant; the householder protects his property from the thief; the servants make ready for an arrival of the master at an unknown time; planning for the future becomes a matter of coping with uncertainty. Can you imagine what it will be like when such 'end times' arrive in your district?

Do you think that society and science are able to take such control of our lives that talk of the 'end times' is irrelevant? What do we make of the prophecies of doom that are issued by the scientists and the sociologists about global warming, failure of water supplies, massive droughts, ethnic wars, global financial collapse and the breakdown of all family relationships?

It is easy to dismiss 'end times' as 'past times' in an organized international society. It is equally as easy to equate 'end times' with 'our times', when chaos seems to reign instead of the rule of God. What is our message for the church in the face of the current state of affairs and the possibility that these will soon get worse? What does 'readiness' mean when we cannot be sure of what we will have to face?

Does Apocalyptic literature always defy logic or does it have a logic of its own? What do you think? Why is such literature so prominent in the New Testament?

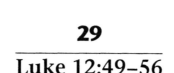

29

Luke 12:49–56

⁴⁹'I came to bring fire to the earth, and how I wish it were already kindled! ⁵⁰I have a baptism with which to be baptized, and what stress I am under until it is completed! ⁵¹Do you think that I have come to bring peace to the earth? No, I tell you, but rather division! ⁵²From now on, five in one household will be divided, three against two and two against three; ⁵³they will be divided:
father against son
    and son against father,
mother against daughter
    and daughter against mother,
mother-in-law against daughter-in-law
    and daughter-in-law against mother-in-law.'
⁵⁴He also said to the crowds, 'When you see a cloud rising in the west, you immediately say, "It is going to rain"; and so it happens. ⁵⁵And when you see the south wind blowing, you say, "There will be scorching heat"; and it happens. ⁵⁶You hypocrites! You know how to interpret the appearance of earth and sky, but why do you not know how to interpret the present time?'

Context

This passage continues the collection of Jesus' teaching about the 'end times'. Decisions must be made in response to the words and actions of Jesus. Such decisions will bring division and suffering: for Jesus at his 'baptism' on the cross and for us as we see the signs of good and evil and choose between them. We need to interpret such things correctly.

Sensing

Stand in the crowd milling around Jesus as he becomes fired up about his mission. People keep bumping into one another (Luke 12:1). Feel the pressure in the crowd and the beginning of arguments. Everyone has a different opinion about Jesus. Things are heating up in every direction. This is not a very comfortable place to be.

Feel the tension within yourself. You have come to listen to Jesus because you have heard about his message of love. You have heard that he is a good man who healed the sick and the mentally disturbed. He brought peace in the storm. But now in this seething crowd things are different from these expectations. There is no talk of healing. There are few signs of peace. There is tension and division in all directions.

Look among the crowds. People are in a heated argument about who Jesus is. Watch as the argument of the tongue is overtaken by the fighting of fists. A burning energy of antici-pation seems to be spreading like fire. People's emotions are being ignited.

Feel yourself being caught up in the argument about Jesus. Is he just a pleasant person with a charming message that overlooks the reality of the situation? Or does he tackle evil head on like a person on fire with righteousness? When he starts talking about hypocrites and fools he can hardly expect a cool response. He is certainly a stirrer. If he did not believe there must be a struggle between the forces of good and evil, why did he challenge those who thought they governed the truth? Why did he show the sort of determination that led to his 'baptism' on the cross?

The saying is sure: 'truth divides'. Be careful on which side you stand.

Intuition

Who are the hypocrites today, so wise about the weather yet so foolish about the truth?

You hear them at dinner parties or across the meal table.

They lecture one another on the evils in society. They decry road rage and child abuse, and then roar at their own children for disturbing their meal with requests for help with homework. They condemn drug addicts for their addiction, and then rush to the TV to watch the weekly lottery draw, waving their tickets with excitement or disappointment. You hypocrites!

You hear them in the workplace attacking the bosses for their lack of commitment to the workers, while they search the papers to see what 'better' jobs are on offer. You hypocrites!

You hear them in the church arguing over the position of the furniture or the times of the services, while they condemn those who clash over cultural issues in their community. You hypocrites!

You hear them in the sports stadium deriding the players for brawling, while they laugh at a punch-up between the fans as they argue over how to get the best seats. You hypocrites!

You hear them demanding better values in society from the politicians, while they find ways of adjusting their tax return to lessen the tax bill. You hypocrites!

You hear them praising the Christian ethic, while they debunk faith in Jesus as the Son of God. You hypocrites!

You hear yourself retelling the story of the good Samaritan, while you pass by the collection box for the Red Cross society. You hypocrite!

You see yourself filled with joy as Christ forgives your sins, while you retain your hardness of heart against a difficult neighbour. You hypocrite!

You hypocrites, so wise about everything, can you not see the truth about yourself in the mirror? Hypocrisy is so obvious except to those who shut their eyes to the truth. Only the wind of the Spirit can lift the smokescreen. Only the fire of Christ can burn away the dross to reveal the gold. Let the truth divide good from evil, right from wrong, and the gospel of Christ from talk about the weather.

Feeling

Sit in a home where there is an argument about religion. Some say religion is about truth, others about commitment. Such an argument catches the emotions and engages the mind. Feel the tensions in the family when members differ from one another. We are embarrassed by the strains and dislike the discomfort.

We want families to be places where we can relate at our best, where love suffers long, and where we can learn tolerance and respect. As you experience the tensions you may want to ban religion and politics from family conversations.

Sit in a home where the family prefers apathy to the truth. Truth tends to divide. It tends to set passions on fire. It is a threat to relationships. Apathy dulls the senses, cools the tempers and deadens the conscience. Truth establishes values and shapes a way of life. It divides because it sorts out the good from the bad, the worthy from the worthless and wisdom from falsehood. Feel the struggle to decide whether the truth is worth the cost of division; whether it is better to be alive in the struggle than dead in the muddle.

Sit in a home where the family tries to promote both love and the struggle for truth. They try to respect the contribution of each person to the sharp debate. Jesus warns us that the truth about himself will divide families. Decide whether the warning is fatalistic or realistic.

Sit in a home where the members of a family say that loyalty to Jesus is more important than loyalty to the family. Do the younger members find it easier in the rebellious years of youth to let the truth divide? Do the older members protect the fragile family to avoid the pain of division?

Listen to the words of Jesus, 'I came to bring fire to the earth.' Do these words stir you to burn with passion for Christ or cause you to be burnt by the pain of division? This is a hard saying of Jesus.

Thinking

This is another of those apocalyptic sayings. It has all the tones of crisis. When judgements must be made, then of course the truth is important. To stand up for Jesus when you are pushed into a corner is very different from having to live things out in a balanced way over a long period of time. Passion is all very well as a push to action but it can also lead to bigotry. The burning truth has been known to result in the burning of martyrs. Raised to fire, passion can result in riots. Religious fervour has some equally strange results. Modern society is so fragile that outbursts of religious fanaticism can cause people to reject the gospel altogether. We have to learn to handle fire or else it gets out of control and becomes destructive. How do you think the church should handle strength of conviction and passion for Christ? What do you think is the difference between respect for truth and apathetic tolerance?

What do you think was Luke's purpose in including the reference here to 'baptism'? It seems to be a pointer to the suffering and cross of Jesus. Do we see our baptism as a challenge to the evil in us and our society? What is the connection for us between our baptism and the truth that divides? Do we see baptism as marking us out as different in society? Does it cause divisions in our relationships? What do you think?

Some in the church have insisted that those who are baptized must be fully convicted of their sinfulness and of their faith in Jesus Christ as Saviour. They deny baptism to children on the grounds that they cannot declare this conviction. They put a fence around the font to see that no unworthy person can get to the waters of baptism. Such a baptism makes a division between those who have expressed faith and those who have not expressed faith. What do you think about such divisions?

Have you the wisdom to interpret the 'present times'? On what basis do you put forward your arguments about the best course of action? How do you discern the truth and present it so that it has the sharpness of a challenge? We must use our minds as well as our emotions to reach judgements about the truth.

30
Luke 13:1–9

[1]At that very time there were some present who told him about the Galileans whose blood Pilate had mingled with their sacrifices. [2]He asked them, 'Do you think that because these Galileans suffered in this way they were worse sinners than all other Galileans? [3]No, I tell you; but unless you repent, you will all perish as they did. [4]Or those eighteen who were killed when the tower of Siloam fell on them – do you think that they were

worse offenders than all the others living in Jerusalem? ⁵No, I tell you; but unless you repent, you will all perish just as they did.'

⁶Then he told them this parable: 'A man had a fig tree planted in his vineyard; and he came looking for fruit on it and found none. ⁷So he said to the gardener, "See here! For three years I have come looking for fruit on this fig tree, and still I find none. Cut it down! Why should it be wasting the soil?" ⁸He replied, "Sir, let it alone for one more year, until I dig round it and put manure on it. ⁹If it bears fruit next year, well and good; but if not, you can cut it down." '

Context

A note of urgency runs through this section of Luke's gospel. The kingdom of God is at hand and people must respond by changing their lives to conform to the will of God. Sin and disaster were linked in the minds of some people but Jesus points out that all need to repent for the day of judgement is here. There may be one further chance but that will be the final opportunity.

Sensing

Listen to the news reports coming through to you. Face the revulsion as you hear that the governor Pilate has had a group of Galilean pilgrims slain in the temple at Jerusalem. Pilate has always been insensitive to Jewish religious feeling and has a reputation for great cruelty.

Feel the terror at another atrocity. Listen to the details. The Roman soldiers have mixed the blood of their victims with the blood of the sacrifices they were offering in the temple. Try to hold back your horror and your queasy stomach. Let the anger rise inside you. Cry out to God in bewilderment. Run to find Jesus, the Galilean, to tell him about it.

'Why did it happen?' Ask him the hard question: 'Why did the God of Justice allow these people to suffer at the very time when they were worshipping him? Suffering is for sinners. Disaster strikes those who do evil. Is not that the rule of our God?'

See Jesus shake his head. Hear him pick up your questions and put them to the crowd. Listen as he gives a warning to everyone. 'All will perish unless the ways of the world are turned upside down. Violence at every level must be replaced by reconciliation. Otherwise we will all perish.' Now is the time for repentance.

Watch as another member of the crowd comes forward with news of another disaster. There has been a construction accident during the building of the reservoir at Siloam. Part of the construction has caved in and fallen on the workers. Eighteen have been killed. It is a terrible tragedy. Hear the crowd ask the questions again: 'Were these workers more wicked than others? Why did they die while the others were saved? Is there any justice in life?'

Listen carefully as Jesus clearly says, 'No, tragedy does not strike the wicked like that. We all have to take responsibility for one another. We are all sinners. Unless we take care of one another, we will all perish. Greed and carelessness are double forces of evil. Repent while there is time. All must enter into a new way of living.'

Feel the personal challenge. Now is the time for action and repentance.

Intuition

We all like another chance. The parable that Jesus told seems a relief to the warning he had just given. There should always be time for repentance. After all, we are weak and sin comes so easily. Lent can be oppressive with its dire warning about the consequences of sin. Yes, this parable comes as a relief. There is always next Lent to respond to the challenge to repent.

Yes, I know that we have been saying that for three years (or more). Yet it is God's responsibility to give us more time. Any God of love would give us a carrot as well as a stick. We need warnings but we also need another opportunity. The gardener has a better attitude than the owner of the property. Surely God is responsible for making our growth possible. We need help. We need strength. We need the right conditions for making the best of our lives. Maybe Jesus is the gardener who knows us better than God. Next Lent we will be ready to repent.

What was it we said to ourselves last year? We said we needed another year. Did we not promise to change those attitudes if we had one more year in which to do it? Next year we will reform our lives and root out the evil. Jesus said, 'If it bears fruit next year, well and good. If not, you can cut it down.' Have we had our year of grace? When will we act? The consequences of our sins will catch up with us all too soon. Can we put off the decision to repent and reform our lives? The water will boil over in the pot if the fire is left burning beneath it. Who will clear up the mess? Will it be this year or the next?

If there is one more year, how will you use God's grace to make your life fruitful? Will you let the Holy Spirit rid you of staleness and renew you with strength? How much time do you need to make a timely repentance?

Feeling

Put yourself in the place of those who have been struck by disaster. Feel their bewilderment and pain. They ask, 'Are we guilty? Are we partly responsible for what has happened? Must we shoulder part of the blame for our misfortune?'

Put yourself in the place of those who are quick to shift the blame on to others. Hear them say about those who have been hurt in a drunken brawl that they should not have been drinking in the first place. Listen to their remarks that if those drunks had not been at the party they would not have been near enough to be struck with a bottle in the face.

Put yourself in the place of those who accept some responsibility as a member of the whole community for any tragedy. They look for ways in which to promote change to make it safer for all to live their lives. They accept part of the blame and seek a change of attitude in society before all perish.

Put yourself in the place of those who are quick to take action to prevent a repetition of every disaster. They use the time before something similar could occur again to make changes in their own lives and in the life of society. Hearing of the rising death toll on our roads they press for changes now in attitudes, actions and the law. They look at their behaviour in aggressive driving and road rage. They take responsibility in such matters. They declare that now is the time to change the way we all act before everyone is in danger of perishing. Timely repentance should lead to timely action.

Put yourself in the place of those who have suffered a national disaster overseas. How do you show your compassion? Do not thank your lucky stars that it did not strike you, but use

Lent to put aside resources to respond to the needs of others to show your care and God's love. In the face of disaster, timely repentance should lead to timely generosity.

Thinking

What do we think is the purpose behind Jesus' words about judgement?

To shock people into repentance can cause them to act out of fear, but we know that fear on its own is not a good motivation for righteous living. That was the way of the old school regime: 'Correct your behaviour or it will be beaten out of you.' That kind of policy is no longer in favour with leading thinkers in educational method. To use the threat of disaster to change behaviour also seems to have its faults. It may prevent us from taking certain actions but it will often give negative rather than positive results. We can become frozen in our actions. Talk of violence in the streets may prevent the elderly from venturing out, unable to make any contribution towards the removal of the causes of violence.

How do you think that we can best create changes for good in the lives of individuals and society? How do we achieve a balance between warnings about the consequences of evil and encouragement to do something good? Is there a parallel here between giving things up for Lent and doing more positive things during Lent?

Luke in his composition of the gospel recognizes this need for a both/and approach to repentance. He includes Jesus' words of warning about the responsibility we all have to repent, and then follows it with a parable which gives us encouragement to bear good fruit in our actions through the grace of God. Timely repentance is the first step towards growth. Luke insists that we are given time to put into practice our new way of life. There can be no growing without a radical rethink about our way of life. There is no evidence of repentance unless it is shown in a life of goodness. Luke's gospel shows Jesus as a man of action. He is the model for our changes of behaviour. Lent gives us an opportunity to consider this carefully and to act sensibly.

31
Luke 13:10–17

¹⁰Now he was teaching in one of the synagogues on the sabbath. ¹¹And just then there appeared a woman with a spirit that had crippled her for eighteen years. She was bent over and was quite unable to stand up straight. ¹²When Jesus saw her, he called her over and said, 'Woman, you are set free from your ailment.' ¹³When he laid his hands on her, immediately she stood up straight and began praising God. ¹⁴But the leader of the synagogue, indignant because Jesus had cured on the sabbath, kept saying to the crowd, 'There are six days on which work ought to be done; come on those days and be cured, and not on the sabbath day.' ¹⁵But the Lord answered him and said, 'You hypocrites! Does not each of you on the sabbath untie his ox or his donkey from the manger, and lead it away to give it water? ¹⁶And ought not this woman, a daughter of Abraham whom Satan bound for eighteen long years, be set free from this bondage on the sabbath day?' ¹⁷When he said this, all his opponents were put to shame; and the entire crowd was rejoicing at all the wonderful things that he was doing.

Context

For Luke, Jesus' consistent presence in the synagogue on the Sabbath confirms his firm commitment to working within the established framework. On this occasion Jesus causes controversy by healing a crippled woman on the Sabbath.

Sensing

Recall Luke's first words about the ministry of Jesus after he emerged from those forty days in the wilderness,

> Jesus began to teach in their synagogues
> and was praised by everyone.

Now begin a tour of those synagogues.

Start your journey in chapter four and arrive on the Sabbath in the synagogue at Nazareth. See there the attendant fetch the scroll of scripture and hand that scroll to Jesus. See Jesus sit down to teach. Sense how all the attention is focused on Jesus. Hear Jesus proclaim, 'Today this scripture has been fulfilled in your hearing.'

Now suddenly the atmosphere changes. Hackles rise and the people rebel. See them drive Jesus out of the synagogue, out of the town, to the very brow of the hill. When Jesus began to teach in their synagogue, praise turned to criticism.

Continue your journey through chapter six and arrive on another Sabbath in another synagogue. See there a man whose right hand is so withered he is quite unable to use it. See Jesus stand up to heal him. Sense how all the attention is focused on Jesus. Hear Jesus proclaim, 'Come and stand here. Stretch out your hand.'

Now suddenly the atmosphere changes. Hackles rise and the people rebel. See them huddle in corners and hear them discuss with one another what they might do to Jesus. When Jesus began to teach in their synagogues, praise turned to criticism.

Continue your journey through chapter thirteen and arrive on another Sabbath in another synagogue. See there a woman whose back is so bent she is quite unable to stand up straight. See Jesus lay his hands on her. Sense how all the attention is focused on Jesus. Hear Jesus say, 'Ought not this woman be set free from this bondage on the Sabbath day?'

Now suddenly the atmosphere changes. Hackles rise and the people rebel. But now they rebel against those who criticize Jesus and rejoice with the woman who was healed. So recall Luke's first words about the ministry of Jesus after he emerged from those forty days in the wilderness,

> Jesus began to teach in their synagogues
> and was praised by everyone.

Intuition

Jesus' actions said to the woman, 'Stand up straight. Be released from your bondage.'

Picture those today who are pinned down in the bondage of fear, whose lives are crippled by debilitating dread. To them Jesus longs to proclaim the message, 'Stand up straight. Be released from your bondage.' How can you help that message to get through?

Picture those today who are pinned down in the bondage of poverty, whose lives are crippled by lack of resources. To them Jesus longs to proclaim the message, 'Stand up straight. Be released from your bondage.' How can you help that message to get through?

Picture those today who are pinned down in the bondage of loneliness, whose lives are crippled by debilitating isolation. To them Jesus longs to proclaim the message, 'Stand up straight. Be released from your bondage.' How can you help that message to get through?

Picture those today who are pinned down in the bondage of despair, whose lives are crippled by debilitating hopelessness. To them Jesus longs to proclaim the message, 'Stand up straight. Be released from your bondage.' How can you help that message to get through?

Picture those today who are pinned down in the bondage of addiction, whose lives are crippled by uncontrollable dependency. To them Jesus longs to proclaim the message, 'Stand up straight. Be released from your bondage.' How can you help that message to get through?

Jesus' actions said to the woman, 'Stand up straight. Be released from your bondage.' And listen carefully, for Jesus is trying to get that message through to you as well.

Feeling

For eighteen years this woman had been bent double and was quite unable to stand upright. Put yourself in her position and see the world from her perspective.

Here is a woman whose mobility was restricted. She was no longer able to walk around freely and quickly. She was no longer able to get easily where she wanted. Put yourself in her position and see the world from her perspective.

Here is a woman whose activities were restricted. She was no longer able to carry her shopping. She was no longer able to move things around her house as she wanted. Put yourself in her position and see the world from her perspective.

Here is a woman whose self-esteem was battered. She was no longer able to hold her head high. She was no longer able to keep up with her friends and neighbours. Put yourself in her position and see the world from her perspective.

Here is a woman whose public image was damaged. Her

physical deformity made her stand out in the crowd. The culture in which she lived associated deformity with possession. Put yourself in her position and see the world from her perspective.

Here is a woman who after eighteen years was set free from Satan's bondage. She was no longer held captive to fear. Put yourself in her new position and see the world from her new perspective.

Here is a woman who after eighteen years was cured of her physical deformity. She was no longer bent double but could once again stand tall. Put yourself in her new position and see the world from her new perspective.

Here is a woman who after eighteen years had her self-image restored. She no longer felt despised and rejected by the people around her. Put yourself in her new position and see the world from her new perspective.

Here is a woman who after eighteen years stood up straight and began praising God. She no longer felt excluded from God's grace and care. Put yourself in her new position and see the world from her new perspective.

Thinking

Some might say that Jesus was simply asking for trouble. After all, he knew the rules, he knew how his actions would be interpreted, he knew the consequences.

Some would say that Jesus was simply asking for trouble. But there was a lot at stake. There was a lot at stake for the poor woman who had been crippled for eighteen years. Surely it would not have been fair to ask her to wait one day longer. She had already suffered more than enough. Clearly there were matters of fairness and justice to be properly considered. So perhaps it was worth asking for trouble.

Some would say that Jesus was simply asking for trouble. But there was a lot at stake. There was a lot at stake for the proper interpretation of the Sabbath. Surely the Sabbath was instituted as a sign of liberation, not as a sign of oppression. The Sabbath reminded the people of God of their release from captivity, not of new captivity. Clearly there were matters of truth and accuracy to be properly considered. So perhaps it was worth asking for trouble.

Some would say that Jesus was simply asking for trouble. But there was a lot at stake. There was a lot at stake for the proper recognition of the presence of the kingdom of God. Surely where God reigns, the presence of Satan is banished. And is not the Sabbath a foretaste of the reign of God? Clearly these were matters of theology and revelation to be properly considered. So perhaps it was worth asking for trouble.

Some would say that Jesus was simply asking for trouble. After all, he knew the rules, he knew how his actions would be interpreted, he knew the consequences. Some would say that Jesus was simply asking for trouble. But what would you say?

32
Luke 13:31–35

³¹At that very hour some Pharisees came and said to him, 'Get away from here, for Herod wants to kill you.' ³²He said to them, 'Go and tell that fox for me, "Listen, I am casting out demons and performing cures today and tomorrow, and on the third day I finish my work. Yet today, tomorrow, and the next day I must be on my way, because it is impossible for a prophet to be killed away from Jerusalem." ³⁴Jerusalem, Jerusalem, the city that kills the prophets and stones those who are sent to it! How often have I desired to gather your children together as a hen gathers her brood under her wings, and you were not willing! ³⁵See, your house is left to you. And I tell you, you will not see me until the time comes when you say, "Blessed is the one who comes in the name of the Lord."'

Context

In Luke chapter nine, on the mount of transfiguration, Moses and Elijah spoke with Jesus about his departure (exodus) in Jerusalem. Now, on the journey to Jerusalem, Jesus underlines the significance of that city.

Sensing

Here is a passage of sharp contrasts. Picture them in your mind.

Here is a passage full of brutality. See the people of Jerusalem rise up in rage. See them challenge the prophet of God sent to proclaim God's word. See them pick up stones from the ground and hurl them relentlessly. See the people of Jerusalem cast those stones at the prophet of God sent to proclaim God's word.

Here is a prophecy full of brutality. Look into the future and see the people of Jerusalem rise up in rage. See them challenge the anointed Messiah of God sent to inaugurate God's kingdom. See them pick up the cross from the ground and hurl insults relentlessly. See the people of Jerusalem crucify the anointed Messiah of God sent to inaugurate God's kingdom.

Here, too, is a passage full of tenderness. See the mother hen gather her brood under her wings. See her offer shelter and security to the young chicks too weak and inexperienced to care for themselves. See the mother hen go out of her way to protect her young.

Here, too, is a passage full of tenderness. Look into the future and see the anointed Messiah of God lifted high on the cross. See him stretch wide his hands to embrace the people of the world. See him offer shelter and security to all who will but turn to him. See him go to his death to bring salvation to many.

Here is a passage of sharp contrasts. Picture them in your mind.

Intuition

Jesus lived in a world rooted in nature. What do you lose when you lose touch with such a world?

Jesus lived in a world where hens roamed free. He observed the hens' characteristic way of life. What do you lose when you lose touch with the hen?

Jesus lived in a world where hens laid their eggs, where hens brooded on their nests, where hens hatched their young into life. What do you lose when you lose touch with the hen?

Jesus lived in a world where hens scratched for their food, where hens protected their young chicks, where hens spread wide their wings to shelter their brood. What do you lose when you lose touch with the hen?

Jesus lived in a world where watching the hen could spark

new insight into the loving nature of the King of kings, where watching the hen could give birth to a parable about the nature of the Messiah. What do you lose when you lose touch with the hen?

Jesus lived in a world where foxes roamed untamed. He observed the fox's characteristic way of life. What do you lose when you lose touch with the fox?

Jesus lived in a world where foxes laid in wait for their prey, where foxes tore their prey limb from limb. What do you lose when you lose touch with the fox?

Jesus lived in a world where foxes terrified the neighbourhood, where foxes attacked the hen's chicks, where foxes savaged the sheep. What do you lose when you lose touch with the fox?

Jesus lived in a world where watching the fox could spark new insight into the cunning nature of the earthly ruler, where watching the fox could give birth to a parable about the nature of Herod. What do you lose when you lose touch with the fox?

Jesus lived in a world rooted in nature. What do you lose when you lose touch with such a world?

Feeling

The images people choose to talk about themselves are not neutral. Images give a powerful clue to self-understanding.

When, in John's gospel, Jesus spoke of himself as the good shepherd, he chose a familiar and well-understood image. Put yourself in the shoes of the shepherd, for here is an image of masculinity.

The shepherd lives a rough and solitary life on the hillside. The shepherd challenges the prowling wolf and the cunning fox. The shepherd lifts the wounded sheep from the deep pit and carries it to safety on his broad shoulders. Here is an image of masculinity.

The shepherd lives a rough and solitary life on the hillside. The shepherd challenges the roaming thief and the travelling bandit. The shepherd fights to protect the life of his lambs. Here is an image of masculinity.

The images people choose to talk about themselves are not neutral. Images give powerful clues to self-understanding.

When, in Luke's gospel, Jesus spoke of himself as the mother hen, he chose a familiar and well-understood image. Put yourself in the shoes of the mother hen, for here is an image of femininity.

The mother hen lives a rough and communal life in the courtyard. The mother hen hatches her chicks. The mother hen nurtures her young. The mother hen feeds her brood. Here is an image of femininity.

The mother hen lives a rough and communal life in the courtyard. The mother hen stretches out her wings to provide shelter for her young. The mother hen protects her brood from harm. Here is an image of femininity.

The images people choose to talk about themselves are not neutral. Images give a powerful clue to self-understanding.

Thinking

In Luke's gospel, how fair do you think Jesus really is to the Pharisees?

In chapter eleven, on the journey to Jerusalem, a Pharisee invited Jesus to dine with him. Here was a generous act, worthy of a generous response. Jesus accepted. But Jesus failed to observe the expected custom. Jesus failed to wash before dinner. Jesus deliberately antagonized the hospitable Pharisee. How fair do you think Jesus really is to the Pharisees?

In chapter eleven, on the journey to Jerusalem, Jesus rounds on the Pharisee for such commitment to the ritual washing before dinner. 'Now', he said, 'you Pharisees clean the outside of the cup and of the dish, but inside you are full of greed and wickedness.' How fair do you think Jesus really is to the Pharisees?

After dinner when Jesus went outside, the Pharisees began to be very hostile towards him. Can you blame them?

In chapter thirteen, on the journey to Jerusalem, some Pharisees came to warn Jesus that Herod was out to kill him. Some Pharisees came to warn Jesus to escape. Here was a generous act, worthy of a generous response. But Jesus failed to heed their warning or failed to take their warning seriously. How fair do you think Jesus really is to the Pharisees?

In chapter thirteen, on the journey to Jerusalem, Jesus rounds on the Pharisees for their deference to Herod. 'Go', he said, 'and tell that fox Herod for me [that] it is impossible for a prophet to be killed outside of Jerusalem.' How fair do you think Jesus really is to the Pharisees?

33

Luke 14:1, 7–14

¹On one occasion when Jesus was going to the house of a leader of the Pharisees to eat a meal on the sabbath, they were watching him closely.

⁷When he noticed how the guests chose the places of honour, he told them a parable. ⁸'When you are invited by someone to a wedding banquet, do not sit down at the place of honour, in case someone more distinguished than you has been invited by your host; ⁹and the host who invited both of you may come and say to you, "Give this person your place", and then in disgrace you would start to take the lowest place. ¹⁰But when you are invited, go and sit down at the lowest place, so that when your host comes, he may say to you, "Friend, move up higher"; then you will be honoured in the presence of all who sit at the table with you. ¹¹For all who exalt themselves will be humbled, and those who humble themselves will be exalted.'

¹²He said also to the one who had invited him, 'When you give a luncheon or a dinner, do not invite your friends or your brothers or your relatives or rich neighbours, in case they may invite you in return, and you would be repaid. ¹³But when you give a banquet, invite the poor, the crippled, the lame, and the blind. ¹⁴And you will be blessed, because they cannot repay you, for you will be repaid at the resurrection of the righteous.'

Context

The Sabbath meal in the house of a leader of the Pharisees provides the context for a healing, two examples of teaching and a parable.

Sensing

When Jesus went out to dinner it was not always easy to know who was doing the watching and who was being watched.

Remember the day when one of the Pharisees asked Jesus to eat with him. See how Jesus went into the Pharisee's house and how he took a place at the table. See how a woman in the city, who was a sinner, brought an alabaster jar of ointment. See how she stood behind Jesus, weeping, and how she began to bathe his feet with her tears and to dry them with her hair. See how she kissed his feet and anointed them with the ointment. All the time the Pharisees were doing the watching and Jesus was being watched.

But remember, too, how Jesus observed the observers. See how Jesus went into the Pharisee's house and how he took a place at the table. See how, on his arrival, the host gave Jesus no water for his feet. See how, on his arrival, the host gave Jesus no kiss of welcome. See how, on his arrival, the host did not anoint Jesus' head with oil. All this time Jesus was doing the watching and the Pharisees were being watched.

Now remember another day when Jesus went to the house of a leader of the Pharisees to eat a meal on the Sabbath. See how Jesus went into the Pharisee's house and how he took a place at the table. See how in front of them all there was a man who had dropsy. Hear how Jesus asked the Pharisees, 'Is it lawful to cure people on the Sabbath, or not?' Hear how the Pharisees kept silent. See how Jesus approached the sick man and healed him. See how the sick man walked away healed. All this time the Pharisees were doing the watching and Jesus was being watched.

But remember, too, how Jesus observed the observers. See how Jesus went into the Pharisee's house and how he took a place at the table. See how the other guests all arrived one by one. See how the arrogant guests came and sat in the places of honour. See how the host moved them down the table. See how the humble guests came and sat in the lowest place. See how the host moved them up the table. All this time Jesus was doing the watching and the Pharisees were being watched.

When Jesus went out to dinner it was not always easy to know who was doing the watching and who was being watched.

Intuition

It is all too easy to be seduced by places of honour.

Take, for example, the subtle allure of social recognition. Imagine the attraction of social recognition held out to guests at a first-century Palestinian wedding banquet. How easy it is to believe that you could be the most important guest to be invited. How easy it is to assume that the place of honour at the table has been reserved for you. When in your life have you succumbed to the subtle allure of such social recognition?

Take, for example, the subtle allure of personal satisfaction. Imagine the attraction of personal satisfaction held out to the public speakers at a first-century Palestinian wedding banquet. How easy it is to believe that you could produce the best wedding speech ever to be uttered. How easy it is to assume that you have perfected the greatest skill with words. When in your life have you succumbed to the subtle allure of such personal satisfaction?

Take, for example, the subtle allure of moral superiority. Imagine the attraction of moral superiority held out to the religious leaders in first-century Palestine. How easy it is to believe that your obedience to the law of God could be so perfect that you remain blameless before the heavenly court. How easy it is to assume that you stand head and shoulders above the moral heights reached by your compatriots. When in your life have you succumbed to the subtle allure of such moral superiority?

Take, for example, the subtle allure of spiritual pride. Imagine the attraction of spiritual pride held out to the religious leaders in first-century Palestine. How easy it is to believe that you stand closer than other men and women to the heart of God. How easy it is to assume that you are the only one who really counts in the eyes of the great divine creator. When in your life have you succumbed to the subtle allure of such spiritual pride?

It is all too easy to be seduced by places of honour.

Feeling

As always, Jesus displays a very keen eye for the values which lie at the heart of human interaction and relationships.

Some people come across as being so proud, so full of pride. But put yourself in their shoes and peel away the outer skin. The proud person arrives at the wedding feast ready to make a grand entry on to the stage before the public gaze. The proud person arrives ready to command respect and public attention. But peel away the outer skin. Inside may be the all-consuming fear of inadequacy and rejection. Inside may be fundamental insecurity and self-doubt.

Some people come across as being so humble, so full of

humility. But put yourself in their shoes and peel away the outer skin. The humble person arrives at the wedding feast ready to slip in by the back door, well away from the public gaze. The humble person arrives ready to be unobserved and unnoticed. But peel away the outer skin. Inside may be the quiet confidence and clear knowledge of self-sufficiency. Inside may be fundamental security and confidence.

Some people come across as being so altruistic, so full of altruism. But put yourself in their shoes and peel away the outer skin. The altruistic person arrives at the wedding feast always ready to put others first. The altruistic person holds open the door and ushers others into the limelight of attention. But peel away the outer skin. Inside may be the manipulative knowledge that altruism leads to its own public recognition and to its own direct rewards. Inside may be hopes for more than meets the eye.

Some people come across as being so self-centred, so full of self-concern. But put yourself in their shoes and peel away the outer skin. The self-centred person arrives at the wedding feast ready to push others into the background. The self-centred person steps through the open door and walks straight into the limelight of attention. But peel away the outer skin. Inside may be the deep hurt of rejection. Inside may be the lasting wound of alienation.

As always, Jesus displays a very keen eye for the values which lie at the heart of human interaction and relationships.

Thinking

For some people God's promises always remain in the future. For other people God's promises are delivered and fulfilled in the present. Do you see the tension between these two views? For some people God's kingdom is always round the corner. For other people God's kingdom was fully initiated in the person of Christ. Do you see the tension between these two views?

There are some people who take the lower table now, that they might be called to the higher table when the kingdom fully dawns. Their hope is in the future. There are other people who take the lower table now because that is how they are called to live when the power of God's reign is fully acknowledged. Their hope is in the present. Do you see the tension between these two views?

There are some people who humble themselves now, that they might be exalted when the kingdom fully dawns. Their hope is in the future. There are other people who humble themselves now because that is how they are called to live when the power of God's reign is fully acknowledged. Their hope is in the present. Do you see the tension between these two views?

There are some people who invite to their banquet the poor, the crippled, the lame and the blind, so that they might be repaid when the kingdom fully dawns. Their hope is in the future. There are other people who invite to their banquet the poor, the crippled, the lame and the blind, because that is how they are called to live when the power of God's reign is fully acknowledged. Their hope is in the present. Do you see the tension between these two views?

For some people God's kingdom is always round the corner. For other people God's kingdom was fully initiated in the presence of Christ. Which view do you consider is more faithful to the gospel?

34
Luke 14:25–33

²⁵Now large crowds were travelling with him; and he turned and said to them, ²⁶'Whoever comes to me and does not hate father and mother, wife and children, brothers and sisters, yes, and even life itself, cannot be my disciple. ²⁷Whoever does not carry the cross and follow me cannot be my disciple. ²⁸For which of you, intending to build a tower, does not first sit down and estimate the cost, to see whether he has enough to complete it? ²⁹Otherwise, when he has laid a foundation and is not able to finish, all who see it will begin to ridicule him, ³⁰saying, "This fellow began to build and was not able to finish." ³¹Or what king, going out to wage war against another king, will not sit down first and consider whether he is able with ten thousand to oppose the one who comes against him with twenty thousand? ³²If he cannot, then, while the other is still far away, he sends a

delegation and asks for the terms of peace. [33]So therefore, none of you can become my disciple if you do not give up all your possessions.'

Context

As Jesus continues on his journey toward Jerusalem, a large number of people travel with him. Jesus warns his followers of the true cost of discipleship.

Sensing

So often Jesus went out of his way to make sure that his followers knew the real cost of being his disciples. 'Sit down', he said, 'and work it out beforehand.' So often, Jesus drove his point home by telling a powerful tale or two.

Listen to the story about the owner of a vineyard who decided to build a watchtower to protect his crop. See the owner look round his estate to choose the best location. Hear the owner describe his vision to the surveyor and to the architect. See the architect draw up the plans. See the surveyor order the materials. See the carts come loaded with the stone and the wood.

Listen to the story about the owner of a vineyard who decided to build a watchtower to protect his crop. See the labourers busy digging the foundations and building up the walls. See the walls grow as high as the workmen's knees, as high as the workmen's waists, as high as the workmen's chests. Then see the workmen go away, the job unfinished. See the tower left half-built. See the building materials left unused, to decay. Hear the local people say, 'This is the fellow who began to build but who could not afford to finish the job.'

Listen to the story about the king who decided to wage war against another king. See the king recruit his soldiers. See the king gather his store of food to feed the army. See the king build up his supply of weapons to arm the men. See the captains train their new recruits in the ways of war. See the new recruits exercising on the hillside.

Listen to the story about the king who decided to wage war against another king. See the king lead his men into battle. See the enemy advance with an army twice the size, with fighting equipment twice as good, with captains twice as clever. Then the king's army is quickly dispersed, their weapons are abandoned in the battlefield. See the king, himself, captured and led away prisoner. Hear the local people say, 'This is the king who began to fight but who could not finish the job.'

So often, Jesus went out of his way to make sure that his followers knew the real cost of being his disciples. 'Sit down', he said, 'and work it out beforehand.'

Intuition

It is sometimes all too easy to forget just how costly true Christian discipleship can be. How willing are you to bear that cost?

Jesus warned his followers that true commitment to him could bring them into conflict with their own parents; their mothers and fathers. How willing are you to bear such a cost?

Jesus warned his followers that true commitment to him could bring them into conflict with their own spouses; their husbands and wives. How willing are you to bear such a cost?

Jesus warned his followers that true commitment to him could bring them into conflict with their own children; their sons and daughters. How willing are you to bear such a cost?

It is sometimes all too easy to forget just how costly true Christian discipleship can be.

Jesus told his followers to pick up their cross and to carry its weight; to bear its load upon their stooping shoulders. How willing are you to carry such a load?

Jesus told his followers to pick up their cross and to endure the contempt of those who derided their burden; to embrace the ridicule of those who scorned their load. How willing are you to carry such a load?

Jesus told his followers to pick up their cross and to face the ultimate penalty of crucifixion; to lose their lives in his service. How willing are you to carry such a load?

It is sometimes all too easy to forget just how costly true Christian discipleship can be. How willing are you to bear that cost?

Feeling

The closer that Jesus came to Jerusalem, the clearer he became about the demands of discipleship. Put yourself in Jesus' shoes and see how he came to expect more and more of those who stayed with him on that journey.

The conflict with the Jewish leaders grew day by day. When Jesus worshipped in the synagogue he was confronted by sick people shouting out to be healed. Jesus healed the sick and flouted the Sabbath rules. Put yourself in Jesus' shoes and sense the growing opposition. The closer Jesus came to Jerusalem the clearer he became about the demands of discipleship. He came to expect more and more of those who stayed with him on that journey.

The conflict with the Jewish leaders grew day by day. When Jesus dined in the homes of Pharisees he was confronted by sinners shouting out to be forgiven. Jesus forgave the sinners and flouted the religious rules. Put yourself in Jesus' shoes and sense the growing opposition. The closer Jesus came to Jerusalem the clearer he became about the demands of discipleship. He came to expect more and more of those who stayed with him on that journey.

The conflict with the Jewish leaders grew day by day. When Jesus taught in public he was confronted by behaviour that shouted out to be reformed. Jesus used his teaching to criticize and, in doing so, offended the religious leaders. Put yourself in Jesus' shoes and sense the growing opposition. The closer Jesus came to Jerusalem, the clearer he became about the demands of discipleship. He came to expect more and more of those who stayed with him on that journey.

Thinking

Sometimes, puzzles raised by one gospel are illuminated by one of the other gospels. According to Luke, Jesus said, 'Whoever comes to me and does not hate father and mother cannot be my disciple.' Is this the kind of teaching you expect from a faith that teaches respect for parents?

According to Luke, Jesus said, 'Whoever comes to me and does not hate wife and children cannot be my disciple.' Is this the kind of teaching you expect from a faith that teaches commitment to family life?

According to Luke, Jesus said, 'Whoever comes to me and does not hate brothers and sisters cannot be my disciple.' Is this the kind of teaching you expect from a faith that teaches love of neighbour and love for the stranger?

According to Luke, Jesus said, 'Whoever comes to me and does not hate even life itself cannot be my disciple.' Is this the kind of teaching you expect from a faith that brings life; life in all its abundance?

According to Matthew, Jesus' stark Semitic saying should have been translated rather differently. According to Matthew, Jesus said, 'Whoever loves father and mother more than me is not worthy of me.' But then true love for Jesus demands true respect for parents.

According to Matthew, Jesus said, 'Whoever loves son and daughter more than me is not worthy of me.' But then true love for Jesus demands true commitment to family life.

According to Matthew, Jesus would have said, 'Whoever loves brothers and sisters more than me is not worthy of me.' But then true love for Jesus demands love of stranger, love of neighbour and love of closest family.

According to Matthew, Jesus would have said, 'Whoever loves life itself more than me is not worthy of me.' But then true love for Jesus demands the full acceptance of life; life in all its abundance.

According to Matthew, Jesus' stark Semitic sayings should have been translated rather differently. So perhaps it is just as well that Jesus' teaching has been preserved by more than one evangelist.

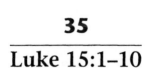

35
Luke 15:1–10

¹Now all the tax-collectors and sinners were coming near to listen to him. ²And the Pharisees and the scribes were grumbling and saying, 'This fellow welcomes sinners and eats with them.'

³So he told them this parable: ⁴'Which one of you, having a hundred sheep and losing one of them, does not leave the ninety-nine in the wilderness and go after the one that is lost until he finds it? ⁵When he has found it, he lays it on his

shoulders and rejoices. ⁶And when he comes home, he calls together his friends and neighbours, saying to them, "Rejoice with me, for I have found my sheep that was lost." ⁷Just so, I tell you, there will be more joy in heaven over one sinner who repents than over ninety-nine righteous people who need no repentance.

⁸'Or what woman having ten silver coins, if she loses one of them, does not light a lamp, sweep the house, and search carefully until she finds it? ⁹When she has found it, she calls together her friends and neighbours, saying, "Rejoice with me, for I have found the coin that I had lost." ¹⁰Just so, I tell you, there is joy in the presence of the angels of God over one sinner who repents.'

Context

When the Pharisees and scribes complained that Jesus associated with sinners, Jesus told three parables: the lost sheep, the lost coin and the lost son. God searches for those who are lost.

Sensing

Listen to the Pharisees grumbling among themselves. 'This Jesus', they say, 'welcomes sinners and eats with them!' Now listen to Jesus' reply.

Picture, if you will, a shepherd. The shepherd has just rounded up his sheep and counted them. He has counted them three times and now his face looks sad and worried. One sheep from the flock has gone missing.

Picture that shepherd as he searches high and low, out on the mountainside, across the dangerous terrain. See him peer into the deep ravine. See him search the hidden places. Picture the sense of relief as that shepherd finds the missing sheep and carries it safely to the fold.

'Your God', says Jesus, 'is like that shepherd who rejoices over the one sheep which was lost and now is found.'

Listen to the Pharisees grumbling among themselves. 'This Jesus', they say, 'welcomes sinners and eats with them!' Now listen to Jesus' reply.

Picture, if you will, a woman. This woman has just sorted out her silver coins and counted them. She has counted them three times and now her face looks sad and worried. One silver coin from the collection has gone missing.

Picture that woman as she searches high and low, throughout the dark house. See her sweep through the dried reeds and rushes on the floor. See her search the hidden places. Picture the sense of relief as that woman finds the missing coin and places it safely with the others.

'Your God', says Jesus, 'is like that woman who rejoices over the one coin which was lost and now is found.'

Listen to the Pharisees grumbling among themselves, 'This Jesus', they say, 'welcomes sinners and eats with them!'

Intuition

Sometimes it is all too easy to give up looking for what has been lost.

Imagine the tired and weary shepherd. A flock of a hundred sheep is far too many for one tired and weary shepherd to accept responsibility. Leaving ninety-nine sheep to fend for themselves while searching for one missing animal makes little sense. Searching all night long with little real hope of success is indeed a thankless task. Sometimes it is all too easy to give up looking for the lost sheep. But give thanks that your God is not that way inclined.

Imagine the tired and weary woman. One small insignificant coin is far too little for one tired and weary woman to worry over. Leaving the other more pressing work of the day to go looking for a needle in a haystack makes little sense. Searching all day long with little real hope of success is indeed a thankless task. Sometimes it is all too easy to give up looking for the lost coin. But give thanks that your God is not that way inclined.

Imagine the tired and weary father. One small insignificant son is far too little for one tired and weary father to worry over. Leaving the other more promising and loyal son to go looking for the prodigal's return makes little sense. Searching all life long with little real hope of success is indeed a thankless task. Sometimes it is all too easy to give up looking for the lost son. But give thanks that your God is not that way inclined.

Feeling

Luke tells three stories which take us right into the heart of God.

The first story explores the motivations and the feelings of an ordinary everyday workman, a shepherd. Here is a man who really cares for his sheep. Here is a man whose heart is broken when one of his sheep wanders off into the darkness. Here is a man who struggles day and night to find the sheep that was lost. The anguish of this shepherd takes us right into the heart of God.

Here is a shepherd who really cares for his sheep. Here is a man whose heart is restored the moment the lost sheep is found. Here is a man who rejoices night and day having found the sheep that was lost. The joy of this shepherd takes us right into the heart of God.

The second story explores the motivations and feelings of an ordinary everyday woman, a housewife. Here is a woman who really cares for her property. Here is a woman whose heart is broken when one of her coins falls into the darkness. Here is a woman who struggles day and night to find the coin that was lost. The anguish of this woman takes us right into the heart of God.

Here is a woman who really cares for her property. Here is a woman whose heart is restored the moment the lost coin is found. Here is a woman who rejoices night and day having found the coin that was lost. The joy of this woman takes us right into the heart of God.

The third story explores the motivations and feelings of an ordinary everyday parent, a father. Here is a father who really cares for his sons. Here is a father whose heart is broken when one of his sons wanders off into the darkness. Here is a father who pines day and night until the son that was lost is found. The anguish of this father takes us right into the heart of God.

Here is a father who really cares for his sons. Here is a father whose heart is restored the moment the lost son is found. Here is a father who rejoices night and day having found the son that was lost. The joy of this father takes us right into the heart of God.

Luke tells three stories which take us right into the heart of God, a divine heart which knows both anguish and joy.

Thinking

Luke tells three stories which illuminate the doctrine of divine grace.

According to the first story, the initiative lay entirely in the hands of God. Here God, in the guise of the hardworking housewife, searched diligently high and low to seek and to find the coin that went missing. As far as we know, the coin took no initiative of its own either to return to the woman's treasury of its own accord or even to respond actively to the woman's insistent attempts to find it. On this account, the road to salvation lay entirely with the Lord who chooses and with the Lord who seeks. Do you find this a wholly satisfactory theology?

According to the second story, the initiative still lay entirely in the hands of God. Here God, in the guise of the hardworking shepherd, searched diligently high and low to seek and to find the sheep that went missing. As far as we know, the sheep took no initiative of its own either to return to the shepherd's fold of its own accord or even to respond actively to the shepherd's insistent attempts to find it. Yet it is likely that the sheep's natural instinct would have set it on the path towards the field and even more likely that the sheep would have responded to the shepherd's familiar cry and call. On this account, the road to salvation starts with the Lord who seeks, but is clearly aided by the soul who responds. Do you find this a wholly satisfactory theology?

According to the third story, the initiative seems to have slipped further away from the hands of God. Here God, in the guise of the prodigal's ageing father, waits patiently at home while the adventurous son learns about the chances and fortunes of life in some far-off country. As far as we know, the son might never have come to his senses. Yet one day, unexpectedly, the realization dawned. The prodigal son repented of his ways and set off towards home, saying, 'Father, I have sinned against heaven and before you; I am no longer worthy to be called your son.' On this account, the road to salvation seems to start with the soul who repents, but is clearly aided by the God who welcomes such repentance and who rehabilitates the penitent. Do you find this a wholly satisfactory theology?

Luke tells three stories which illuminate the doctrine of divine grace. What do you make of those stories?

36
Luke 16:1–13

¹Then Jesus said to the disciples, 'There was a rich man who had a manager, and charges were brought to him that this man was squandering his property. ²So he summoned him and said to him, "What is this that I hear about you? Give me an account of your management, because you cannot be my manager any longer." ³Then the manager said to himself, "What will I do, now that my master is taking the position away from me? I am not strong enough to dig, and I am ashamed to beg. ⁴I have decided what to do so that, when I am dismissed as manager, people may welcome me into their homes." ⁵So, summoning his master's debtors one by one, he asked the first, "How much do you owe my master?" ⁶He answered, "A hundred jugs of oil." He said to him, "Take your bill, sit down quickly, and make it fifty." ⁷Then he asked another, "And how much do you owe?" He replied, "A hundred containers of wheat." He said to him, "Take your bill and make it eighty." ⁸And his master commended the dishonest manager because he had acted shrewdly; for the children of this age are more shrewd in dealing with their own generation than are the children of light. ⁹And I tell you, make friends for yourselves by means of dishonest wealth so that when it is gone, they may welcome you into the eternal homes.

¹⁰'Whoever is faithful in a very little is faithful also in much; and whoever is dishonest in a very little is dishonest also in much. ¹¹If then you have not been faithful with the dishonest wealth, who will entrust to you the true riches? ¹²And if you have not been faithful with what belongs to another, who will give you what is your own? ¹³No slave can serve two masters; for a slave will either hate the one and love the other, or be devoted to the one and despise the other. You cannot serve God and wealth.'

Context

One of the constant themes in Luke's gospel is the use of wealth. This passage collects together three teachings by Jesus on different aspects of wealth. The first is a parable about quick thinking, the second a saying about faithfulness and the third a teaching about God and wealth.

Sensing

Put yourself in the place of the manager who is about to lose his job because he has been too slack about money.

Sit in the office as the owner walks in. You know what will be said. You have seen last year's results and realize that things have not gone well. You were far too easy and slack with the debtors. Wait for the words of the owner, 'Make the accounts up to date, and go.' You have that sinking feeling inside. Debate what you will do next. Manual labour is out of the question. You will need friends to get another job.

See the owner off the property and return to your desk. Pick up the telephone and dial the number of the debtors, one by one. Be ready to do a deal to receive payments in kind. Act quickly, there is no time to lose. Cut out all the margins for yourself and insist on prompt payments.

Watch as the debtors come to you one by one with the goods. You usually make 100 per cent profit on the olive oil but there will be no margin for you in this account. Your owner will take it all. After delivery, the olive oil merchant slaps you on the back for such a discount and invites you back to his shop any time you like.

You usually make 20 per cent profit on the wheat but there will be no margin for you on this account. Your owner will take all. The farmer is very pleased with the discount and calls you his friend. So it goes on all day. Night comes; you have no wealth but many friends.

There, it is done! Are you pleased with yourself? You have been decisive and smart, even under pressure. Everyone is a winner. The owner has received some return, the debtors have a good discount, you have little money but you do have some friends. In the end friendship is more important than wealth.

Intuition

Wealth: does it terrify you or entice you? How do you measure it?

Money is a strange object. In itself it is nothing but a balance in the bank or a few notes or coins in the pocket. It is only when you come to spend it that it judges you. The amount of money that you spend is not the issue. You can have a lot of money and spend large sums, or you can have little and spend small sums. The amount is not the issue but the object of your spending is.

Do you use your wealth to give you status? Do you splash out in order to impress others? Do you hoard up what you have to try to provide you with security? Do you spend your money on yourself or others? What do you really want from your wealth?

What is the priority you set between your material and spiritual wealth? Can the attitude to the one affect the other? Is it more comfortable being a rich Christian or a poor Christian? All of us have to handle wealth in one way or another. If we do so with faithfulness and honesty, it will reveal something important about ourselves to others. They will trust us not only with earthly matters but also with spiritual issues. Our use of material things is a test of our spiritual gifts.

Little things show the measure of a person. How do you measure yourself when it comes to writing a brief note to those in times of turmoil? Do you say that the postage will cost too much? How do you measure yourself when it comes to buying a bunch of flowers for someone in mourning? Do you say that they will cost too much? Little things show the measure of a person.

How do you measure yourself when it comes to filling in your tax return or putting money in the parking meter? Would you say that you were totally honest? Little things show the measure of a person.

How do you handle your wealth? If you are a Christian leader, can we trust you with money matters and with the spiritual riches with which you have been entrusted, not for yourself but for the good of God's community? The measure of the one will be the measure of the other.

Feeling

Put yourself in the position of a slave. A slave is the object of another person's demands and commands. You have no life of your own. You belong to someone else. You have no right to make choices; these are made for you by others. You can be bought or sold like a household appliance. You are useful as long as you do the assigned work. You are a slave.

Put yourself in the position of a slave with more than one boss. You are pulled apart trying to satisfy and please a couple of people or organizations at the same time. It is almost impossible to treat both equally or for them to treat you fairly. Your loyalty is split in two.

Put yourself in the position of being driven by two opposing principles. Try to manage the conflicts without always making compromises. You will have to choose to follow one and then the other, hoping to balance both demands, even though you know that they are mutually opposed. You are torn in two by opposing principles.

Jesus said, 'You cannot serve God and also an attitude towards money which sees it as an end in itself.' Feel the tension in those words. Wealth can entice us into self-satisfaction and selfishness. God has no part in such attitudes. God calls for the opposite, for people to live for community and God's kingdom. With the misuse of money you can only be friends with yourself. With the use of God's wealth you can be friends with God and with all the community.

In your position are you a slave or a friend of God? Are you a friend or a slave of money? Jesus calls on us to choose between them. Otherwise we will be torn apart and destroy not only ourselves but those around us. To be a slave to God is to be set free to serve. To be a slave to money is to be trapped in poverty towards God and others. You choose!

Thinking

The parable about the owner and the manager has left many people in confusion. It seems to be illogical to praise dishonesty and then go on to teach about faithfulness and honesty. Surely God is not applauding sharks in the business world, who give away what belongs to others.

When you examine the passage carefully some of this confusion is created by our own approach to parables. We want to equate each character with someone, even God. We equate the owner with God and the manager with a Christian. This is a misunderstanding of a parable. A parable is a story which illustrates the punch line within it. This parable is about quick thinking and smart action. The manager takes a quick decision in an extreme situation. Similarly, the early church lived in a time when swift and courageous action had to be taken in extreme situations, situations such as persecution, expulsion from the family, calls to service in the cause of the kingdom. We know that some put off key decisions because they were tied up with financial affairs. Jesus' call and the call of the leaders of the early church was to decisive action along with a certain amount of shrewdness. In the disturbed world of our times, Christians may once again see the point of the story: act now even if you have to cut your losses. In the end you will have to rely more on friendship than on wealth. The welcome of friendship is always superior to the welcome of wealth. True friends value us for who we are, not for what we have. Is not this the way with God?

When you think about it, Jesus' saying about it being impossible to be a slave to two masters is logical. You cannot have two people trying to run a business with opposing points of view. You cannot have two people trying to drive a car in opposite directions. You cannot hoard wealth and make good use of it at the same time. The sayings and the parable do make sense.

37
Luke 16:19–31

¹⁹'There was a rich man who was dressed in purple and fine linen and who feasted sumptuously every day. ²⁰And at his gate lay a poor man named Lazarus, covered in sores, ²¹who longed to satisfy his hunger with what fell from the rich man's table; even the dogs would come and lick his sores. ²²The poor man died and was carried away by the angels to be with Abraham. The rich man also died and was buried. ²³In Hades, where he was being tormented, he looked up and saw Abraham far away with Lazarus by his side. ²⁴He called out, "Father Abraham, have

mercy on me, and send Lazarus to dip the tip of his finger in water and cool my tongue; for I am in agony in these flames." 25But Abraham said, "Child, remember that during your lifetime you received your good things, and Lazarus in like manner evil things; but now he is comforted here, and you are in agony. 26Besides all this, between you and us a great chasm has been fixed, so that those who might want to pass from here to you cannot do so, and no one can cross from there to us." 27He said, "Then, father, I beg you to send him to my father's house – 28for I have five brothers – that he may warn them, so that they will not also come into this place of torment." 29Abraham replied, "They have Moses and the prophets; they should listen to them." 30He said, "No, father Abraham; but if someone goes to them from the dead, they will repent." 31He said to them, "If they do not listen to Moses and the prophets, neither will they be convinced even if someone rises from the dead."'

Context

This story illustrates only too well the point that Jesus has already made in this chapter, that the wrong attitude to wealth causes a great chasm to form between a person and God. The rich man has cut himself off from others by his attitude to wealth, while Lazarus has no friend but Abraham in heaven.

Sensing

Dream that you are a person who has all the money you could ever want in life. The rich are happy. Dream on! You have enough money to buy all the smart clothes you want with the most exclusive labels. Imagine walking down the street. Watch the crowds turn in admiration.

See yourself in the best restaurant. The waiter shows you to the best seats. Look at the menu but not the prices. Anything that you want you can afford. Eating and drinking are not to satisfy hunger for food but hunger for pleasure and status. Call to the waiter for another bottle of the best wine. Love the attention and the servitude that money can buy.

Leave the restaurant. There is a beggar on the steps. What you left on your plate would satisfy him for a day. Tell yourself he should get a job and earn his living. You feel for him but there is a great gulf between his lifestyle and yours. You cannot understand his need. Tell yourself that there is nothing you need to do to bridge the chasm.

Go home and open your mail. There is your latest bank statement. The total for this month is more than at the end of last month. The balance keeps growing. You will want for nothing. You can even afford a grand funeral when you die. Imagine how it feels to be that rich. You are a great distance from those who are at the other end of the scale. There is a great chasm fixed between you and them.

Imagine you are rich. Listen to the ten commandments of Moses with their call to live as a community under God. Listen to the prophets' call for mercy, justice and truth. Do not close your heart to the real condition in which others find themselves. If you cannot hear Moses or the prophets or your heart speaking, can you believe in the upside-down voice of resurrection? Your money can create a great chasm between you and the truth. Imagine such a situation and take stock.

Intuition

What makes people change in their attitude to others? In this story the rich man goes on seeing himself in a position of power over others. He is just as bad in death as in life. In life he ignores the needs of the hungry. In death he sees the poor man as his servant to alleviate his discomfort. Do you treat other people as objects for your satisfaction or as fellow human beings whom you can help?

Are funerals displays of wealth and poverty? This rich man had all the trimmings and all the trappings of a full funeral. Is that the fashion with funerals in your area? Do we fix a great chasm between rich and poor, not only in life but in death? Is there pressure on the grieving family to splash out on a funeral and sink further into debt later? The church once had a strict policy of one standard funeral for all. Would this help to remove the great chasm between rich and poor at the time of death? What instructions have you left for your funeral?

Are you frightened by this story of life and death? Do you see the future as a time of judgement when roles will be reversed? Does resurrection change your attitude to life, making you see more clearly the needs of your poor neighbours? Can you see from the prophets' message what selfishness does to the soul, hardening it so much that everyone is seen as its servant? Does believing in resurrection change your life so that it conforms to the true servanthood of Jesus?

Can the love of God help you build a bridge over the chasm now, so that your resources are seen as gifts for all, not just for yourself? Moses would teach you that. Abraham would teach you that. Jesus would teach you that. Is it not true that only love can fill up the chasms we create?

Feeling

Feel good about being Lazarus in the story. You may be poor now but you are in for a good time later. You may have a dog's life now but after death Abraham will be your friend and the angels will be your guardians. That should make you feel better!

In your new-found comfort how do you feel towards the rich man? There was a great gulf fixed between the two of you during your lifetimes. You had nothing. He had it all. Do you feel sorry for him or sorry for yourself? After death the story says that the roles are reversed. He has the burning thirst and you have the water. How do you feel about that? Do you want to help if you could, or is such a change of attitude out of your reach?

In your new-found comfort how do you feel about the rich man? Do you consider that he deserves the disaster he has got into? Are you just as hard in your attitude as he is? Does belief in resurrection help you bridge the gap? Will you be able to relate differently in life eternal? We must all leave behind the fixed attitudes we have to one another, the poor for the rich and the rich for the poor. Something must create a change.

This story seems to imply that God tells us it is good to be poor. As the poor person, does this make you feel angry? The story seems to confirm the attitude of 'the rich man in his castle and the poor man at his gate', a type of determinism. Surely God understands that the poor need feeding now; that we cannot wait for death and resurrection.

In your position take a look at God's economy. Do you believe that God says it is better to be poor than to be rich? Is it enough knowing that after death the poor will have a comfortable time in the presence of God? Surely the poor seek to free themselves from poverty, otherwise they will fall into the same chasm that swallows up the rich. The great chasm between the rich and the poor can only be filled with a new kind of caring, a miracle of resurrected love.

Thinking

Some commentators think that the last verse was added on to the story to express the frustration that many felt in the early church. The evidence of the resurrection would seem to be the church's trump card in convincing people of the new way of life in Christ. Surely the resurrection is good news for all. Surely it is enough to convince us that there is a God who breaks down the old order of decay and brings life and light to the world.

In our post-Christian society the debate has almost moved from one of how the resurrection could possibly be true to one in which it does not seem to matter whether it happened at all. A great gulf seems to be fixed between believers and those who just do not care about such things any more. What is your contribution to such a debate?

Do you think that the last verse is true, that those who cannot see the point in the teaching of Moses and the prophets will never be convinced by the resurrection? Do we have to begin with the moral issues before we can move on to any consideration of a life after death? Thinking about it, the story considers in depth the moral attitudes between the rich and the poor. Both attitudes need to be radically transformed by a different view of life and relationships. The rich must limit their consumption of the resources of the world. It is still true that what is thrown away by the rich would be enough to provide for the needs of the poor in their society. There is enough work if we restored the balance between the overworked and the underemployed. Keeping the Mosaic commandments would restore a sense of community in society. The prophets help us to see that duty to God and duty to neighbour are one. The resurrection allows Christ's Spirit to empower us so that we can put the teaching into practice. The gulf can be bridged. Is that how you see it?

38
Luke 17:5–10

⁵The apostles said to the Lord, 'Increase our faith!' ⁶The Lord replied, 'If you had faith the size of a mustard seed, you could say to this mulberry tree, "Be uprooted and planted in the sea", and it would obey you.

⁷'Who among you would say to your slave who has just come in from ploughing or tending sheep in the field, "Come here at once and take your place at the table"? ⁸Would you not rather say to him, "Prepare supper for me, put on your apron and serve me while I eat and drink; later you may eat and drink"? ⁹Do you thank the slave for doing what was commanded? ¹⁰So you also, when you have done all that you were ordered to do, say, "We are worthless slaves; we have done only what we ought to have done!"'

Context

As Jesus begins the journey to Jerusalem to face the climax of his ministry, Luke collects a series of lessons about faith and service. These are the basics of discipleship. We cannot be given an increase in faith. We have to exercise faith to make it stronger. There is no reward for service. It is the outcome of our love for God.

Sensing

Walk with Jesus on his journey to Jerusalem. You are wondering when the climax of all his teaching and ministry will come to a head. You hope that God's kingdom of peace and love may arrive soon. Maybe it will be this year in Jerusalem. We have told one another that Jesus is the Messiah. We say that we believe in him, but when will the time of perfection come? When will the kingdom of God arrive?

Tell Jesus of your hopes and worries. 'Jesus, I do believe but I find it hard to keep up my faith.' You find it easy to say such words. The other disciples are expressing similar thoughts. Tell

Jesus again of your faith but also of your hesitancy and your lack of certainty. 'I believe, help my unbelief.'

Expect a sympathetic response from Jesus. He is so understanding, so loving, so kind. The hope is rising in your heart that Jesus will make it all come true for you. Reach out your hand to touch his. Look into his eyes and tell him the longings of your heart. 'Increase my faith. You can do it Lord. You are the one who fixes everything. You are the one who can make me perfect.'

Watch Jesus to your astonishment draw you aside and stare you straight in the eye. His look is stern and serious. Listen as he speaks firmly to you: 'You ask me to do everything for you. Faith is not like that. Faith is your response to my challenge. It is your "yes" to our partnership. Faith only grows as you put it into practice. Try it out and see what happens. If you want big things to happen, take big steps of faith.'

Feel the sting in your heart. You wanted Jesus to do it all for you but he calls on you to put your faith into action and act. This road to Jerusalem gets tougher and tougher. Where will it end? For what is to come, I will need even more faith than it takes to uproot a mulberry tree, that's for certain!

Intuition

When you use the word 'discipleship', what springs to mind? Is it commitment, undying love, care for others, faith in Jesus, working with God? What is your score when it comes to being a good disciple: five out of ten; ten out of ten? Do you consider yourself as quite good, not bad or not yet perfect? What reward do you expect for a score like yours?

What score would God give you for being a good disciple? Would God rate you more or less than you rate yourself? Should you get a reward for your level of discipleship? Maybe you hope to hear, 'Well done, good and faithful servant.' What do you expect your reward to be; a top position in the organization, a word of special praise at the annual church meeting, many favourable speeches at your funeral, a secure place in eternal life? Surely good service justifies top rewards.

What a shock to be told we have only done what was expected of us. We find it hard not to want to be rewarded for duty. We do our job as a Christian and then we are told that we just did our duty. That sounds like the attitude in many congregations. All that hard work never seems to be recognized. All our giving is seen as part of our duty. No one makes a fuss of us. No one says that we are special for doing the basic essentials. No one seems to give us our due reward.

Without a reward is it all worth it? How often have we asked that question? But surely we know that discipleship is the outpouring of our love in response to the greatest reward of all, our relationship with God. Discipleship is our commitment to service. What more do we want but the chance to put service into practice?

Love responding to love looks for nothing more than love in return.

Feeling

Stand still on the road and feel Jesus' rebuke and challenge. Will you break off the relationship and go away and sulk? Can you accept the rebuke and see the point of the remark? Will you move on again facing the challenge, and with renewed energy get stuck into the task?

Stand still before a friend whom you respect. Surely rebukes and challenges will enhance the relationship. When love is firm between you, you will be proud to be considered strong enough to be corrected by the other party.

Stand still in shock when you do not receive what you wanted. Feel the anger rising and face the temptation to give up the task in hand. But have you considered whether what you asked for was helpful or possible? Stand there and sort out your feelings when you do not receive what you wanted.

Stand still and receive your voluntary tasks as part of your duty as a citizen. Are you expecting to receive special thanks for putting the rubbish out at the edge of the footpath? Are you hoping to be thanked for keeping within the speed limit in your car? Are you expecting extra praise or pay for doing something practical for your community? Stand there and sort out your feelings about rewards for service.

Listen as the local authorities remind you that you have only done what was expected of you. Are you going to become upset and withdraw, or do you feel that you have the privilege of service? In our society no one seems prepared to do community building and caring without the promise of a reward. We need to hear more of the words,' 'We have only done what we ought to have done.' Standing there, how do you feel repeating those words?

Stand and listen to those who say that a financial payment is a better reward than the acknowledgment of grateful appreciation for Christian witness and service. What value system do you hold as a disciple? What reward do you expect for faith and service in practice?

Thinking

When you think about it, these are harsh sayings by Jesus to his disciples. It would seem that the thought of the clashes that were inevitable in Jerusalem and which would lead finally to the cross, were already throwing their shadows on the journey. There is a new toughness about Jesus' approach in this passage. What do you think were the causes? Is there any logical explanation which helps us interpret the 'mood'?

Why do you think Jesus chose such a difficult example of what might be done through faith? Moving a mulberry tree is both impractical and impossible. There is no advantage to anyone in having a mulberry tree planted in the sea. Why link that sort of useless task to faith? Is this a 'tongue in cheek' saying by Jesus to force us to think what we really need to achieve through faith? Too many people expect to be given faith to achieve the impossible, as if that would prove how much faith they had. Is not that putting God to the test? Miracles of that kind are just for show and aggrandizement. Surely we do not want that sort of faith, even if we were given it for nothing.

Can you define what you need faith to achieve? Most of the things we have to do through faith are quite straightforward, though still tough. We have to forgive our enemies, care for the poor, give respect to all people whether we like what they say or not, declare the truth and tell others what Jesus has done for them and us. That is the work of the servant of Christ and the servant of humanity in Christ's name.

The sort of faith that we need for that work is a trust that God's Spirit will stir up the gifts we have and give us courage to use them. It is straightforward to see how we achieve that sort of faith, by putting what faith we have into practice. As we use the faith we have, we will be given more.

Work it out for yourself. It is perfectly logical when you think about it.

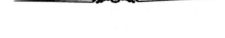

39
Luke 17:11–19

¹¹On the way to Jerusalem Jesus was going through the region between Samaria and Galilee. ¹²As he entered a village, ten lepers approached him. Keeping their distance, ¹³they called out, saying, 'Jesus, Master, have mercy on us!' ¹⁴When he saw them, he said to them, 'Go and show yourselves to the priests.' And as they went, they were made clean. ¹⁵Then one of them, when he saw that he was healed, turned back, praising God with a loud voice. ¹⁶He prostrated himself at Jesus' feet and thanked him. And he was a Samaritan. ¹⁷Then Jesus asked, 'Were not ten made clean? But the other nine, where are they? ¹⁸Was none of them found to return and give praise to God except this foreigner?' ¹⁹Then he said to him, 'Get up and go on your way; your faith has made you well.'

Context

For his journey to Jerusalem Jesus had to pass through the borderlands between south Galilee and Samaria. The people of the two lands keep their distance from one another. Lepers had to keep their distance from non-lepers. When free of the disease, the priests returned them to the community. Healing restores the physical condition. Thanksgiving reaffirms the relationship with God. Jesus is disappointed that those healed missed out giving the thanks which would have proved that they were whole.

Sensing

Wake up one morning and look at your feet. See the tell-tale signs of decaying skin. Feel the numbness when you put one of your feet to the ground. Come to the chilling realization that you have leprosy. Feel the tears rolling down your face as you bid farewell to your family. You will live outside your community for fear of infecting others. The pain drives hope from your heart. Feel the numbness in your mind concerning what you can do. Wander off lost into the edge of the wasteland. Sit down on the ground in a daze.

Wake up to the sound of voices. People are coming close. You must run away. Hear them calling you back, 'It's all right. We are lepers too. Come and join us.' Sit down again as each of the nine introduce themselves. Eight, like you, are Jews, but one is a Samaritan. Search the eyes of the others and see them affirm that the Samaritan is welcome. Feel the confusion in your heart – Jews do not mix with Samaritans; lepers cannot mix with other human beings. In sickness one barrier is down and another is raised. Strange isn't it?

Take your place in the group as they share a simple meal together, left by some kind people on the edge of the village. Listen to the gossip that has been picked up by the shouts across the divide: 'Jesus is coming this way tomorrow.' What shall we do? Isn't Jesus a healer? How can we see if he can help us? Can the Samaritan come too?

The decision is made. We will hail him from a distance as he approaches the village. We will ask for mercy, anything that he can do to help.

Listen as he tells you what to do. 'Trust that you are healed and show yourself to the priest.' Feel the power returning to your feet. You hobble no longer. You run. You race to find the priest. You are so excited. You just cannot wait to prove that you are healed. You can go back to the old life, pick it up again where you left off.

Turn round and notice that the Samaritan is missing. He has gone right up to Jesus. We have got what we needed, what more does he want? Is there anything more important in life than healing? What is this talk of thanksgiving?

Intuition

What things keep you apart from your family or community? Do you see examples of people being treated as outcasts? Nowadays researchers have found drugs to cure leprosy. Society has places where the sick are treated with understanding and care.

But there are many other things which cause people to be driven out of society. Ethnic divisions make people outcasts. Mental illness can banish some people to the 'edge of the desert'. AIDS makes it hard to live with those who reject the lifestyle as well as fear the disease. Family breakdowns mean some children feel that the house is no longer their home. There are many things which keep us apart from one another.

Where are the means of healing for these causes of stigma and shame? What part can faith in Christ play in such healing? People still cry out in agony, 'God, have mercy on us.' How will they receive mercy in your community? Who listens and acts in the name of Christ?

What keeps us apart from our relationship with God? Have we cut ourselves off from God, thinking that we are too foul to go near the throne of grace? Does our attitude to our neighbour cut us off from God? If 'those' people believe in God, then I will not have anything to do with God. Is that why we are absent from God's assembly? Do we want a great demonstration of God's power to believe we can be healed by God? Can we cope when we are simply asked to trust that we will be restored to health?

What holds us back from acknowledging that all healing is part of God's activity? Do we take all of modern medicine for granted? Have we lost the art of saying thank you since we grew out of childhood? Can we really be a whole person until we have learnt to say thank you to God and our neighbour? Is that what holds us back, our failure to recognize that without God we are not whole? So what part does thanksgiving play in your life?

Feeling

Put yourself in the place of the Samaritan. Recognize the two things which changed your whole attitude to life: the wonder of the companionship of sickness and the wonder of the relationship with God through thanksgiving and faith. Translate these feelings into your own experience.

Remember the experience of companionship in a hospital ward. The barriers of class and race fall away. We share what we can with one another: the conversation, the hope, the laughter and the tears. Everyone's family is our family. We live in community at our point of need.

Remember your experience in times of sickness. Some people isolate you, others share with you their faith and love. Some tell you that Jesus is near by and pray with you. What were your feelings towards the visitors?

Remember your experience in times of recovery when you knew that your body was healing steadily. You felt close to Jesus and wanted to express to him the joy in your heart. You gratefully said a prayer of thanksgiving.

Remember your experience in times of prayer. Regular thanksgiving affects your relationship with God. Do you express gratitude to God without grovelling? Do you feel that saying thank you to God is out of place because it should be said to the human beings who have helped you day by day?

There are many causes of joy in your life; some expected and some unexpected. Remember your experiences and give thanks for them all. Then you will be whole in your relationship with God.

Thinking

Sometimes we consider demonstrations of joy to be rather embarrassing. The Samaritan praised God at the top of his voice. Why do you think people act like that? He had not even been to the priest to be affirmed as healed.

Do you think that it was unreasonable of Jesus to criticize the other nine? They only did what they were told to do; to go to the priest to be cleared for their return to the community. Why was Jesus so disappointed in them?

Logic often works against the best choice on occasions. Sometimes the heart must rule the head. This is difficult advice for those with a strong logical preference. But when you think about it, it was only right that once the lepers felt the healing occur they should give thanks to God. It is sad we do not do that more often. In this secular age we take most things as our 'right'. We consider that doctors and nurses are there to get us back to health. How many of us telephone the doctor's surgery to pass on a message of thanks when we are fully recovered? How many of us offer a special prayer of thanks to Christ when we are restored to health? If our health is not improving we are quick to telephone the doctor and to earnestly pray to God for healing. But thanksgiving. . .

Not understanding the place of thanksgiving in our lives, we tend to blame others when things do not lead to recovery and restoration. We perceive that they have failed in their duty towards us. When things do not turn out right it is their fault. When things improve it is in accordance with our rights that it should be so. Have you ever thought that way?

Can you see why wholeness depends on a proper understanding of the place of thanksgiving in our lives? Thanksgiving builds up the relationship between the people involved. It puts everything in the right perspective. It leads at times to that exuberant shout of joy: 'God, all is restored, all is whole, my joy is complete.'

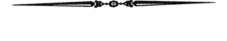

40
Luke 18:1–8

¹Then Jesus told them a parable about their need to pray always and not to lose heart. ²He said, 'In a certain city there was a judge who neither feared God nor had respect for people. ³In that city there was a widow who kept coming to him and saying, "Grant me justice against my opponent." ⁴For a while he refused; but later he said to himself, "Though I have no fear of God and no respect for anyone, ⁵yet because this widow keeps bothering me, I will grant her justice, so that she may not wear me out by continually coming."' ⁶And the Lord said, 'Listen to what the unjust judge says. ⁷And will not God grant justice to his chosen ones who cry to him day and night? Will he delay long in helping them? ⁸I tell you, he will quickly grant justice to them. And yet, when the Son of Man comes, will he find faith on earth?'

Context
Luke's gospel has a variety of passages about prayer. This further instruction amplifies the call for perseverance. Such persistence is encouraged by the assurance that God's will for all is justice, the sorting out of what is true and good in society. Such a

purpose requires our cooperation and our faith in God and in one another.

Sensing

Take the role of the widow in the story. You have been oppressed by a neighbour who has taken advantage of your circumstances. You are on your own and need someone to stand up for you. You know your community. Its law is dedicated to support the weak.

Go along to your local law court. Explain your grievance to the official in the small claims tribunal. Feel your anger at being put off and told to come back when things are less busy. Go again the next week, only to be told you have not filled in the form properly.

Go again the next week feeling disappointed at your treatment but still determined to have justice. Hand over the forms and sit down when you are told to wait. After an hour go back to the counter again. Demand to see someone in authority. Feel the frustration when told that everyone is at afternoon tea. Sit down again and think it over. Is it worth the hassle and the wait? Why not give up, go home and mourn your husband? If he had been alive none of this would have happened.

Put these thoughts behind you and go to the counter the moment you see people leaving the tea room. Raise yourself to your full height and say very firmly, 'The fabric of society depends on justice. It is your responsibility and mine. It is time you did your task now.'

See the look of surprise as your request is acted on immediately. Feel proud that you did not give up but kept going to the end. Thank God for the faith that kept you going. Surely God does listen to our cry for justice.

Ask yourself what you would have done if you had been told that no one cares about justice any more and that you would have to fight it out yourself with your neighbour. How long would you have kept up your call for your rights to be supported? Could you have kept it up if you did not know that God was on your side?

Intuition

Perseverance is an important aspect of faith in God and in society. If you participate in the system of justice in your country, you will need faith and perseverance. Nothing is simple; everything is costly. You need to be tough and determined. You need faith that God works for a just society and that God is on your side as you try to establish your rights. The whole system is cumbersome and slow. In civil cases the process tries to force the parties to settle matters between themselves by compromise or exhaustion. If you want justice you will need to have faith and perseverance.

If you try to work for change in an unjust society, you will need faith and perseverance. The entrenched positions will be hard to shift. Economic advantage or privilege will make many defend the current situation. The network of injustice is hard to penetrate. The mixed motives of people are hard to unravel. You will need faith and perseverance even to begin to gather the momentum necessary for change. On the journey you will doubt that God cares about fairness. Jesus' story both warns and encourages us. You will need to keep it up.

If you try to resolve a conflict in your family circle, you will need faith and perseverance. Broken relationships are hard to mend. People do not like admitting that they might have been in the wrong. It is hard to discover the truth as everybody has their own version of it. You will need to pray about the situation and rebuild faith in God and in people that there is a way forward to reconciliation. When you try to help your family you will have to be ready to keep it up.

If you expect God to have a quick fix for the troubles of the world, look at the cross. God knows it must be taken that seriously. God knows that justice, truth and reconciliation are costly. God knows that you have to endure to the end. Jesus did not give up. Neither can we. We will need perseverance in faith and prayer to be there at the end.

Feeling

Stand in line in the bank while people keep you waiting. Do you feel frustrated and angry? People are taking little notice of you. Others are served first and no one supports you in your rights. Do you demand your rights or do you feel like quitting when no one joins you in fighting for your place?

Take your place and stand up for Jesus when people say that they have no respect for your religion. Can you relate to those who say that they have no respect for what you hold dear? Do your feelings get the better of you so that you become angry and walk away?

On your knees at prayer, how do you relate to God when you do not see things change for the better, when injustice continues to oppress people in your society? Do you become angry and tell God that you will not believe any more? How do you feel about God at these times?

When you see the situation as bad as ever, do you blame God and dismiss God as irrelevant? Do you lose your faith that God cares and acts? Can you see what *would* change the situation? Do you place the blame on other human beings? How do you feel about others at these times?

When nothing seems to work, how do you feel about yourself? Do you become depressed and cease to pray or work for your goals?

In the story Jesus makes it clear that God does care, that God is on the side of justice and truth. God keeps it up despite continuing rejection by humanity. God calls for our prayers, commitment and persistence. How do you feel about God's call to keep it up?

Thinking

Sometimes it is not easy to work out the point in these stories by Jesus. In their transmission to us we would love to know more about the context and the background to the story. The introductory verses here look like an editor's commentary, and it is likely that the story existed separately. No doubt Luke fitted it into his fabric when he deemed it appropriate.

Ask yourself, does it fit here? This section looks like a preparation for the conflicts in Jerusalem. Jesus is giving final instructions to his closest disciples. He knows that their expectations of a clear victory for God ignore the hardness of the human heart and the entrenched nature of evil. If any of his followers expect an easy ride they will be painfully disillusioned. What Jesus needs is a group of disciples with determination in faith, prayer and action. The arrival of the kingdom of God will not mean immediate justice and truth. It will take time to achieve those goals, time to gain the transformation of people and society. What will come is a reversal of the usual order of affairs. The victory of love can only come through endurance even unto death.

This story of challenge and encouragement was just as necessary in the early church after the first wave of enthusiasm. The expected return of Christ in glory, and the implementation of the kingdom of God in the victory of justice and truth, did not come as soon as they hoped. Some began to doubt God's promises and God's empowerment. In such a setting the story would have been remembered. Luke reminds them of the challenge: would they be found faithful when the Lord came?

The story illustrates the contrast between the judge who had no respect for God or humanity, and the God of justice and compassion who was always acting with speed to help the faithful. The judge would respond to persistence. God would respond to perseverance in faith. Is this how we see God? Justice and truth will only come when we work for it with determination and with faith. We too must keep it up to the end.

When you think about it this story fits very well into the context of the journey to Jerusalem. Our journey takes us down the same road to the cross and the resurrection; to the ascension and the empowering of the Spirit. With Christ we can keep up the journey to the end.

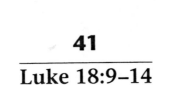

41

Luke 18:9–14

⁹He also told this parable to some who trusted in themselves that they were righteous and regarded others with contempt: ¹⁰'Two men went up to the temple to pray, one a Pharisee and the other a tax-collector. ¹¹The Pharisee, standing by himself, was praying thus, "God, I thank you that I am not like other people: thieves, rogues, adulterers, or even like this tax-collector. ¹²I fast twice a week; I give a tenth of all my income." ¹³But the tax-collector, standing far off, would not even look up to heaven, but was beating his breast and saying, "God, be merciful to me, a sinner!" ¹⁴I tell you, this man went down to his home justified rather than the other; for all who exalt themselves will be humbled, but all who humble themselves will be exalted.'

Context

At this stage on the road to Jerusalem, Jesus offers two parables on prayer. The first parable is about the unjust judge. The second parable contrasts the Pharisee and the tax-collector.

Sensing

Follow Jesus into the temple in Jerusalem. Slip in at the back and watch the people who come to pray.

Follow Jesus into the temple in Jerusalem. Slip in at the back and keep your eyes on that Pharisee. Look at the way that Pharisee walks with his eyes looking straight ahead. Look at the way he holds his head high in the presence of God. Here is a man who is clearly doing God a favour when he comes into the temple to pray.

Keep your eyes on that Pharisee. Look at the way that Pharisee looks down on the other people in the temple. Sense his self-confidence. Sense his self-assurance. Sense his arrogance. Here is a man who clearly has nothing to fear when he comes into the temple to pray.

Keep your ears on that Pharisee. Listen to the way in which he opens his mouth to pray,

> God, I thank you that I am not like other people: thieves, rogues, adulterers, or even like this tax-collector. I fast twice a week; I give a tenth of all my income.

Listen to the way in which he addresses the almighty God.

Follow Jesus into the temple in Jerusalem. Slip in at the back and keep your eyes on that tax-collector. Look at the way he walks with his eyes staring down to the floor. Look at the way he holds his head low in the presence of God. Here is a man who clearly expects no favours when he comes into the temple to pray.

Keep your eyes on that tax-collector. Look at the way he looks up to the other people in the temple. Sense his lack of confidence. Sense his lack of assurance. Sense his humility. Here is a man who clearly has everything to fear when he comes into the temple to pray.

Keep your ears on that tax-collector. Listen to the way in which he opens his mouth to pray,

God, be merciful to me, a sinner!

Listen to the way in which he addresses the almighty God.

Follow Jesus into the temple in Jerusalem. Slip in at the back and watch the Pharisee and the tax-collector who come to pray. Then decide which example you wish to follow.

Intuition

Suppose someone was watching you when you go into church to pray. What clues would they pick up?

What clues would they pick up from the way you dress? Do you take trouble to dress up to come into the presence of God? Or do you reckon that God should take you as you are?

What clues would they pick up from your footsteps? Do you come into the house of God with an attitude of hushed reverence? Or do you continue as if in the everyday world?

What clues would they pick up from the look in your eyes? Do your eyes sparkle with anticipation and joy as you come into the presence of God? Or do your eyes glaze over with the dullness of routine?

What clues would they pick up from the posture of your body? Do you adopt a special position for prayer, with bended knees or with upraised hands? Or do you reckon that the body is not really part of prayer?

Suppose someone were reading your thoughts when you go into church to pray. What clues would they pick up?

What clues would they pick up from your prayers of adoration? Do you allow yourself to become absorbed in the wonder of God? Or do you find yourself repeating secondhand shouts of praise?

What clues would they pick up from your prayers of contrition? Do you really experience sorrow and contrition for your sins? Or do you find yourself relying on the general confession?

What clues would they pick up from your prayers of thanksgiving? Do you really give thanks to God out of your personal experience of God's goodness? Or do you find yourself drawing heavily on the experiences of others?

What clues would they pick up from your prayers of supplication? Do you focus your requests on the immediate needs of self? Or do you share in God's great work of prayer for the salvation of the world?

Suppose someone were watching you and reading your thoughts when you go into church to pray? What clues would they pick up?

Feeling

The prayer, 'God, be merciful to me, a sinner!' can be said in many different tones of voice. Try out the different voices.

Put yourself in the shoes of the drowning man who has never known for himself the power of God. All around the sea is swirling and the waves are beating. Your arms have grown weary from swimming against the tide and against the odds. All your past life flashes before your eyes. Hopeless and grasping the last straw of hope, you cry aloud, 'God, be merciful to me, a sinner!' Here is the voice of desperation.

Put yourself in the shoes of the anxious child who has grown up in awe of the exacting justice of God. All around are the little temptations of life, the white lie, the moment of laziness, the broken fast in the middle of Lent. All your peccadillos in life flash before your eyes as you draw near to the presence of God. Worthless and grasping little hope, you cry aloud, 'God, be merciful to me, a sinner!' Here is the voice of fear before the judgement throne of God.

Put yourself in the shoes of the God-fearing adult who has grown up aware of the infinite mercy of God. All around are the very real occasions when you have fallen short of the standards of love exemplified by the kingdom of God. All your shortcomings in life flash before your eyes as you draw near to the presence of God. Full of hope and secure in the divine love, you cry aloud, 'God, be merciful to me, a sinner!' Here is the voice of confidence before the mercy seat of God.

Put yourself in the shoes of the tax-collector who has seen the errors of his ways. All around are the signs of having forgotten the God of his fathers. There in the temple you resolve to put the past behind you and to embrace a new future holding the hand of God. In confidence you pray, 'God, be merciful to me, a sinner!' In confidence you walk away forgiven. Here is the voice of the forgiven sinner.

The prayer, 'God, be merciful to me, a sinner!' can be said in many different tones of voice. Try out the different voices and pray that your voice may be in tune with the voice of God.

Thinking

The Pharisee and the tax-collector believed in very different kinds of God. Can you perceive the difference?

For the Pharisee, God has very clearly defined standards and God expects men and women to live up to those standards. Surely this is a reasonable enough faith to hold?

For the Pharisee, God rewards those men and women who strive hard to match the standards that God requires of them. Surely this is a reasonable enough faith to hold?

For the Pharisee, God delights in those men and women who have shown in their lives great devotion to the law of God. Surely this is a reasonable enough faith to hold?

For the Pharisee, God is exalted and praised through the recitation of those virtues which love for God has cultivated. Surely this is a reasonable enough faith to hold?

The Pharisee and the tax-collector believed in very different kinds of God. Can you perceive the difference?

For the tax-collector, God has a very generous and very forgiving heart. God expects men and women to turn to the love of God when they see the folly of their ways. Surely this is a reasonable enough faith to hold?

For the tax-collector, God accepts and forgives men and women who turn to the love of God with penitent and contrite hearts. Surely this is a reasonable enough faith to hold?

For the tax-collector, God delights in those men and women who have such confidence in the love of God that they throw themselves on the divine mercy. Surely this is a reasonable enough faith to hold?

For the tax-collector, God is exalted and praised through the humble acceptance of the forgiveness and mercy which God extends. Surely this is a reasonable enough faith to hold?

The Pharisee and the tax-collector believed in very different kinds of God. Can you perceive the difference?

42
Luke 19:1–10

¹He entered Jericho and was passing through it. ²A man was there named Zacchaeus; he was a chief tax-collector and was rich. ³He was trying to see who Jesus was, but on account of the crowd he could not, because he was short in stature. ⁴So he ran ahead and climbed a sycamore tree to see him, because he was going to pass that way. ⁵When Jesus came to the place, he looked up and said to him, 'Zacchaeus, hurry and come down; for I must stay at your house today.' ⁶So he hurried down and was happy to welcome him. ⁷All who saw it began to grumble and said, 'He has gone to be the guest of one who is a sinner.' Zacchaeus stood there and said to the Lord, 'Look, half of my possessions, Lord, I will give to the poor; and if I have defrauded anyone of anything, I will pay back four times as much.' ⁹Then Jesus said to him, 'Today salvation has come to this house, because he too is a son of Abraham. ¹⁰For the Son of Man came to seek out and to save the lost.'

Context
The long journey towards Jerusalem, begun at chapter nine and verse 51, now draws to a close. As Jesus enters Jericho, he meets with Zacchaeus. Zacchaeus' life is changed by the meeting.

Sensing
Sometimes the stories Luke tells are pure pantomime. Steal away to join the crowd in the market square at Jericho. Picture what is going on and allow yourself to be carried away by the changing responses of the crowd.

Today Luke introduces to the pantomime a little fellow called Zacchaeus. See the little fellow push his way into the crowd. He is so short that he stands no chance at all of catching even a glimpse of Jesus. See the little fellow run hither and thither trying to see over the heads of people so much taller than him. You and the crowd cheer his antics.

Today Luke introduces to the pantomime a little fellow

called Zacchaeus. Hear the rumours run swiftly through the crowd. He is a chief tax-collector. He is very rich. He has amassed his wealth by colluding with the occupying army. Feel the mood of the crowd change. You and the crowd boo his presence.

Today Luke introduces to the pantomime a little fellow called Zacchaeus. Undeterred by the crowd he scrambles up a sycomore tree, a comical sight indeed. You and the crowd cheer his disregard for public protocol.

Today Luke introduces to the pantomime a little fellow called Zacchaeus. Watch Jesus make a bee-line straight for that sycomore tree. You and the crowd hush. Hear Jesus shout up into the tree,

> Zacchaeus, hurry and come down; for I must stay at your house today.

Feel the mood of the crowd change. You and the crowd boo Jesus for welcoming sinners.

Today Luke introduces to the pantomime a little fellow called Zacchaeus. Watch as Zacchaeus drops down from the tree. Listen as Zacchaeus makes public his speech to Jesus,

> Look, half of my possessions, Lord, I will give to the poor;
> and if I have defrauded anyone of anything, I will pay back four times as much.

You and the crowd cheer his generous spirit.

Sometimes the stories Luke tells are pure pantomime. Steal away to join the crowd in the market square at Jericho. Picture what is going on and allow yourself to be carried away by the changing response of the crowd.

Intuition

The real hero of the story is, of course, the sycomore tree. Without the sycomore tree Zacchaeus would never have come face to face with Jesus. How willing are you to plant sycomore trees around your church?

For Zacchaeus there were clearly physical challenges which made his journey to Jesus unnecessarily difficult. A short person simply could not see what was going on. So what physical challenges get in the way of people meeting with Jesus in your church today and how can you overcome those challenges? What kind of sycomore trees need to be planted there?

How easy is it for disabled people to get in and out of your church, to sit comfortably and inconspicuously in your church, to make their way to receive communion? Is there a need for a sycomore tree here?

How easy is it for the partially sighted to read the service sheet or to use the books in your church? How easy is it for those with hearing difficulties to follow the service and to hear the officiant? Is there a need for a sycomore tree here?

For Zacchaeus there were clearly social challenges which made his journey to Jesus unnecessarily difficult. A tax-collector simply was not made welcome. So what social challenges get in the way of people meeting with Jesus in your church today and how can you overcome these challenges? What kind of sycomore trees need to be planted there?

How easy is it for people of different social and racial backgrounds to come into your church, to sit comfortably and inconspicuously in your church, to feel at home with the predominant culture? Is there a need for a sycomore tree here?

How easy is it for people who are unaccustomed to living in a world of books and printed texts to follow your services? How easy is it for people who are unaccustomed to the musical culture of the church to enter into your traditions of worship? Is there a need for a sycomore tree here?

The real hero of the Zacchaeus story is, of course, the sycomore tree. How willing are you to plant sycomore trees around your church?

Feeling

The story of Zacchaeus is a profound drama about a changed human life, a drama in four acts. Let that profound human drama change your view of life.

In act one, Zacchaeus is building a life for himself. He is ambitious, well motivated, hardworking and unscrupulous. He is a man who sees himself and his own family at the centre of the universe. The taxation system operating within the Roman empire affords him all the opportunities he needs. In act one, he climbs to the very top of his chosen career and becomes a chief tax-collector. In act one, he becomes very rich and surrounds himself with all the luxury money can buy. Here is Zacchaeus the contented man.

In act two, Zacchaeus is exploring the value of the life he has made for himself. He is lonely, hated, ostracized and an outcast in his own community. He is a man who begins to look for more in life than wealth and possessions. In act two, he climbs to the very top of the sycomore tree to look for something better in life. In act two, he becomes very unsettled and sees through the folly of his lifestyle. Here is Zacchaeus the unsettled man.

In act three, Zacchaeus is seeking a new life for himself. He is open, honest, sorrowful and penitent about the past. He is a man who seeks to make amends for his sins, when he sees himself as he really is in the eyes of Jesus. In act three, he repents and publicly confesses his guilt, resolving to make a new start. In act three, he demonstrates a change of heart by giving one half of his possessions to the poor and by dedicating the other half to repay those whom he has defrauded. Here is Zacchaeus the repentant sinner.

In act four, Zacchaeus lives the new life claimed in the name of Jesus. He is accepted, forgiven, restored and loved. He is a man who was lost and now is found. In act four, salvation has come to his house and has come to stay. In act four, he sits and eats in the company of Jesus. Here is Zacchaeus the restored man.

The story of Zacchaeus is a profound drama about a changed human life, a drama in four acts. Let that profound human drama change your view of life.

Thinking

Do you recognize a recurrent motif in Luke's theology?

In chapter five Luke sets the scene. Here Jesus saw a tax-collector named Levi, sitting at the tax booth. Jesus said to Levi, 'Follow me.' Then Levi gave a great banquet for Jesus in his house. The Pharisees and the scribes complained, saying, 'Why do you eat and drink with tax-collectors and sinners?' Jesus replied, 'I have come to call not the righteous but sinners to repentance.' Do you spot the theme?

In chapter fifteen Luke tells a story about a remarkable shepherd. Here the shepherd leaves the ninety-nine sheep in the wilderness while he goes off in search of the one sheep that was lost until he finds it. Jesus said, 'There is more joy in heaven over one sinner who repents than over ninety-nine righteous people who need no repentance.' Do you spot the theme?

In chapter fifteen Luke tells a story about a remarkable woman. Here this woman lights the lamp, sweeps the house and searches diligently for the coin that was lost until she finds it. Jesus said, 'There is joy in the presence of the angels of God over one sinner who repents.' Do you spot the theme?

In chapter fifteen Luke tells a story about a remarkable father. Here the father welcomes the prodigal son who returns, kills the fatted calf and orders a feast of celebration. Jesus echoes the father's words, 'We had to celebrate and rejoice, because this brother of yours was dead and has come to life; he was lost and has been found.' Do you spot the theme?

In chapter nineteen Luke completes the scene. Here Jesus saw a tax-collector named Zacchaeus stuck up a tree. Jesus said to Zacchaeus, 'Hurry and come down.' Then Zacchaeus invited Jesus into his home as an honoured guest. Then all who saw this happen complained, saying, 'He has gone to be the guest of one who is a sinner.' Jesus replied, 'The Son of Man came to seek out and to save the lost.' Do you spot the theme?

Now do you recognize a recurrent motif in Luke's theology? And why do you think Luke emphasizes the theme so strongly?

43

Luke 19:28–40

²⁸After he had said this, he went on ahead, going up to Jerusalem.

²⁹When he had come near Bethphage and Bethany, at the place called the Mount of Olives, he sent two of the disciples, ³⁰saying, 'Go into the village ahead of you, and as you enter it you will find tied there a colt that has never been ridden. Untie it and bring it here. ³¹If anyone asks you, "Why are you untying

it?" just say this: "The Lord needs it."' ³²So those who were sent departed and found it as he had told them. ³³As they were untying the colt, its owners asked them, 'Why are you untying the colt?' ³⁴They said, 'The Lord needs it.' ³⁵Then they brought it to Jesus; and after throwing their cloaks on the colt, they set Jesus on it. ³⁶As he rode along, people kept spreading their cloaks on the road. ³⁷As he was now approaching the path down from the Mount of Olives, the whole multitude of the disciples began to praise God joyfully with a loud voice for all the deeds of power that they had seen, ³⁸saying,

'Blessed is the king
    who comes in the name of the Lord!
Peace in heaven,
    and glory in the highest heaven!'

³⁹Some of the Pharisees in the crowd said to him, 'Teacher, order your disciples to stop.' ⁴⁰He answered, 'I tell you, if these were silent, the stones would shout out.'

Context

The long journey to Jerusalem now draws close to its end. For Luke the 'Palm Sunday' narrative is set on the Bethany to Jerusalem road as Jerusalem comes into sight by the Mount of Olives.

Sensing

Actions often speak louder than words. Come and join the action.

Today you are drawing very close to Jerusalem. Sense the excitement in the air. The pilgrim road is now quite crowded with people anxious to arrive in the holy city itself. Sense the anticipation in the air. Only a few more twists and turns in the road hold you back from your first glimpse of the city of God. Sense the expectation in the air.

Today you are drawing very close to Passover time. Sense the excitement in the air. The pilgrim road is now quite crowded with people anxious to celebrate the Passover feast. Sense the anticipation in the air. Only a few more hours and days in the calendar hold you back from the moment when the people of God expect the new beginning. Sense the expectation in the air.

Today you are drawing very close to the time of year when

tradition says God will send the Messiah. Sense the excitement in the air. The pilgrim road is now quite crowded with people talking about Jesus of Nazareth and the claims to messiahship. Sense the anticipation in the air. Only a few more hours and days of uncertainty separate you from knowing whether this year the Messiah will come. Sense the expectation in the air.

Actions often speak louder than words. Come and join the action.

Today you see the disciples bring a colt to Jesus and you see Jesus mount the colt. Sense the excitement in the air as the people recall the prophecy of Zechariah 9:9,

> Lo, your king comes to you:
> triumphant and victorious is he,
> humble and riding on a donkey,
> on a colt, the foal of a donkey.

Today you see Jesus riding as king on that donkey down from the Mount of Olives. Sense the anticipation in the air as the people recall the prophecy of Zechariah 14:4 looking to the coming Messiah,

> On that day his feet shall stand on the Mount of Olives.

Today you see people spreading their cloaks on the road as Jesus rides past. Sense the expectation in the air as connections are drawn with the enthronement rite of Jehu in 2 Kings 9:13,

> Then hurriedly they all took their cloaks and spread them for him on the bare steps; and they blew the trumpet, and proclaimed, 'Jehu is king.'

Actions often speak louder than words. Come and join the action.

Intuition

The unsung hero of the story is clearly the owner of the colt. Could that hero be you?

Imagine how implausible it is. A short time before the Passover festival, the busiest time of the year, Jesus calls out for a colt. Everyone else is looking for a lamb for the Passover meal but Jesus demands a colt. What implausible requests does Jesus make of you?

Imagine how inconvenient it is. A short time before the

Passover festival, the busiest time of the year, Jesus requires your colt for a pantomime procession. The transport industry is at breaking point, carrying food and people into the city. What inconvenient requests does Jesus make of you?

Imagine how mysterious it is. A short time before the Passover festival, the busiest time of the year, Jesus requisitions your colt without so much as an explanation. You have no idea for what the colt is required or when you will see it again. It makes further advanced bookings so very difficult. What mysterious requests does Jesus make of you?

Imagine how incriminating it is. A short time before the Passover festival, the busiest time of the year, Jesus wants to be seen in public on your colt. You know how much the authorities are gunning for Jesus. You know how vulnerable this makes Jesus' disciples and followers. Now you will be aiding and abetting the most hunted person in Jerusalem. What incriminating requests does Jesus make of you?

Imagine how demanding it is. A short time before the Passover festival, the busiest time of the year, Jesus demands your colt with the imperious command, 'The Lord needs it.' You are not offered the opportunity to refuse. The choice is somehow taken out of your hands. What demanding requests does Jesus make of you?

The unsung hero of the story is clearly the owner of the colt. Could that hero be you?

Feeling

For the Jesus of Luke's gospel the descent towards Jerusalem from the Mount of Olives came at the end of a long and deliberate journey started in chapter nine verse 51 when 'he set his face to go to Jerusalem'. This last leg of the journey to Jerusalem was undertaken riding on the back of a colt. Try to get inside Jesus' feelings.

Here is a well-organized Jesus. Nothing is left to chance. Careful arrangements have been made well in advance for a colt to be ready in the next village. The colt has been specially and symbolically chosen as one that has never previously been ridden. A password has been carefully arranged with the owner, who releases the colt when he hears the words, 'The Lord needs it.' Jesus is well organized.

Here is a very courageous Jesus. The long journey towards

Jerusalem had been well and truly overshadowed by the sense of growing opposition and impending doom. Back in chapter thirteen Jesus lamented, 'Jerusalem, Jerusalem, the city that kills the prophets and stones those that are sent to it!' Jesus has no illusions about the kind of welcome that awaits him. As a man whose life was under threat he would have done well not to draw attention to himself. Jesus is very courageous.

Here is a very deliberate Jesus. The statements which Jesus makes are unambiguously messianic. He chose to ride towards Jerusalem on a colt in fulfilment of prophecy. He chose to begin his journey from the Mount of Olives in fulfilment of prophecy. He rode along a path strewn with cloaks, proclaiming royal acclaim. He accepted the chant of the people,

> Blessed is the king
> who comes in the name of the Lord!

Jesus is very deliberate.

Here is a generous Jesus. Back in chapter thirteen Jesus proclaimed of Jerusalem, 'How often have I desired to gather your children together as a hen gathers her brood under her wings!' Now, riding towards Jerusalem, Jesus offers the city one more chance to 'recognize on this day the things that make for peace'. Jesus remains generous.

This last leg of the journey to Jerusalem was undertaken riding on the back of a colt. Try to get inside Jesus' feelings.

Thinking

Matthew, Mark and Luke all present the account of Jesus riding towards Jerusalem on the colt in a slightly different way. What do you make of Luke's perspective on the story?

Mark tells us that, as Jesus rode along, 'Many people spread their cloaks on the road, and others spread leafy branches that they had cut in the fields.' Those leafy branches immediately linked Jesus' entry to Jerusalem with the triumphal entry of Simon Maccabaeus into Jerusalem recorded in 1 Maccabees 13:51. Luke tells us that, as Jesus rode along, 'people kept spreading their cloaks on the road'. In other words, Luke omits the whole tradition of the 'palm branches'. What do you make of that? Is it pure chance that Luke is playing down the political threat posed by Jesus?

Mark tells us that Jesus rode right into Jerusalem on the colt, symbolically entering and claiming the city as king. Matthew goes one step further and describes how, when Jesus entered Jerusalem, the whole city was in turmoil. Luke tells us that Jesus stopped before reaching the city and wept over it. What do you make of that? Is it pure chance that Luke is playing down the political threat posed by Jesus? Mark tells us that, as Jesus rode along, the crowds shouted out,

> Blessed is the coming kingdom of our ancestor David!
> Hosanna in the highest heaven!

That Hosanna immediately linked Jesus' entry to Jerusalem with God's intervening hand of victory. Luke tells us that, as Jesus rode along, the crowds shouted out,

> Peace in heaven,
> and glory in the highest heaven!

What do you make of that? Is it pure chance that Luke is playing down the political threat posed by Jesus?

Matthew, Mark and Luke each presents the account of Jesus riding towards Jerusalem on the colt in a slightly different way. What do you make of Luke's perspective on the story?

———————————❯❯·◎·❰❰———————————

44

Luke 20:27–38

²⁷Some Sadducees, those who say there is no resurrection, came to him ²⁸and asked him a question, 'Teacher, Moses wrote for us that if a man's brother dies, leaving a wife but no children, the man shall marry the widow and raise up children for his brother. ²⁹Now there were seven brothers; the first married, and died childless; ³⁰then the second ³¹and the third married her, and so in the same way all seven died childless. ³²Finally the woman also died. ³³In the resurrection, therefore, whose wife will the woman be? For the seven had married her.'

³⁴Jesus said to them, 'Those who belong to this age marry and are given in marriage; ³⁵but those who are considered

worthy of a place in that age and in the resurrection from the dead neither marry nor are given in marriage. [36]Indeed they cannot die any more, because they are like angels and are children of God, being children of the resurrection. [37]And the fact that the dead are raised Moses himself showed, in the story about the bush, where he speaks of the Lord as the God of Abraham, the God of Isaac, and the God of Jacob. [38]Now he is God not of the dead, but of the living; for to him all of them are alive.'

Context

Having arrived in Jerusalem, Jesus taught in the temple. At this point Luke records two questions put to Jesus to catch him out. The first question was political (about taxes), the second question was theological (about life after death).

Sensing

Politics and religion are the real stuff of controversy. Come to the temple in Jerusalem and see how the troublemakers tried to embroil Jesus in the controversy of politics and in the controversy of theology.

Watch the political trap being set. See a Pharisee step forward. Hear the Pharisee clear his throat and listen attentively as he poses his question,

Is it lawful for us to pay taxes to the emperor, or not?

Watch the Pharisee step back and wait for the controversy to flare up.

Hear the whispering in the background. If Jesus argues against paying taxes to the Roman authorities, there is a clear case against him as a political rebel. The Romans will hate him. If Jesus argues in favour of paying taxes to the Roman authorities, there is a clear case against him as a traitor to the Jewish people. All who seek liberation from Roman rule will hate him. Hear the whispering in the background.

Now listen to Jesus' reply as he carefully takes the question apart and lays the pieces on the table. 'Give to the emperor', he says, 'the things that are the emperor's, and to God the things that are God's.' Hear the sharp intake of breath from the crowd. The political trap has been sprung, but its prey has got away.

Watch the theological trap being set. See a Sadducee step forward. Hear the Sadducee clear his throat and listen attentively as he poses his question,

In the resurrection whose wife will the woman be? For the seven had married her.

Watch the whispering in the background. A lot of bad feeling already exists between Sadducees and Pharisees. The Sadducees based their theology on the five books of Moses alone. The Pharisees took a much wider view of the scriptures and the traditions. The question makes the Pharisees' belief in resurrection look so silly. Hear the whispering in the background.

Now listen to Jesus' reply as he carefully takes the question apart and lays the pieces on the table. He says that the question is based on a wrong view of resurrection, and even the five books of Moses attest to the fact of resurrection. Hear the sharp intake of breath from the crowd. The theological trap has been sprung but its prey has got away.

Politics and religion are the real stuff of controversy. Come to the temple in Jerusalem and see how Jesus extricates himself from the traps.

Intuition

Here is a story about the continuity of the people of God. How conscious are you of that sense of continuity?

Conjure up in your mind images of three Old Testament prophets, Amos, Hosea and Isaiah. Let their preaching fire your imagination. How conscious are you of living your Christian life in their presence?

Conjure up in your mind images of three New Testament disciples, Peter, James and John. Let their discipleship fire your imagination. How conscious are you of living your Christian life in their presence?

Conjure up in your mind images of three early Christian fathers, Ambrose, Augustine and Athanasius. Let their teaching fire your imagination. How conscious are you of living your Christian life in their presence?

Conjure up in your mind images of three leaders of the Protestant Reformation, Luther, Calvin and Zwingli. Let their zeal fire your imagination. How conscious are you of living your Christian life in their presence?

Conjure up in your mind images of three founders of Anglicanism, Laud, Hooker and Cranmer. Let their doctrine fire your imagination. How conscious are you of living your Christian life in their presence?

Conjure up in your mind the countless generations of Christian men and women who have witnessed tirelessly to the love of God in our own communities throughout the ages. Let their devotion fire your imagination. How conscious are you of living your Christian life in their presence?

Here is a story about the continuity of the people of God. How conscious are you of that sense of continuity?

Feeling

Here is a story about friendship, about real friendship that really lasts.

Take, for example, the bond of friendship between the patriarch Abraham and the Lord his God. Recall how God called Abraham away from his roots and set him on the journey of a lifetime. Recall how God stood by Abraham and nurtured him on the journey. Here is a story about friendship, about real friendship that really lasts. Friendship like this cannot be destroyed by death.

Take, for example, the bond of friendship between the patriarch's son Isaac and the Lord his God. Recall how God called Isaac into being when his parents were so very old. Recall how God redeemed Isaac from the sacrificial fire. Recall how God stood by Isaac and nurtured him on the journey. Here is a story about friendship, about real friendship that really lasts. Friendship like this cannot be destroyed by death.

Take, for example, the bond of friendship between the great teacher Moses and the Lord his God. Recall how God protected Moses as an infant. Recall how God called Moses away from the flock of his father-in-law Jethro and sent him to lead the Israelite people to a new beginning. Recall how God stood beside Moses at the edge of the Red Sea. Here is a story about friendship, about real friendship that really lasts. Friendship like this cannot be destroyed by death.

Take, for example, the bond of friendship between Peter, James, John and Jesus their Lord. Recall how Jesus called each one of them away from their roots and set them on a journey of a lifetime. Recall how Jesus stood by them and nurtured them on their journey. Here is a story about friendship, about real friendship that really lasts. Friendship like this cannot be destroyed by death.

When pressed to make a case for the resurrection of the dead, Jesus pointed precisely to the indestructible friendship that exists between God and the people of God. For our God is not the God of the dead but the God of the living. Here is a story about friendship, about real friendship that really lasts.

Thinking

Here is a story about how to use scripture and about how to misuse scripture. What do you think?

Were the Sadducees correct in the way in which they read the levirate law of marriage set down in the books of Moses? According to Deuteronomy 25:5, if a man died childless, his brother must marry the widow and beget children to carry on the line. What do you think?

Were the Sadducees correct in the way in which they applied the levirate law of marriage to the quotation concerning the resurrection? What assumptions were they making when they applied a passage of scripture about marriage and family to a question about life beyond death? What do you think?

Were the Sadducees correct in their belief that the five books of Moses held the key to theological truth? What do you think?

Here is a story about how to use scripture and about how to misuse scripture.

Was Jesus correct in the way in which he began his case? Jesus did not refute the text of scripture but challenged the assumptions on which the text was applied to the question of resurrection. What do you think?

Was Jesus correct in drawing a picture of the resurrection which he did not anchor in scripture? 'Those who are considered worthy of a place in that age', he claimed, 'neither marry nor are given in marriage.' What do you think?

Was Jesus correct in deflecting his questioners from the details of their precise question to the issue underlying it, the resurrection of the dead? What do you think?

Was Jesus correct in searching the books of Moses for a text which supported the resurrection of the dead? And was Jesus totally successful in his choice of text? What do you think?

Here is a story about how to use scripture and about how to misuse scripture. What do you think?

45

Luke 21:5–19

5When some were speaking about the temple, how it was adorned with beautiful stones and gifts dedicated to God, he said, 6'As for these things that you see, the days will come when not one stone will be left upon another; all will be thrown down.'

7They asked him, 'Teacher, when will this be, and what will be the sign that this is about to take place?' 8And he said, 'Beware that you are not led astray; for many will come in my name and say, "I am he!" and, "The time is near!" Do not go after them.

9'When you hear of wars and insurrections, do not be terrified; for these things must take place first, but the end will not follow immediately.' 10Then he said to them, 'Nation will rise against nation, and kingdom against kingdom; 11there will be great earthquakes, and in various places famines and plagues; and there will be dreadful portents and great signs from heaven.

12'But before all this occurs, they will arrest you and persecute you; they will hand you over to synagogues and prisons, and you will be brought before kings and governors because of my name. 13This will give you an opportunity to testify. 14So make up your minds not to prepare your defence in advance; 15for I will give you words and a wisdom that none of your opponents will be able to withstand or contradict. 16You will be betrayed even by parents and brothers, by relatives and friends; and they will put some of you to death. 17You will be hated by all because of my name. 18But not a hair of your head will perish. 19By your endurance you will gain your souls.'

Context

As Jesus' teaching in Jerusalem draws to a close before the beginning of the passion narrative, the three synoptic gospels present teaching about the future. This section in Luke is often known as the 'eschatological discourse'.

Sensing

It is all too easy to build a false sense of security in bricks and stones.

Picture the great temple in Jerusalem. See how it is adorned with beautiful stones and gifts dedicated to God. See how strongly and solidly it has been built. See how the people admire the great temple. Feel how the people draw a sense of security from the great temple. Hear Jesus say, 'Not one stone will be left upon another; all will be thrown down.'

Picture the great cathedral which you know best. See how it is adorned with beautiful stones and gifts dedicated to God. See how strongly and solidly it has been built. See how people admire that great cathedral. Feel how the people draw a sense of security from that great cathedral. Hear Jesus say, 'Not one stone will be left upon another; all will be thrown down.'

Picture the great parish church which you know best. See how it is adorned with beautiful stones and gifts dedicated to God. See how strongly and solidly it has been built. See how the people admire that great parish church. Feel how the people draw a sense of security from that great parish church. Hear Jesus say, 'Not one stone will be left upon another; all will be thrown down.'

Picture the most humble village chapel which you know well. See how even here that chapel is adorned with wood and stone and with gifts dedicated to God. See how strongly and solidly it has been built. See how the people admire that humble village chapel. Feel how the people draw a sense of security from that humble village chapel. Hear Jesus say, 'Not one stone will be left upon another; all will be thrown down.'

It is all too easy to build a false sense of security in bricks and stones.

Intuition

Sometimes it would be really useful to be able to peer round the corner of time and to see into the future. The trouble is that life is just not like that.

Imagine what it would be like if your horoscope really could predict the days when things will go well for you and the days when it would be better simply to stay in bed. The trouble is that life is just not like that.

Imagine what it would be like if a fortune-teller really could predict the business deals to go for and the deals it would simply be better to avoid. The trouble is that life is just not like that.

Imagine what it would be like if there was a foolproof way of telling which horse would win the 2.30 and when it was best to place no bet. The trouble is that life is just not like that.

Imagine what it would be like if our dreams could really predict the dangers that lie ahead for us and when it is best to leave the car in the garage. The trouble is that life is just not like that.

Imagine what it would be like if we knew from the day we were born how long we had to live and when we were going to die. The trouble is that life is just not like that.

Sometimes it would be really useful to be able to peer round the corner of time and to see into the future. The disciples asked Jesus to help them do precisely that.

The disciples wanted to know when the temple would be destroyed. Imagine what it would have been like to know the answer. The disciples wanted to know when the day of the Lord would come. Imagine what it would have been like to know the answer. The disciples wanted to know when the Messiah would return. Imagine what it would have been like to know the answer.

Sometimes it would be really useful to be able to peer round the corner of time and to see into the future. The disciples asked Jesus to help them do precisely that. The trouble, said Jesus, is that life is just not like that.

Feeling

Jesus warned his disciples that the future would hold wars, earthquakes, famines and plagues. These warnings were not concerned with the end of the world but about the world in which Christian men and women continue to live. Open your hearts to let God's love into this world.

Switch on the television and see the pictures of war. Turn on the radio and listen to the stories of war. Open the papers and read the news of war. See how human lives are torn apart by the destruction of war. Feel for the human pain caused by the suffering of war. Open your hearts to those whose lives are caught in the drama of war. Pray that the church of Christ is there alongside the pain and the suffering.

Switch on the television and see the pictures of earthquakes, floods and storms. Turn on the radio and listen to the stories of earthquakes, floods and storms. Open the papers and read the news of earthquakes, floods and storms. See how human lives are torn apart by natural disasters. Feel for the human pain caused by the suffering such disasters bring. Open your hearts to those whose lives are caught in the drama of natural disasters. Pray that the church of Christ is there alongside the pain and the suffering.

Switch on the television and see the pictures of famine and drought. Turn on the radio and listen to the stories of famine and drought. Open the papers and read the news of famine and drought. See how human lives are torn apart by the shortage of food and water. Feel the human pain caused by the suffering of hunger and thirst. Open your hearts to those whose lives are caught in the drama of famine and drought. Pray that the church of Christ is there alongside the pain and the suffering.

Switch on the television and see the pictures of plague and disease. Turn on the radio and listen to the stories of plague and disease. Open the papers and read the news of plague and disease. See how human lives are torn apart by the devastation of illness. Feel the human pain caused by the suffering of illness. Open your hearts to those whose lives are caught in the drama of plague and disease. Pray that the church of Christ is there alongside the pain and the suffering.

Jesus warned his disciples that the future would hold wars, earthquakes, famines and plagues. These warnings are about the world in which Christian men and women continue to live. Open your hearts to let God's love into this world.

Thinking

Luke's own voice is heard most clearly in the material which he adds to his main source, the gospel of Mark. In this, Jesus' final teaching before the passion narrative, Luke adds material which will prepare the early followers of Jesus for what awaits them. Do you understand what is going on?

In Luke's gospel Jesus warns his followers that they will be arrested and persecuted. According to the Acts of the Apostles, Peter and John were arrested and brought before the Jewish rulers, elders and scribes. According to the Acts of the Apostles, Stephen was stoned to death. According to the Acts of the Apostles, James, the brother of John, was killed with the sword. Do you think Luke had this in mind?

In Luke's gospel Jesus warns his followers that they will be handed over to synagogues and prisons. According to the Acts of the Apostles, the high priest and the Sadducees, filled with jealousy, arrested the apostles and put them in the public prison. During the night an angel of the Lord opened the prison doors and set them free. Do you think Luke had this in mind?

In Luke's gospel Jesus warns his followers that they will be brought before kings and governors. According to the Acts of the Apostles, when Gallio was proconsul of Achaia, the Jews brought Paul before the tribunal. According to the Acts of the Apostles, Paul was brought before the governor Felix and later before Festus and then before King Agrippa. Do you think Luke had this in mind?

In Luke's gospel Jesus promises his followers that he will give them words and wisdom that none of their opponents will be able to withstand or contradict. According to the Acts of the Apostles, when Peter was arrested, he spoke full of the Holy Spirit and those who heard him were amazed. Do you think Luke had this in mind?

Luke's voice is heard most clearly in the material which he adds to his main source, the gospel of Mark. It is perhaps no accident that the writer of Luke's gospel also wrote the Acts of the Apostles.

46

Luke 21:25–36

25'There will be signs in the sun, the moon, and the stars, and on the earth distress among nations confused by the roaring of the sea and the waves. 26People will faint from fear and foreboding of what is coming upon the world, for the powers of the heavens will be shaken. 27Then they will see "the Son of Man coming in a cloud" with power and great glory. 28Now when these things begin to take place, stand up and raise your heads, because your redemption is drawing near.'

29Then he told them a parable: 'Look at the fig tree and all the trees; 30as soon as they sprout leaves you can see for yourselves and know that summer is already near. 31So also, when you see these things taking place, you know that the kingdom of God is near. 32Truly I tell you, this generation will not pass away until all things have taken place. 33Heaven and earth will pass away, but my words will not pass away.

34'Be on guard so that your hearts are not weighed down with dissipation and drunkenness and the worries of this life, and that day does not catch you unexpectedly, 35like a trap. For it will come upon all who live on the face of the whole earth. 36Be alert at all times, praying that you may have the strength to escape all these things that will take place, and to stand before the Son of Man.'

Context

Following the prophecy of the destruction of Jerusalem, Luke gathers three teachings of Jesus about the coming of the Son of Man. At his coming, God's power and glory, and the kingdom of God, will be revealed. The kingdom will come out of chaos and the disciples must be ready to welcome it with alertness, confidence, soberness and prayer.

Sensing

It is Passover time in the season of spring. There is a freshness in the air. This is the time for new beginnings. This is the season of new growth.

Let yourself be a pilgrim in Jerusalem, here for the festival. You have travelled through the countryside and noted the first signs of spring. The branches of the fig tree, like bare arms, are sprouting the tips of the first leaves.

Listen as Jesus tells a parable about the fig tree. Yes, your eyes have seen it too. The first leaves are the definite sign that summer will be here soon. It will indeed come, but now it is only the tips of the leaves that show us that this will be so.

Listen as Jesus speaks about the kingdom of God. Hear the tone of confidence in his voice. He seems to be saying, 'As spring is to summer; as beginning is to fulfilment; so these signs that I do will blossom into fullness in the kingdom of God.'

All around you people are becoming excited. The questions, 'When?', 'How?', 'How long?' buzz around you like the first flies of the day as the sun warms the Temple Mount. The prophets have been telling us of the coming day of the Lord for so long. Advent is a long time coming.

Listen to Jesus as he responds to the murmured questions about time and about urgency. He seems to be saying, 'This generation, every generation, will see God's activity. The signs are about you as always. Distress among the nations is always the outcome of evil, can't you see that? When I stand up to evil, when you stand up to evil, whatever the cost, then the dawn of the kingdom will turn into day. Whenever truth exposes the lie, whenever prayer turns despair to hope, whenever love raises the head above water, whenever life is stronger than every kind of death, then the kingdom of God is near and your redemption has drawn nigh.'

Listen as Jesus confirms our hopes. He seems to be saying, 'Change and decay in all around I see, but my words remain for those who believe in me.'

Do you welcome these signs of new beginnings? Have you caught the confidence in these words of Christ?

Intuition

Do you dream dreams? Our dreams might be nightmares of disaster or idyllic dreams of paradise and perfection.

The nightmares are a reality for some people. The distress of nations is near at hand for them. There is political turmoil, open warfare, massive dislocation of life, fleeing in the night under the threat of the gun, job loss, road death and violence in the streets and in the home. These nightmares are in our waking moments, not in the illusions of sleep. 'Where is God in all this?' we cry. 'How can we stand up and raise our heads in such turmoil? Surely it is best to lie low and keep your head down when the flak is flying? Do not ask me to save others when I can hardly save myself.'

Our nightmares trap us in despair. We feel we have lost control of events. We are as helpless as the plastic bottle in the sea, tossed by every tide and drifting with every current. There is no point of reference any more, no sense of decision making, no stability in the structures. The heavens have fallen in and the depths rise up to swallow us. Where is redemption now?

Faced with such dreams, what is wrong with a drug to obliterate the pain, to suppress our worries? We cannot live with the nightmare in the daytime. We cannot sleep with the depression in the night-time. Where is redemption now?

In the lull between the nightmares we fall into daydreaming: 'Wouldn't it be nice if . . .?' We dream of structures to support community, of governments providing healthcare, of neighbours caring and sharing, of the old-time Christmas spirit, of judgement day for the wicked, of God's coming to restore justice, peace and truth. We know that the nightmare can become reality. Can the daydream come true as well?

Wake up to the advice of the Son of Man and let these be your goals: readiness to seize the opportunities for good, prayer to strengthen us in times of distress and a willingness to stand with Christ. Is not this the message of Advent?

Feeling

Do you feel that you can trust God? The gospels are full of promises for improvements. Each Advent is a sign of new beginnings and our hopes rise again. We repeat to ourselves, 'Maybe this year the promise will come true. Maybe this year the Christmas spirit will really take a firm hold on us all.'

Do you feel that you can trust God enough to raise your head in hope? On a personal basis we know we fail so often to live up to what we hope for ourselves, never mind what hope God has for us. We know that Advent is a time for taking stock. How do we feel about ourselves and our need for redemption? Can we trust God to give us a new beginning, to defeat the sin that besets us and spoils our relationship with God and others?

Do we feel our redemption drawing nigh? Can we rise from our knees, begging for mercy, and begin the journey to Christmas?

Do we feel that we can trust God enough to bring about a new world? We are tired of the old world. The old century was a triumph of technology and a disaster in tolerance and respect. Is Advent but an illusion to dash our hopes yet once more?

Do we feel that we can trust our neighbours enough to invite them to celebrate Christmas without causing social strains and road carnage? Have we the confidence in one another to rise to the occasion and seize the opportunity to celebrate being fully human? Advent is about developing our feelings of trust, trust in ourselves, in God and in one another. In Jesus, God showed us how to trust, how to hope that humanity could reach its potential, how to draw the very best out of each other. Advent is God's sign of trust in us. Advent is our sign that we will trust God for the future. Let us journey in trust together.

Thinking

The early church blossomed in times of social instability and unrest. We often think that it would be simple to be a Christian in times of stability and security. Historical research, however, seems to show that the Christian witness is most effective when the need for it is most obvious.

We know people often find redemption when they are facing some personal crisis. They open themselves to God's healing strength because they acknowledge their own frailty. Convicted of sin they seize the opportunity with joy to hear God's word of forgiveness. The kingdom of God is near.

Isn't it true that when social structures fall apart Christians often see the need for God's spirit to recreate community? In such a community, caring is both needed and given. When the contrasts between good and evil are obvious people can recognize the need for some better way. The kingdom of God is near.

When war has destroyed the myth of humanity's inevitable progress, nations are driven again to work out the necessary foundations for peace. Reconciliation, justice and respect stand out as the virtues needed for life. Christians astound the world with Christ's command to go beyond this and love our enemies. The kingdom of God is near.

When faced with the exploitation of children and recruitment of the young to fight the adult's war, the challenge of the child of Bethlehem touches the hearts of many and causes them to offer protection to the young. The kingdom of God is near.

When we consider it carefully, people in these situations are driven to awake out of the sleep of apathy into the reality of daylight. What practical steps can you see that might drive this message home this Advent? How can you tip the balance in favour of the kingdom? Wise thinking can result in just action. Then, indeed, the kingdom of God is near.

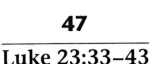

47

Luke 23:33–43

³³When they came to the place that is called The Skull, they crucified Jesus there with the criminals, one on his right and one on his left. [³⁴Then Jesus said, 'Father, forgive them; for they do not know what they are doing.'] And they cast lots to divide his clothing. ³⁵And the people stood by, watching; but the leaders scoffed at him, saying, 'He saved others; let him save himself if he is the Messiah of God, his chosen one!' ³⁶The soldiers also mocked him, coming up and offering him sour wine, ³⁷and saying, 'If you are the King of the Jews, save yourself!' ³⁸There was also an inscription over him, 'This is the King of the Jews.'

³⁹One of the criminals who were hanged there kept deriding him and saying, 'Are you not the Messiah? Save yourself and us!' ⁴⁰But the other rebuked him, saying, 'Do you not fear God, since you are under the same sentence of condemnation? ⁴¹And we indeed have been justly condemned, for we are getting what we deserve for our deeds, but this man has done nothing wrong.' ⁴²Then he said, 'Jesus, remember me when you come into your kingdom.' ⁴³He replied, 'Truly I tell you, today you will be with me in Paradise.'

Context

The journey to Calvary, the place of The Skull, is complete, and with great simplicity and pathos Luke records that 'they crucified Jesus there with the criminals'. The remainder of the passage shows how Jesus reigns from the cross, committed to saving the world and not himself. Salvation begins with forgiveness for all, illustrated by the gift of Paradise for an individual who trusts in his Saviour. The kingdom of God is dawning even in the darkness.

Sensing

Put yourself in the place of the second criminal. You have been realistic all along about your fate. In a rush of passion and anger you had killed a soldier. At the time you believed you were doing the right thing. You were a Jew, he was a Gentile. He was deriding you about your religion, mocking what you held most dear. Surely God would be on your side and give you a martyr's reward? There would be Paradise for the righteous. You struck him dead, and Paradise turned into hell.

Feel the pain now; the pain of disgrace, the pain of defeat and the pain of death. Suffer with dignity, knowing you deserve this death. In a way it is your victory of defiance.

Listen to the shouting. It is not about you but about Jesus. He is the centre of attention. You are hardly noticed. You are a little jealous. He is not the sort of martyr that you are. He has not killed anyone. As far as you can tell he has done nothing wrong. You have heard that he has a strange philosophy of treating everyone as an equal, and telling folk to love their enemies. Why should anyone like that find himself on a cross?

Your strength is ebbing away. You want to get this over as soon as possible and die. In the background you hear new shouting. It is the third man on a cross. He is bitter and twisted in his agony. He attacks Jesus: 'What's the use of being the Messiah and not being able to save yourself and us too? You are an impostor!'

Gather your strength. You cannot remain silent in the face of injustice. Take a deep breath though it hurts on the cross. Defend the innocent. Honour God. Admit your sin. Seek God's will: 'Jesus, remember me when you are king.' What are you saying? How can the dying Jesus rule from the cross?

Give your life away again. Let death relieve you of pain. Listen, Jesus is speaking quietly to you: 'Today we will both be in Paradise, resting in the home of the righteous awaiting resurrection.'

God's promise is true. God does reward the faithful with eternal life. God's kingdom has come.

Intuition

This is a crisis situation.

When you are in a crisis, what do you really want from God? It is natural to yell and scream and to seek to be saved from the mess. We want a saviour who will come to the rescue. We pray for someone to take away the pain. Do you clamour for an interventionist God?

When someone else is in a crisis, we can so easily join in the crowd's words of hurtful mockery. We love the superiority it brings. Our sadistic thoughts add fire to the bully within us. A little malicious gossip, a few taunting words, our tongue used as a sword to cut the other person down to size; in a crisis we can employ them all.

In a crisis we can take advantage of another person's misfortune. We can pick up what they have left behind. The gap they leave may be to our advantage. Their possessions may even come our way. Around the world we witness scenes of looting after shopkeepers have been driven out or killed.

In a crisis how can God take control? When good is suppressed, evil flourishes. What will bring humanity back to decency and dignity?

In a crisis the shock of seeing others suffer may awaken our conscience. In a crisis the words of the righteous may recall us to act justly. In a crisis a sudden realization of the consequences of evil may drive us to silent shame. In a crisis we need a sacrificing saviour to make us take responsibility for our actions. Only then will the kingdom of God come.

Feeling

Do you dread reading this part of the gospel of Luke? Does the death of Christ make you feel ashamed or miserable or plain terrified? How do you relate to Christ's death?

His death seems to defeat the kingdom of God that he had promised. Empathize with Jesus. All he had worked for was in ruins. He preached love of friends and enemies, and it had

failed. No one had learnt the lesson until it was too late. His
friends had betrayed or deserted him. His enemies had gained
power to eliminate him. Have you feelings of sorrow for Jesus
in the midst of failure?

Share your feelings with Jesus at his death. Tell him you
pinned your hopes on his teaching, that you were ready to walk
with him to glory when all of humanity would find peace and
justice, that you longed for the end of evil but now fear that his
death is the end of goodness. Does his death kill what hope you
had of living a better life?

Do you feel his death is a warning signal to those who stick
their necks out and try to change their community for the
better? You have seen so many others hurt by mockery and
jealousy. What about yourself, do you feel that it might happen
to you?

Tell Jesus that his death is a secret warning to you about
your own mortality. It reminds you that we all have to die. Tell
Jesus about the fear you have of your own death. Tell him of
your hopes as well as your fears.

When you read these verses in the gospel do you ask, 'O
God, where is your kingdom? O God, where is your victory?' Is
this your cry of hope or your cry of despair?

'And he loved them unto the end', and the end is not death
but eternal life. The God-fearing criminal holds on to the
promise of Paradise. With God there is no end to love. That is
the rule of the kingdom.

Thinking

The text here parallels that in the other gospels. It is the core of
the Christian tradition about Jesus. In his death all that the
Messiah revealed proved to be true. The forces of evil gathered
all their strength to put out the light of God's love, and failed.

A criminal, the centurion, some of the crowds, all were
transformed by this death. Luke carefully points out the contrasts. Salvation comes to those who have eyes to see what is
happening, and who take responsibility for responding to God.

Luke highlights the issues by making us clarify what kind of
salvation we want. The contrast is between the call to save
yourself and the call to give your life away in sacrifice for others.
You cannot do both. For Jesus to save himself and avoid the
cross meant that he would not expose evil fully. Neither would

he show that God's love endures all things. No doubt Jesus could have avoided death. He could have retired to the safety of Galilee and allowed the rulers of Jerusalem to persist in the distortion of theology and the destruction of peace. But God cannot compromise with evil. Evil must be exposed, even if this entails suffering.

Luke's account of the cross shows that salvation is always corporate. I am never saved in isolation. The salvation of Christ is both for the world and for each person within it. An individual can reject it, as one criminal did on the cross. Another can embrace it even in death, as the other criminal discovered to his salvation.

Luke shows that God's rule operates within the structures of the world, not outside them. The cry of the crowd to Jesus was to come down from the cross, avoid the conflict and walk away from reality. That would not be a sign of God's kingdom in action.

Paradise for many people is an unworldly place where life is perfect. The word Paradise in Hebrew thought stood for the 'Garden of Eden', a place where God's will is done willingly. 'Paradise' represents the place where God reigns. The criminal shows that he is ready to share in the kingdom of God. His commitment to justice and his trust in the justice of God is recorded by Luke. Salvation is open to all. That is the point Luke makes about the kingdom of God in action.

48

Luke 24:1–12

¹But on the first day of the week, at early dawn, they came to the tomb, taking the spices that they had prepared. ²They found the stone rolled away from the tomb, ³but when they went in, they did not find the body. ⁴While they were perplexed about this, suddenly two men in dazzling clothes stood beside them. ⁵The women were terrified and bowed their faces to the ground,

but the men said to them, 'Why do you look for the living among the dead? He is not here, but has risen. ⁶Remember how he told you, while he was still in Galilee, ⁷that the Son of Man must be handed over to sinners, and be crucified, and on the third day rise again.' ⁸Then they remembered his words, ⁹and returning from the tomb, they told all this to the eleven and to all the rest. ¹⁰Now it was Mary Magdalene, Joanna, Mary the mother of James, and the other women with them who told this to the apostles. ¹¹But these words seemed to them an idle tale, and they did not believe them. ¹²But Peter got up and ran to the tomb; stooping and looking in, he saw the linen cloths by themselves; then he went home, amazed at what had happened.

Context

Luke's gospel closely follows the record of Mark. He adds some material which parallels that in John's gospel. All the gospels record that the resurrection happened on the 'first day of the week'. After that there are minor variations which show that no attempt was made to create a 'standard version'. The accounts of the eye-witnesses were remembered and treasured, for the story can never be fully understood or explained. We are still left surprised, excited and amazed.

Sensing

Imagine yourself as one of the women who went to the tomb that first Easter morning.

The first shafts of light are streaking the sky. Hurry to the tomb before the first light of day exposes you to the danger of being seen. Feel the sadness that the whole Sabbath had to pass before you could complete the proper care of the Master's body. Remember the place where you laid him. In the spring the cold of the tomb will stop the decay happening too quickly. Take out the ointments and the spices, ready to use them in accordance with the ritual.

Hear the worried question of Mary Magdalene: 'Did we not see the stone firmly in place when we left?' Look at one another in confusion. 'Yes, yes', you reply, 'what's wrong?' 'The stone has moved. The body has been moved. It is not here. See for yourself.'

Go into the tomb and let your eyes get used to the semi-darkness. The body is *not* here. What has happened?

Go out into the sun. It has risen and is shining on two figures. They are men. They see your perplexed looks. Listen as they speak in clear direct tones: 'What are you doing, looking for the living among the dead? Do you not remember what he told you in Galilee: "On the third day I will rise again"?'

Look at one another in the group. 'He did tell us; but who would believe it?' Discuss the experience as you stand there beside the empty tomb. 'Yes, he did tell us, but who would believe it? Let's go and tell the men.'

Return to the city. Find the apostles and the other disciples. Why will they not believe what you are saying? They must remember!

Watch Peter listen with the others and then, as impetuous as ever, rush out of the door. He is off to see for himself. Wait with the rest of the group for his return. Discuss your experience as you respond to questions. Do you remember? Do you remember?

Peter returns home. The whole group becomes silent. 'What did you see, Peter?'

Listen as he tells of his experience: 'The tomb is empty. The linen clothes are folded. Jesus said he would rise on the third day.' This will be a day to remember!

Intuition

What do you remember about Easter services in the past? What is there about this festival that stirs strong memories of life and hope?

Do you remember the hymns and the music? Do the words 'Jesus Christ is risen today' bring to mind the message of new hope after suffering and pain? Does some modern hymn recall an experience of God as risen amongst us now? What music makes Easter stand out in your mind?

Do you remember the symbols and flowers at Easter? The contrast between the stark sparseness of Lent and the scented beauty of the decorations at Easter recalls the theme of death and life. What do Easter flowers mean for you?

What symbols of Easter do you recall? The resurrection candle, the new fire and the empty tomb in the garden bring to mind the Easter dawn. What other symbols evoke Easter for you?

What words shine out in your mind when you remember Easter? These words may ring true for you:

On the third day he will rise again.
Why do you look for the living among the dead?
He is not here; he is risen.

Or are our hearts as stone dead as the closed tomb? Are our minds shut to any new ideas about what might have happened? Are we so perplexed that we cannot imagine the resurrection ever taking place? Have we nothing to remember but fear, fear that death finished off our final hopes about Jesus, fear that death will be the end of us and those we love, fear that Easter memories will die like the Easter flowers? Or are our hearts open to greet the risen Christ this Easter? Can we see Easter this year as a time for the resurrection of our faith, our hopes, our zest for living?

Remembrance can fix us in the past or it can build a foundation for a new experience. Look for new life in this Easter, this table, this word of the Lord: 'He is risen indeed!'

Feeling

You must have had many new experiences in your life. Have you responded to them with eagerness or shut them off out of fear? Easter is always about new experiences. It breaks out from the old into the new. The rest of the year is never the same after the Easter event. Hope is rekindled, a new confidence arises in the Easter people. We are ready for a new blossoming of our faith. At this vigil feast what expectations have you of a new experience for Easter?

When did you last have a new experience of the risen Lord? Some people are amazed by that question, but it should not take us aback on Easter Day. Have you buried Jesus long ago? Are you surviving on just a memory? Or are you open to resurrection experiences and eager for a new experience of Christ?

The disciples had many experiences of being with Jesus. Be a disciple, commit yourself to his group, walk with him into new territory, listen to his challenging and comforting words, share the last fellowship meal, witness his love, even to death. His disciples had related in all these ways to Jesus over a span of some three years. Yet they were open to new experiences after the resurrection. On this Easter Day feel close to Jesus in a new way. Do not bury Jesus in the past and look for the living among the dead. Look for a new experience of Christ. Relate to Jesus as your risen Lord.

The day is dawning. The risen Christ greets us anew. Let a new relationship with Christ begin.

Thinking

Maybe your reaction to Easter is similar to the disciples' first reaction to the women's message:

These words seemed to them an idle tale;
and they did not believe them.

When you think about this story it is good to see such an honest record. We would be suspicious if the story had been easily accepted. We would be on our guard if such a difficult concept as resurrection had been accepted with ease. It is good that the account is so full of honest reaction and amazement, even disbelief. It allows us to tussle with the ideas and the news.

So we can ask ourselves, 'Is resurrection possible?' Resurrection seems to break all the rules of observation. Death is an end and we must not pretend it is otherwise. Observation tells us so. Luke in his gospel affirms this is so. Jesus is dead and buried, and there is no doubt about it.

But Luke tells us that there was a further experience of Jesus which was just as amazing and just as real for the first disciples. It was an experience which was beyond the restricted view of life that most people hold as 'factual'. The experience was a break-out situation for them. It moved them over a barrier into a future which was scary yet exciting. The experience was hard to believe, impossible to explain, but it could not be ignored. The only way of describing it was to speak of a new quality of life, a quality which they called resurrection. It was not resuscitation, the return to the old life prior to death. It was resurrection, the advance to a new life beyond death. It was not an idle tale but it took time for the reality to dawn. It could not be dismissed. It had to be detected. Like a detective we too must look at every piece of evidence and come to a conclusion that takes each one of them into account.

How do you make sense of these records of the risen Lord?

Remember what Jesus said. Remember what the disciples said. Remember Luke's account, tested by time. Remember your own experiences. Like a good detective come up with your conclusions.

49

Luke 24:13-35

¹³Now on that same day two of them were going to a village called Emmaus, about seven miles from Jerusalem, ¹⁴and talking with each other about all these things that had happened. ¹⁵ While they were talking and discussing, Jesus himself came near and went with them, ¹⁶but their eyes were kept from recognizing him. ¹⁷And he said to them, 'What are you discussing with each other while you walk along?' They stood still, looking sad. ¹⁸Then one of them, whose name was Cleopas, answered him, 'Are you the only stranger in Jerusalem who does not know the things that have taken place there in these days?' ¹⁹He asked them, 'What things?' They replied, 'The things about Jesus of Nazareth, who was a prophet mighty in deed and word before God and all the people, ²⁰and how the chief priests and leaders handed him over to be condemned to death and crucified him. ²¹But we had hoped that he was the one to redeem Israel. Yes, and besides all this, it is now the third day since these things took place. ²²Moreover, some women of our group astounded us. They were at the tomb early this morning, ²³and when they did not find his body there, they came back and told us that they had indeed seen a vision of angels who said that he was alive. ²⁴Some of those who were with us went to the tomb and found it just as the women had said; but they did not see him.' ²⁵Then he said to them, 'Oh, how foolish you are, and how slow of heart to believe all that the prophets have declared! ²⁶Was it not necessary that the Messiah should suffer these things and then enter into his glory?' ²⁷Then beginning with Moses and all the prophets, he interpreted to them the things about himself in all the scriptures.

²⁸As they came near the village to which they were going,

he walked ahead as if he were going on. ²⁹But they urged him strongly, saying, 'Stay with us, because it is almost evening and the day is now nearly over.' ³⁰When he was at the table with them, he took bread, blessed and broke it, and gave it to them. ³¹Then their eyes were opened, and they recognized him; and he vanished from their sight. ³²They said to each other, 'Were not our hearts burning within us while he was talking to us on the road, while he was opening the scriptures to us?' ³³That same hour they got up and returned to Jerusalem; and they found the eleven and their companions gathered together. ³⁴They were saying, 'The Lord has risen indeed, and he has appeared to Simon!' ³⁵Then they told what had happened on the road, and how he had been made known to them in the breaking of the bread.

Context

This resurrection account is unique to Luke. It was of key importance to the early church, who had two questions: How did the death and resurrection of Jesus fit into the plan of God revealed in the Hebrew scriptures? How did the death and resurrection of Jesus fit into the current experience of the church? This account of the walk to Emmaus responds to their questions, and ours.

Sensing

Set out for Emmaus with Cleopas on that first day of the week. The sun is beginning to decline. The festival is over. It is time to head for home, two hours away.

Set out with a heavy heart. A week ago you came to Jerusalem with high hopes. In seven days they have been dashed. Feel the burning of the sun outside and the heat of despair burning within. Shade your head and shade your eyes as you share your feelings with your companion.

Out of the corner of your eye catch a glimpse of another pilgrim walking alongside you. Hear him ask what you were saying to one another, as he draws parallel to you. Listen as Cleopas explains the events of the past week to this pilgrim: 'We had hoped . . . death . . . empty tomb . . . they did not see him.' Note the disappointment in his voice. It matches your mood too.

Listen to the stranger's lecture: 'Foolish . . . slow of heart . . . necessary . . . Moses and the prophets . . . listen to the scriptures.' You need new ears to listen to this. After an hour of talking, feel the excitement; what he says makes sense. Your heart is warmed, home is near, hope is returning, life begins again. He is good company but where is he going? He seems so far ahead of us.

Open your lips to invite him into your home: 'It's late. Stay with us.' Feel the relief as he agrees. Make the table ready. Put the bread and the wine and the lamb on it. Invite the guest to give thanks for the spring, new life, and God's salvation.

Hear his words of blessing. Watch him break the bread and share it. Who can he be, this fellow pilgrim, this teacher, this friend of God? Feel your heart racing, your mind turning, your lips quivering: 'Yes, it must be! It is! Jesus, it *is* you.' We have new eyes to see you. Stay with us. We want to hold on to you, to keep you, to prove it is true.

Bread that is kept grows stale. It must be new every morning. New ears, new eyes, for a new day – that is resurrection!

Intuition

What do we hope for when we hear again the Easter story?

Do we hope that Jesus will come back to life so that we can listen to his words of wisdom? Do we hope that Jesus can interpret life more meaningfully for us? Do we hope that Jesus can return to heal our sickness? What do we hope will come from our Easter experience?

Do we hope that Jesus will show us how resurrection works? Do we hope that he will give us a demonstration of his new body? Do we hope that he will make death unnecessary? What do we hope will come from our Easter experience?

Do we hope that Jesus will become our house guest? Do we hope that we can keep Jesus for ourselves as our private property? Do we hope that we can put limits on his activity so that he is not so far ahead of us? What do we hope will come from our Easter experience?

Have we new ears to hear the scriptures relating God's plan, not only for yesterday but also for tomorrow? Have we new ears to hear how Easter interprets our living today as well as yesterday? Have we new ears to relate the Easter story to our lives now?

Have we new eyes to see Jesus in the bread of the altar and the bread for the needy? Have we new eyes to see the events of our day transformed into deeds of love to bring Christ's presence in our midst? Have we new eyes to see suffering as shared by God as surely as bread has to be broken to be shared?

What do we hope for, what do we listen for, what do we look for, at the breaking of the bread?

Feeling

Put yourself in the place of Cleopas when Jesus disappears from the table. Immediately afterwards, you feel despondent again and angry that Jesus has departed just as you had new ears and new eyes to take notice of him. Now that he has gone you are unsure whether you want to sit down and treasure the experience, or leap up and share it.

Put yourself in the place of Cleopas when Jesus vanishes from the table. Do you dismiss it all as an illusion, or tell yourself that you have seen the Christ? You feel a mixture of emotions, both joy and frustration.

Cleopas says that he felt his heart burning within him while Jesus was opening the meaning of the scriptures. Share his feelings when you read the bible and see the truth that it reveals. Have we new eyes and new ears to see and hear the word of God?

Put yourself in the place of Cleopas. Do you feel that you must share your news with others despite your weariness from the journey? Let the Easter story give you new energy for witness and service. Feel the new life flowing through you again.

Put yourself in the place of Cleopas. He could not wait to return to the company of the disciples. He wanted to share the account with them, to be part of the community of the risen Lord. Share Cleopas' feelings of excitement about your fellow Christians in the church. Relate to them so that you can each share the experience of the resurrection within the community.

Put yourself in the place of Cleopas. Be convinced that it was the Spirit of Jesus that opened your ears to the scriptures. Be convinced that it was the Spirit of Jesus that was made known to you in the breaking of the bread. Be convinced of the truth about Jesus.

Put yourself in the place of Cleopas. Listen as the disciples tell you, 'The Lord is risen indeed!' Have you new ears to hear and new eyes to see? Be convinced by your experience and the experience of others that Christ is alive, alive for you, for them, this Easter Day.

Thinking

This passage holds together the two ways in which most people experience Christ. It links the scriptures with the sacrament. We need to study the scriptures to hear the truth. We need to experience the sacrament of the eucharist to see the risen Christ.

The scriptures make clear that the account of Jesus is about a person who was rooted in a place and a time in history. They witness to real people and real events. This Jesus was acknowledged as a prophet who declared God's purpose and will in action and teaching. This same man was crucified by a combination of opposing forces: those who had power in religion and in state. The facts are given and the record is clear. The scriptures also record the evidence of the tomb and the first eyewitnesses of resurrection.

We can shut our ears to these records. We can dismiss them as irrelevant. Yet they will not go away. They are told and retold for our good until we have new ears to listen. It is the duty of the Christian community to tell them. We have the opportunity to listen to them until the truth dawns.

The sacrament of the breaking of the bread calls us to have new eyes to see the risen Christ. We experience the same Spirit of Christ in the scriptures and in the sacrament. Words are not tangible, but bread and wine can be touched and felt. We can look at the sacrament with the eyes of logic and see bread. We can look at the sacrament with the eyes of faith and see Christ.

But the sacrament is not illogical. When we think about it, we can see how the tangible can express the intangible. Do not the marks of the words on this page represent the mind of the writer? We often communicate by symbols. The words on the page are not the thoughts in the mind, but they are the means by which those thoughts are conveyed to the reader. The bread is not the Christ, but it conveys the Christ. Sacraments are no more illogical than words. It just takes new eyes to see the meaning.

50
Luke 24:36–48

³⁶While they were talking about this, Jesus himself stood among them and said to them, 'Peace be with you.' ³⁷They were startled and terrified, and thought that they were seeing a ghost. ³⁸He said to them, 'Why are you frightened, and why do doubts arise in your hearts? ³⁹Look at my hands and my feet; see that it is I myself. Touch me and see; for a ghost does not have flesh and bones as you see that I have.' ⁴⁰And when he had said this, he showed them his hands and his feet. ⁴¹While in their joy they were disbelieving and still wondering, he said to them, 'Have you anything here to eat?' ⁴²They gave him a piece of broiled fish, ⁴³and he took it and ate in their presence.

⁴⁴Then he said to them, 'These are my words that I spoke to you while I was still with you – that everything written about me in the law of Moses, the prophets, and the psalms must be fulfilled.' ⁴⁵Then he opened their minds to understand the scriptures, ⁴⁶and he said to them, 'Thus it is written, that the Messiah is to suffer and to rise from the dead on the third day, ⁴⁷and that repentance and forgiveness of sins is to be proclaimed in his name to all nations, beginning from Jerusalem. ⁴⁸You are witnesses of these things.'

Context
On the road to Emmaus the disciples witnessed the presence of Jesus in a *spiritual* way. Now the whole community of disciples is invited to touch the body of Jesus in a *physical* way. Jesus' feet and hands show that the resurrected Christ is the same person as the one who was crucified. They are left wondering about the truth of their experience, but Jesus explains it all from the scriptures. Of this they shall be witnesses to all nations.

Sensing
Imagine yourself standing there when Jesus stood among his disciples. You have just heard the two companions from Emmaus tell their amazing story. Ask them whether they are

certain of their facts. Check out their understanding of what
Jesus told them from the scriptures. Ask them to repeat again
how they knew Jesus at the breaking of the bread.

Look up and see Jesus standing behind them. Gaze into his
eyes and see them affirm his words of peace as you stare at him
in terror. Watch the other disciples shake their heads in disbelief. Hear someone cry out, 'It's a ghost! It cannot be real.' Listen
to Jesus' response, 'Look, touch if you like, see the marks of the
nails. I am no ghost.'

Feel your heart turn from panic into joy. 'It really is Jesus –
but it can't be true, can it?' Watch him take the piece of fish
from the dish and eat it in front of them. He is sitting down
now. 'Don't you remember?' he begins. Follow his argument
about the Messiah's role to suffer and rise from the dead. You
recognize the verses he quotes from the Law, the Prophets and
the Psalms. Yes, Jesus is right about the scriptures; nod your
assent. Will he stay? Can we stay? Isn't this wonderful?

Ask yourself the hard questions: If Jesus is resurrected, how
can we find the words to tell other people? Who will believe us
when we tell them the truth? It is like a dream, but it is *not* a
dream. It is for real.

Listen as he speaks about repentance and forgiveness. Watch
as Peter and the others ask pardon for denying that they knew
Jesus at the time of his death. Go up to Jesus yourself and ask
for forgiveness that you had decided that resurrection was
impossible and so refused to believe the reports from the others.
Pledge your loyalty again that you will be a witness to the truth.

Look at his eyes. They still say, 'Peace be with you.'

Intuition

It is hard to be a witness to the resurrection today. Some people
believe in a continuing spiritual presence of Jesus. They find the
story of the road to Emmaus best expresses the experience of
Easter for them. They can find Jesus in the scriptures. They can
find Jesus in the breaking of the bread. They can witness to an
occasional sharp experience of Jesus before he vanishes again.
But speak of a physical resurrection and they have no room for
it in their scheme of things.

It is hard to be a witness to the resurrection today. Some
people can see the resurrection foreshadowed in the Old Testament. There are glimpses of such a possibility. There are verses

in the Psalms that encourage the thought, but it is the passages in Isaiah about the Suffering Servant which suggest it most clearly. We feel we can touch the cross with confidence, but to touch the wounds of the resurrected body – that is too much.

It is hard to be a witness to the resurrection today. It is easier to believe that the disciples *did* see a ghost or had an hallucination or simply dreamt the whole thing. Don't we often have that sort of experience after a loved one has died? We feel their presence again: coming through the door, sitting in a favourite chair, even in the garden in an old familiar spot. Is this what resurrection means?

It is hard to be a witness to the resurrection today. But if it was not as the disciples said it was, then what have we to gain from our faith? The accounts do not gloss over the difficulties. They tell us how amazed and frightened the disciples were, how hard they found it to believe what was before their eyes. They affirmed that Jesus' body did have a physical form. They could touch as well as see.

It is hard to be a witness to the resurrection today. Yet we can only affirm their story, explain it as the bedrock of our faith, tell others that it assures us of forgiveness and new life, and witness to its living power in our lives.

It may be hard, but that is always the way with the truth.

Feeling

Take the place of Peter among the disciples and see how it feels to be in the room with Jesus. You are well aware of your failure to support Jesus at the times of his trial and crucifixion. You remember well the experience of finding the tomb empty and the linen cloths lying by themselves. You are certain about the time that Jesus appeared to you in his resurrected form.

Take the place of Peter and feel the joy of being able to share the experience with all the rest of the disciples. Feel the restored relationship with Jesus growing stronger. Feel a tinge of satisfaction now that the others know that you were right after all about the resurrection. Feel the growing responsibility of being ready to proclaim the truth that Jesus is the Messiah who has died and is risen.

Take the place of Peter and feel the desire to say sorry and be forgiven and renewed. Is this part of the truth of scripture and the message of the gospel? Feel the glow of rising self-confidence

that Jesus is true to his word, that forgiveness is offered to you
and all nations because of the cross and resurrection.

Take the place of Peter and find the new relationship of
peace with Jesus. Feel the sense of commitment to the Messiah.
Be sure in your heart that Jesus is worthy of this commitment,
that the truth of the gospel is worth living and dying for.

Take the place of Peter and note how the other disciples are
looking to Peter to give them a lead in this relationship with
the risen Christ. Will you touch and see? Will you explain and
witness? Will others follow your example?

Take the place of Peter and feel the commitment to be the
first to witness to the truth about Jesus, that he died for our
salvation, that God raised him from the dead, that this Jesus is
Lord. We have touched. We have seen. Now it is time to be a
witness to the truth.

Thinking

Clearly Luke has included this passage to respond to a number
of questions raised in the early church. Anyone thinking about
the story of the resurrection wants to ask such questions:

- Who saw Jesus in his resurrected form?
- What sort of presence did Jesus have?
- Could it have been a spirit or ghost that the disciples saw?
- What was the link between the crucified Christ and the risen
  Lord?
- Did the disciples find it easy to be convinced about the
  resurrection?
- Did the fellowship that the disciples enjoyed with Jesus over
  meals continue after the resurrection?
- Were the crucifixion and the resurrection in accordance with
  the scriptures?
- What was the message that the first disciples were told to
  proclaim?
- What was the task given by Jesus to the disciples after the
  resurrection?

When you think about it the passage reveals that these key
questions are answered very fully. The disciples were convinced that Jesus' resurrection body had a continuity with his
crucified body, that it was to some extent physical, and that it

was certainly not the same as a ghost. At the end of the resurrection appearances they understood the way that the scriptures pointed forward to the cross and resurrection, and that its message directly offered salvation to them and all people.

When you think about it, the continuing witness of the disciples in the early church was to a well-tested resurrection faith. This had been forged out of amazement, disbelief and a certain amount of fear. The disciples were convinced, but realized that it would not be easy for future generations to come to a strong faith unless the story was told truthfully and carefully. It needed to be kept alive by the continuing witness of the church and the continuing presence of the Spirit of Christ. Future generations would need to touch the story through the witness of the church, and in turn learn to be witnesses to others.

51

Luke 24:44–53

44Then he said to them, 'These are my words that I spoke to you while I was still with you – that everything written about me in the law of Moses, the prophets, and the psalms must be fulfilled.' 45Then he opened their minds to understand the scriptures, 46and he said to them, 'Thus it is written, that the Messiah is to suffer and to rise from the dead on the third day, 47and that repentance and forgiveness of sins is to be proclaimed to all nations, beginning from Jerusalem. 48You are witnesses of these things. 49And see, I am sending upon you what my Father promised; so stay here in the city until you have been clothed with power from on high.'

50Then he led them out as far as Bethany, and, lifting up his hands, he blessed them. 51While he was blessing them, he withdrew from them and was carried up into heaven. 52And they worshipped him, and returned to Jerusalem with great joy; 53and they were continually in the temple blessing God.

Context

Luke brings his gospel to a close with a blessing by Jesus of his disciples before his 'withdrawal' and ascension. This scene is a narrative conclusion to the first part of Luke's story of the church. Jesus had completed his work on earth and is taken into heaven. The disciples on the other hand are given a commission and a promise. The gospel ends on a positive note: the activity is worship, the location is the temple and the emotion is joy.

Sensing

Imagine yourself on the ridge on the top of the Mount of Olives. Ahead of you is Bethany, behind you is the road from Jerusalem. This is the highest spot around. From here on Palm Sunday you had accompanied Jesus into Jerusalem to inaugurate the kingdom of God. Now the journey to heaven is about to be completed. The Father's will has been done, the purpose of the incarnation fulfilled, repentance and forgiveness will open the gateway to heaven for people of all nations, a new power from God has been promised.

Feel the joy rising in your heart. Capture the sense of eagerness to share the story with all around you. You are no longer stunned with amazement, instead you are strengthened with resolve. Everyone must know of this victory of God.

Stand there on the edge of the hillside above Bethany, home to Jesus and his friends on so many occasions. Realize that all he could do and should do has been done. It is time to go home. It is time to say goodbye. It is a sad time for you, but you are happy for Jesus. You trust him, he is in charge; he has given you a promise and he will keep it.

Look at his face. It is a picture of peace, peace stemming from the knowledge that all things have been made whole. Look at his face. It is a picture of confidence in you and those standing with you. Look at his hands. He has lifted them up in blessing. Look at his hands. He is passing responsibility over to you. Look at the clouds. They seem to bow down to enfold Jesus and take him up in their arms to glory. Look at the clouds. They are rising up into the sky, swirling, dancing, racing ahead.

Shout your praise to God as you race down the slope, racing not to Bethany but back to Jerusalem. That is where the people are. That is where the task must begin. You can hardly wait, but you need the promised Spirit first. Jesus' ascension has lifted your spirits up as high as the heavens.

Intuition

When you are writing a book it is hard to know how to bring it to a good conclusion. There is so much more to be written. Have you made everything clear? Will people receive the message? How can you leave your readers eager to know more but feeling satisfied with what they have? Endings are difficult.

When you are saying goodbye to a friend, it is hard to know how to draw the conversation to a close. You have so much more you want to say to them. Will the friendship survive the departure? Will you forget all the times that you have shared together? Will the memories survive, enlivened with your spirit? Endings are difficult.

When you are a teacher and come to the final class with the pupils, it is hard to know how to draw everything to a good conclusion. Have they learnt enough to carry on without you, with only the notes and the memories to answer their future questions? Have they grasped the principles enough to put them into practice on their own? Endings are difficult.

When you are a playwright and you are looking at the details for the final scene, it is hard to know how you can tie all the ends together. You look at the opening scene and see if you can find parallels so that the play fits within a frame. If the play starts in one location, you may want to set the last scene there too. If the play starts with a prophecy you may want to see it fulfilled in the finale. Endings are difficult.

Luke was challenged to find a good ending to his version of the good news about Jesus Christ. He wanted to finish it well, to show how Jesus had said farewell to his friends, to draw to a close Jesus' teaching and, like a good playwright, to tie the end to the beginning. Many say that Luke succeeded in his task. Some endings are brilliant!

Feeling

Be a disciple and kneel to receive a blessing. It will help you feel close in your relationship with God. A blessing is a strengthening of the bond between those concerned. It affirms the love that binds people together. It reinforces the sense of mutual responsibility. It remains a gift from the giver to the receiver, which the memory enlivens every time it is recalled.

Put yourself in the place of a young person leaving home for a new job or a new city. A blessing is especially important when it is a 'final' blessing. Stand and receive a blessing with a hug from a parent. Feel the confidence entrusted in you. Feel the warmth of love which lets you go and empowers you to overcome any sense of loss at the parting. Feel support for the tasks you want to do. Feel an eternal bond forged between you for ever.

Kneel to receive a blessing from a priest after an act of repentance and forgiveness. Feel the flow of confidence and trust that you can get on with a new way of living, free from the burden of guilt. Be assured that the blessing seals the approval of God for the courage you have shown in being honest with yourself before God. Feel the bond between you and God fully restored. Stand up and depart in joy.

Be a disciple in your church and receive a blessing as you commit yourself to a new piece of Christian ministry. Experience an anointing spirit in the pressure of the hands, giving you empowerment for service. Feel an inner glow and an exuberance of joy. This blessing will make you ready to witness and serve your Lord.

Put yourself in the place of one of the disciples as Jesus blessed them before his departure into heaven. Receive his blessing this ascensiontide, holding firm the bond between you, forgiving the past and giving you confidence for your work, filling your heart with joy and your lips with praise. This is a good way to go.

Thinking

This conclusion to Luke's gospel has always raised some difficulties for readers and scholars. It seems strange that Luke, who in all likelihood wrote both the Gospel of Luke and the Acts of the Apostles, should include two versions of the ascension event. The one in the gospel is trimmed to the bone while the account in Acts is so much fuller. There the timing and the location seem to be so different.

Yet, when you think about it, the inclusion of each of the two accounts has a very different purpose. The brief gospel account must be sufficient to round off the gospel without creating such a full stop that the 'second volume' is regarded as totally separate. At the opening of the Acts of the Apostles there must be an explanation for the change in the disciples from a terrified, broken group to a confident, faithful community. Luke therefore deems it necessary to go into fuller details there with explanations about teaching, timing and location.

There are very good reasons why Luke wrote as he did. In this account of the ascension he stresses the sense of plan and purpose behind the event. Jesus has given full teaching about his life, death and resurrection in accordance with the scriptures. He has given the promise and the task to his disciples. Everything is ready for his planned departure. He appears to be on his way home to Bethany but all is ready for his departure to his eternal home. He blesses his friends before being carried 'home'. The disciples recognize that this is how it should be for they now are certain of who Jesus is, that he is one with God.

Instead of leaving them terrified, the departure causes them joy and gives them reason for praise. Surely what is appropriate for them is appropriate for us. We are empowered by Christ's blessing. We are confirmed in our faith. This ending will be the cause of a new beginning. With joy we too can say, 'To God be the glory!'

Further reading

The following books provide further insight into the theory of psychological type underpinning the Myers-Briggs Type Indicator and the relevance of type theory for the Christian community.

Bayne, R., *The Myers-Briggs Type Indicator: a Critical Review and Practical Guide*, London, Chapman and Hall, 1995.

Briggs-Myers, I. and Myers, P. B., *Gifts Differing*, Palo Alto, California, Consulting Psychologists Press, 1980.

Bryant, C., *Jung and the Christian Way*, London, Darton, Longman and Todd, 1983.

Butler, A., *Personality and Communicating the Gospel*, Cambridge, Grove Books, 1999.

Davis, S. and Handschin, B., *Reinventing Yourself: Life Planning after 50*, Palo Alto, California, Consulting Psychologists Press, 1998.

Duncan, B., *Pray Your Way: Your Personality and God*, London, Darton, Longman and Todd, 1993.

Dwyer, M. T., *Wake Up the Sun: an Exploration of Personality Types and Spiritual Growth*, Thornbury, Victoria, Desbooks, 1988.

Faucett, R. and Faucett, C. A., *Personality and Spiritual Freedom: Growing in the Christian Life Through Understanding Personality Type and the Myers-Briggs Type Indicator*, New York, Doubleday, 1987.

Francis, L. J., *Personality Type and Scripture: Exploring Mark's Gospel*, London, Mowbray, 1997.

Goldsmith, M., *Knowing Me: Knowing God*, London, Triangle, 1994.

Goldsmith, M. and Wharton, M., *Knowing Me, Knowing You*, London, SPCK, 1993.

Grant, W. H., Thompson, M. and Clarke, T. E., *From Image to Likeness: a Jungian Path in the Gospel Journey*, New York, Paulist Press, 1983.

Harbaugh, G., *God's Gifted People: Discovering Your Personality as a Gift*, Minneapolis, Augsburg Publishing House, 1990.

Hirsh, S. and Kummerow, J., *Life Types*, New York, Warner Books, 1989.

Innes, R., *Personality Indicators and the Spiritual Life*, Cambridge, Grove Books Ltd, 1996.

Johnson, R., *Your Personality and the Spiritual Life*, Crowborough, Monarch, 1995.

Keating, C. J., *Who We Are is How We Pray*, Mystic, Connecticut, Twenty-Third Publications, 1987.

Kelsey, M., *Prophetic Ministry: the Psychology and Spirituality of Pastoral Care*, Rockport, Massachusetts, Element Inc., 1991.

Kroeger, O. and Thuesen, J. M., *Type Talk*, New York, Delta, 1988.

Kroeger, O. and Thuesen, J. M., *Type Talk at Work*, New York, Delacorte Press, 1992.

Michael, C. P. and Morrisey, M. C., *Prayer and Temperament*, Charlottesville, Virginia, The Open Book Inc., 1984.

Moore, R. L. (ed.), *Carl Jung and Christian Spirituality*, Mahwah, New Jersey, Paulist Press, 1988.

Moss, S., *Jungian Typology*, Melbourne, Collins Dove, 1989.

Osborn, L. and Osborn, D., *God's Diverse People*, London, Daybreak, 1991.

Oswald, R. M. and Kroeger, O., *Personality Type and Religious Leadership*, Washington, DC, Alban Institute, 1988.

Quenk, N. L., *Beside Ourselves: Our Hidden Personality in Everyday Life*, Palo Alto, California, Davies-Black, 1993.

Richardson, P. T., *Four Spiritualities: Expressions of Self, Expressions of Spirit*, Palo Alto, California, Davies-Black, 1996.

Spoto, A., *Jung's Typology in Perspective*, Boston, Massachusetts, Sigo Press, 1989.

Thorne, A. and Gough, H., *Portraits of Type*, Palo Alto, California, Consulting Psychologists Press, 1991.

Williams, I., *Prayer and My Personality*, Bramcote, Grove Books, 1987.

Printed in the United Kingdom
by Lightning Source UK Ltd.
121205UK00001B/453